Clothing the Pacific

Figure I.1 A Rarotongan canoe dance *c*. 1900, reproduced by kind permission of The British Museum (BMOC/B85/6)

Clothing the Pacific

Edited by
Chloë Colchester

Oxford • New York

First published in 2003 by
Berg
Editorial offices:
1st Floor, Angel Court, 81 St Clements St, Oxford, OX4 1AW
838 Broadway, Third Floor, New York, NY 10003–4812, USA

Berg is the imprint of Oxford International Publishers Ltd.

Library of Congress Cataloging-in-Publication Data

A catalogue record for this book is available from the Library of Congress.

British Library Cataloguing-in-Publication Data

A catalogue record for this book is available from the British Library.

ISBN 1 85973 666 1 (Cloth)
1 85973 671 8 (Paper)

Typeset by JS Typesetting Ltd, Wellingborough, Northants.
Printed in the United Kingdom by Biddles Ltd, Guildford and King's Lynn.

www.bergpublishers.com

Contents

List of Illustrations

Preface

Clothing the Pacific is the first publication to emerge from a three-year project funded by the Economic and Social Sciences Research Council (UK). This project, also called 'Clothing the Pacific', set out to examine the multiple histories of cloth and clothing in the contemporary Pacific and to investigate how cloth has facilitated both social innovation and resistance during the colonial and post-colonial periods.

Clothing was one of the key visual markers of the advent of colonialism in the Pacific, and was seen by Europeans as one of the signs of the acceptance of civilization by islanders. However, the way in which foreign clothing was perceived and incorporated by islanders did not necessarily reflect these ideas, but involved the investment of indigenous preoccupations into new materials. The present study thus addresses the place of clothing in colonial and mission history. It investigates what clothing did, but also how it was perceived and reworked by Europeans and Pacific Islanders in often strikingly diverging ways.

The poorly explored history of the place of cloth and clothing in the history of cross-cultural interaction Pacific is addressed by a series of detailed, historically arranged studies which document the continuing preoccupation with both imported and indigenous clothing in exchange and religious practice, in clothing and in the decoration of domestic space, in public political activity as well as in cultural festivals and in the contemporary art scene. A dominant theme of the book is whether missionary and colonial activity, as well as European clothes, altered the way in which clothing registers specific capacities for action, and if so, how Pacific Islanders have responded to this during the centuries that have elapsed since first contact. Read together, it is hoped that the case studies presented here will offer an extended and comparative analysis on the place of material culture in the process of cultural interpretation and appropriation.

Clothing the Pacific presents a perspective on clothing that examines how gestures with clothes amplify physical expression in different social situations: ranging from encounters between Europeans and Pacific Islanders; to ceremonies where clothing is attributed with the power to accomplish certain ends concerning matters of life, health or death; and to the new kinds of social encounter that are taking place in the Pacific diaspora. By focusing upon the way that the interpretation of gestures with clothing affects social interaction, this collection of case studies highlights the need to develop a more integrated account of the place of people's appearance both in art and in every day life.

Susanne Küchler

List of Contributors

Ping-Ann Addo, is a doctoral candidate at the Department of Anthropology at Columbia University. She is currently doing fieldwork research on the changing uses and perceptions of Tongan clothing in the Tongan Diaspora.

Alain Babadzan is Professor of Anthropology at the Université Paul Valéry, Montpellier. His books include, *Les Dépouilles des Dieux: Essai sur la Religion Tahitienne à l'Epoque de la Découverte* (Musée des Sciences de l'Homme 1993).

Lissant Bolton is the Assistant Keeper of Oceania at the British Museum. She has written extensively on the nature of women's kastom in Vanuatu. She has recently published a monograph of her research entitled *Unfolding the Moon Women Kastom and Textiles in Vanuatu* (University of Hawaii Press 2003).

Chloë Colchester is a research fellow in Anthropology at University College, London and is the research associate on Clothing the Pacific: a Study of the Nature of Innovation. She writes on the nature of Pacific modernity.

Susanne Küchler is a Reader in Material Culture in the Department of Anthropology at University College, London. She has worked extensively on issues of remembering and forgetting in relation to Pacific art. She is the Director of the ESRC-funded project on which this volume is based. Her books include *Malanggan: Art Memory and Sacrifice* (Berg 2003).

Rosanna Raymond is one of New Zealand's most celebrated Pacific fashion activists and is a member of the performance group *The Pacific Sisters*. During the 1990s she was the principal organizer of the Pacific fashion show at *Pasifika* in Auckland. She has staged and participated in numerous performances at galleries and arts and cultural festivals in Auckland, Australia and the UK.

Serge Tcherkézoff, is Professor of Anthropology at the Université de Marseille and is the Director of the Centre de Recherches et de Documentation sur l'Océanie (CNRS, EHESS, Université de Provence). His current research involves making an ethno-historical analysis of the various Western inventions of 'Polynesia' as a culture area since the eighteenth century.

Nicholas Thomas is Professor of Anthropology at Goldsmiths College. He has written extensively on art, and on cross-cultural interaction in the Pacific. His books include *Entangled Objects* (Harvard 1991); *Oceanic Art* (Thames & Hudson 1995) and *Possessions: Indigenous Art/Colonial Culture* (Thames & Hudson 1999).

Acknowledgements

I should like to thank the many people who have helped to bring this book to fruition and in particular the other members of the Clothing the Pacific team. Both Nicholas Thomas and Lissant Bolton made insightful comments about several of the papers as well as the introduction that helped to clarify the shape and content of the book. Susanne Küchler encouraged me to reconsider the relationship between cultural translation and humour by drawing attention to the importance of visual analogy in the Pacific. Graeme Were and Susanna Kelly both helped immensely by co-ordinating the illustrations. I would also like to thank the British Museum for their generous support in providing the project with office space and library facilities as well as to the staff of the Department of Ethnography who commented upon early drafts of some of the papers during the weekly material culture seminar. My gratitude is also due to Alain Babadcan and his publishers at La Maison des Sciences de l'Homme for allowing me to translate a large section of his book, *Les Dépouilles des Dieux* and to the Journal of Material Culture for allowing me to reprint Nicholas Thomas' essay, 'The Case of Misplaced Ponchos'.

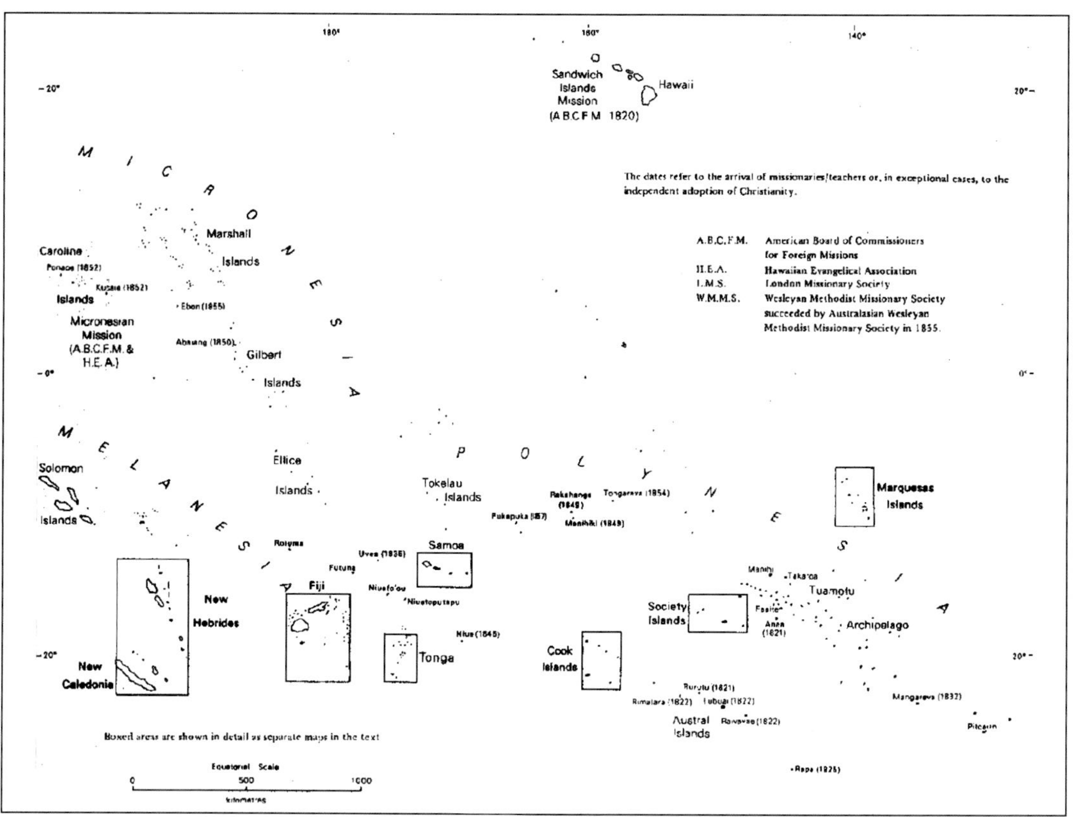

Figure I.2. The Arrival of Church denominations in the Pacific (from Neil Gunson, *Messengers of Grace*).

Introduction

Chloë Colchester

Traces of the material culture associated with nineteenth-century evangelism and colonialism are everywhere in the Pacific. Throughout Polynesia and in many parts of Melanesia, the bold, island-style prints that people wear have been derived by Indian-Fijian traders and Hawaiians from Manchester cottons. These vivid cotton prints of hibiscus flowers are the offshoots of the Victorian 'culture of flowers' that involved the industrial revolution, the expansion of international networks of trade, the establishment of trade stores in many parts of the colonial periphery (Phillips 1998), and the consumption of floral prints by Pacific islanders.

Where the extended influence of Victorian mission to the Pacific is most evident, however, is in Pacific women's contemporary dress. Even today, foreign visitors are often surprised to discover that Pacific women's 'traditional dress' consists of all-concealing tent-like cotton pinafores, known as 'Mother Hubbards', *vinivo* and *mu'umu'u* in Vanuatu, Fiji and Hawaii respectively, which seem stuck in the nineteenth century. They indicate how powerfully Victorian missionary influence continues to be felt in the present. As social life moves on, with growing numbers of Pacific women gaining paid employment, these Victorian-style frocks made from cotton fabric printed with brilliant island designs are an indication of the way that women's dress has lagged behind other social innovations. Recently, however, as American-style modern mass leisurewear has begun to achieve an international following, allowing the physical expression of liberalism to be exported to the Pacific, dress has become a focal point of cultural debate in the islands.

Clothing was one of the most obvious markers of the changes imposed by colonialism and the mission. Richard Eves has shown how in the latter stages of missionary activity in the Pacific, reform was imposed not only through changes in dress but through the use of the drill, the monitoring of domestic activity, and the establishment of Christian sewing clubs and women's institutes (Eves 1996). Like the fire-and-brimstone sermons one still hears old-school Pacific preachers deliver to their congregations, these practices have remained part of the enduring legacy of reformist missionary activity in the Pacific. They reveal how the wives of Protestant evangelists tried to help their husbands in their attempts to transpose redemption to a this-worldly level by circumscribing the instrumentality of objects to *le monde vécu*.

For a distinguishing feature of the Protestant mission to the Pacific, as to other parts of the colonial periphery, was the emphasis placed on defining ordinary everyday activity, a pursuit in which the imposition of foreign practices of domesticity, home-making, dress and deportment were regarded as being as central to conversion as translating the Holy Book (cf. Comaroff 1996).

In *The Ebb-Tide*, a short story derived from his experience in the Pacific, Robert Louis Stevenson's aristocratic character Attwater complains about the parochial interpretation of religion that was implied by the Protestant missionaries' preoccupation with clothing. It illustrates the unease with which any interest in clothing is so often greeted, as if it diminished the gravity of human affairs:

> They go the wrong way to work; they are too parsonish, too much of the old wife and even the old apple-wife. *Clothes, clothes,* are their idea; but clothes are not Christianity, any more than they are the sun in heaven, or could take the place of it! They think a parsonage with roses and church bells, and nice old women bobbing in the lanes, are part and parcel of religion. But religion is a savage thing, like the universe it illuminates; savage, cold, bare, but infinitely strong. (Stevenson, 1979 [1893]: 252–3)

Catholic priests did not share this degree of concern with everyday material things since their approach to the place of objects in worship and religious practice was different, and moreover the impact of Roman Catholics was to remain small compared to that of the Protestant Evangelicals. For Protestant Evangelicals wanted the islanders' to accept not only their faith, but their way of life. Proscribing the use of artefacts in divine mediation, and their attempts to change the economy of devotion, went together with a preoccupation with ordinary, everyday things such as household furnishings and dress.

White lace antimacassars and decorative details executed in ribbons and appliqué (together with a seemingly endless series of covers, tidies and holders) reveal how the wives of missionaries attempted to instil the Victorian virtue of clothing one's family and one's home. They show how humdrum activities such as dressmaking and endless clothes washing came to play an important part in attempts to redefine the effective capacity and significance of the things. Even today, several decades after the islands have achieved political independence, Pacific contemporary Church-based women's organizations still gather to stitch, plait and print cloth for good causes, or to inspect the cleanliness of each other's houses. In addition, the comparative poverty of the early Protestant missions may have played a part, for it meant that in certain instances (as in Tonga for example) missionaries became involved in sanctioning the production of native cloth and trading and bartering exported cottons in order to survive (Rutherford 1996).

Yet the enduring popularity of nineteenth-century-style clothing in the contemporary Pacific does not simply indicate the long reach of Victorian missionary

Figure I. 3 'Then and Now' Bill Bates © Fiji Sun.

influence. In many areas, European clothes were adopted voluntarily. It is also important to note that the conversion of the Pacific was to a large extent achieved by Polynesians, by members of populations who had already been converted, and who had already interpreted or appropriated Christianity in distinctive ways (Gunson 1978). Even today, maintaining missionary-inspired dress has become symptomatic of a certain cultural tenacity, or a preference for formality in the face of more modern alternatives. Both in the islands and in the Pacific diaspora, dress has become a focal point of conflicting values. Surrounded by modern dress-styles, many older Pacific migrants living in Auckland, Sydney and Los Angeles cling to old-fashioned standards of conveying modesty and respect through dress, although they face increasing opposition from younger migrants who wish to liberate themselves from the heavy legacy of missionary morality. The following anecdote from a Samoan museum curator, living in New Zealand, relates to an experience she had in Wellington in the 1990s:

> In an effort to impress my prospective in-laws, a well to-do [Samoan] minister and his wife, I made every effort to dress in what I thought would be appropriate attire for church – a lovely white cotton two-piece suit, a short-sleeved shirt and a long skirt. After the service we were introduced, and as we were talking politely to one another the minister's wife looked me up and down, then leaned over and started buttoning up my blouse, right

> up to the neck! Ten years on, married with a daughter, I still get slapped on the knees when I go to the minister's house with knee-length shorts on, and I'm always told off for wearing trousers to church (Leote-Ete et al 2002).

European perceptions of dress are also subject to time-lag; and in their face-to-face encounters with Europeans, Pacific Islanders can find themselves confronted with stereotypes that became established in the salons of Europe over two hundred years ago, with the dramatic stories of Cook's and Bligh's encounters with Pacific Islanders, long before they were popularized by Hollywood and tourism. This encounter between two Samoan sisters and a Roman market-stall holder, which occurred in the Piazza Campo dei Fiori during the year 2000, is a case in point.

> Eimi and Evotia Tamua are sisters, and they are both professional photographers. One takes 'ethnographic' photographs of the way of life on the islands, and at Pacific cultural festivals. The other works with photographs to make art installations. She is planning to exhibit oversize portraits of Samoans using their German surnames as titles: Zemke White, Pfeiffer, Kurtz and so on. At the moment, however, they are on holiday, travelling around Europe in search of the ultimate food experience: eating chocolates in Brussels, patisserie from a particular Parisian baker and tasting the pasta and coffee from their favourite places in Rome.
>
> Today they are buying fruit in the Campo dei Fiori. The market stall vendor looks at them and asks them where they are from. 'New Zealand' they reply. He looks at them blankly; obviously he can't place them at all. They try again, 'We're from the Pacific, Polynesia.' 'Aah! Polynesie!' he says, pleased that he's got it, and he starts doing a take-off of the hula, swaying his arms and moving his hips jerkily from side to side.
>
> The two sisters look at him. They wonder why he can't see that the image in his mind's eye doesn't fit them at all. For it is autumn, and there is slight a nip in the air, and both sisters are sensibly dressed in trousers, jackets and jumpers, and their hair is cropped fashionably short.

This is of course, a classic example of European Orientalism, and reveals a well-established tendency to see remote peoples as inhabiting a fantasy world that is somehow situated apart from our own, and so denies the history of colonialism, or of the expansion of the Christian community. Hearing this story of an encounter between Pacific Islanders and Europeans from a Pacific viewpoint brings home how distancing these attitudes can be. For after all, this is Rome, and conversion to Christianity has been described as the single most important feature of nineteenth-century Pacific history.

Therefore, as well as analysing the place of clothing in conversion, *Clothing the Pacific* addresses the place of clothing in new encounters of this kind that are taking place in the midst of settler cultures and European cities rather than in remote geographical locations. As Pacific diaspora communities have become entrenched in Auckland, Wellington, Sydney and Los Angeles, the politics of dress has started to come to the fore. The 1990s witnessed the emergence of Pacific fashion activists and performance artists, as well as contemporary artists and designers in Auckland who are conscious of precisely the issues of globalization, identity and postcolonialism that are now of concern to anthropologists. Their work is often overtly critical of missionary and colonial impositions, and thus may be challenging to the status quo of the home country, while also raising important issues about the position of social anthropologists and other cultural commentators as the privileged interpreters of culture.

As a way of developing a distinctive Pacific fashion aesthetic that deliberately flouts Victorian prudishness, some Auckland-based Pacific fashion activists have drawn upon depictions of Pacific costumes in nineteenth-century studio photographs made for the colonial and missionary audience. Yet these photographs are of dubois historical accuracy. Studio portraits were typically highly stage managed. They involved getting islanders to act out savagery or perceptions of native sexuality for the camera in reconstructions of native dress. Other Pacific streetwear designers use modern American genres of T-shirt graphics to challenge Pacific expatriates who are in danger of forgetting their distinctive traditions. One of the aims of this book is to contrast these more recent critical reappraisals of the missionary legacy with other historical case studies, which show the place of clothing in the history of cross-cultural interaction in the Pacific.

I have chosen to begin with these anecdotes because they show some of the ways in which dress – and fabric – have been implicated in Europeans' and Pacific Islanders' responses or reactions to one another. But I have also chosen these examples because they all show how ways of using cloth, or ideas about 'native dress', can serve to *thwart* direct social engagement by establishing distance between people, or between people and a given object of worship. This seems to be worth emphasizing at the outset since much of the anthropological literature has dwelt upon the capacity of cloth to connect – whether this involves binding two people's wrists together in marriage, establishing alliance relations between intermarrying kin, or marking connections between the living, the dead and future generations, or the relationship between a ruler and his or her subjects.

So many of the facial expressions that index emotion are shared worldwide that people have often expected that gestures with clothing would also be mutually intelligible. Yet the history of cross-cultural encounters in the Pacific shows that attempts to communicate using only body language and clothing were often fraught with hazard and misunderstanding. In the early accounts of contact we find that both European voyagers and Pacific Islanders exchanged clothes, and made gestures with clothing to indicate respect, anticipating that these gestures would be understood. Yet the encounters were only partial, being skewed by misunderstanding. What gave rise to these misunderstandings, and how, much later on, clothing and clothing imagery have enabled people to achieve a self-conscious awareness of cultural similarity and difference, provides the main subject matter of this book.

Pacific Clothing

This book's title, *Clothing the Pacific*, might suggest that missionaries introduced clothing to the Pacific, or that they were alone in seeing clothing not merely as a form of protection but as a means of achieving religious conversion – of becoming Christian. If so it is misleading. For clothing was vital to religious and political vision in the Pacific prior to the arrival of the mission.

This was a region where the body provided the main locus of visual and material expression and of ritual-cum-political activity. A whole range of body arts, including diverse forms of clothing, wrappings and coverings – made from materials taken from trees, plants and birds feathers, and embellished with mud, tree sap and soot – were involved. These diverse complexes of body art and clothing are believed to have developed from a common Austronesian cultural substrate, and many 'traits', such as the use of barkcloth, or paper body wraps (made from the felted inner bark of the paper mulberry tree) in ceremonial practice as well as in everyday dress can be traced back to a shared founding 'technology' of dress. Thus body art and clothing – together with the imagery that clothing produced, and as opposed to sculpture, monumental art, or painting – provided the fountainhead for the stylistic development of sacred art and religious-cum-political practice in the region as a whole.

It is an intriguing accident of history that missionaries and Pacific Islanders shared a common preoccupation with clothing; but though this affinity seems to have been sensed, it was not explicitly recognized at the time. We know this because ceremonial practice involving indigenous clothing in the Western Pacific was not upset by missionary activity. It was only in central and Eastern Polynesia, where they found idols and spirit houses, that the missionaries, to borrow Hocart's phrase, 'recognised the religion that they had come to destroy' (Hocart 1952). One can only surmise that ideas regarding the hierarchy of the arts and the nature of images were so entrenched in the nineteenth century that dressmaking and fabric could only be perceived in the contexts of trade and industry, or domesticity and handicraft (Parker, 1983 and Williams in Henderson 1931).

We should not be surprised at this oversight. Similar preconceptions regarding the hierarchy of the arts remained influential to the development of twentieth-century modernist art and architecture – as well as to anthropology. In their polemic against decoration, modernist architects such as Loos went so far as to assert that surface ornament was not merely superficial but that it was a source of moral depravity and barbarism that must be stripped away for true purity of form to be achieved.

Modernist anthropology has also been accused of neglecting the particular aspects of art and presentational practice in order to formulate more abstract models of reality. By editing out the world of appearances and surface embellishment from the understanding of social interaction, modernist models reinforced the conviction that the driving forces of social reality were located beneath the shifting ephemera on the surface of life. Thus, although the exchange of food, clothing and body ornaments in the Pacific Islands inspired much of the most theoretically provocative thinking on person–object relations in twentieth-century anthropological literature, there was a marked tendency to shy away from discussing clothing *per se* by deploying other, more abstract analytical rubrics and models – such as 'The Gift' (see Lévi-Strauss 1966). In the social sciences, to be objectively serious about clothes came to mean studying how they *reflected* other domains of experience: such as social relations, religion or politics, that were somehow perceived as being bracketed off from the world of appearances (see Strathern 1990). In this book we implicitly reject this approach, following Anne Hollander's insight that 'it is in their specific aspect that clothes, like art, have their power. . . and offer a means of seeing' (Hollander 1993: xv). It is a necessarily exploratory approach: even today, we lack an alternative theory of form that would help us to understand the place of clothing and clothing imagery in the envisioning of social relations in the Pacific.

Some provocative ideas have been put forward on the place of body art in the development of social forms in the Pacific. Alfred Gell's two books *Wrapping in Images* and *Art and Agency*, built upon earlier work on Melanesian body art carried out by Marilyn and Andrew Strathern as well as by Michael O'Hanlon, to develop an 'anthropological theory of art' that would address the implications of the centrality of body art to the stylistic development of art and cultural forms in Polynesia. Earlier Marilyn and Andrew Strathern had argued that body decorations in Highland New Guinea were not like masks and costumes in other cultures: that is, they were not a disguise, a means of impersonating some other identity, or of representing some other person, animal or spirit, but a means of achieving 'the aggrandisement of their own' (Strathern and Strathern 1971: 171). A related perspective was developed by O'Hanlon, who argued that, among the Wahgi, ceremonial displays of body art were carefully scrutinized because they 'revealed the status of intragroup and intergroup morality' (O'Hanlon 1989: 124).

From these studies as well as his own research into Polynesian tattooing, Gell sketched out the outlines of an alternative anthropological theory of art and agency, which would be different from the kind of Western secular aesthetic theories that had developed through the contemplation of images and objects hung upon a wall or placed in an architectural setting. Art that amplified the agency of a person, he argued, placed it in the thick of social interaction, it implied some form of exchange. Other questions followed. All things not being equal, in a region famous for its political hierarchies, it was pertinent to ask whose body the imagery emanated from, what it *did,* and how other people stood in relation to it.

One of the aims of gathering together material for this book has been to collate material relating to clothing that was either influential to the development of Gell's theory, or which tackles some of the issues that he raised in a new way. While certain chapters are broadly supportive of the instrumental approach to adornment put forward by Gell, others draw attention to people's response to performances featuring clothing – to clothing imagery. Our argument is simply that in order to address the place of clothing in colonial and mission history it is essential to investigate not only what clothing did, but also how it was *perceived* by Europeans and Pacific Islanders – how the people wearing clothes were supposed and believed to look and how clothing was used to create images of sociality.

More generally this book aims to fill a gap in the existing literature on the Pacific. For it should be pointed out that the place of cloth and clothing in colonialism and mission history has been poorly explored in the literature on the Pacific, in contrast to work carried out in Africa and India. (See for example Bayly 1983; Cohn 1989; Comaroff 1996; Hendrickson 2000 on the relationship between colonialism and clothing in India and Africa).

A theme running throughout the book is whether missionary and colonial activity as well as European clothes altered the way in which clothing registered specific capacities for action and if so, how Pacific Islanders have responded to this. Polynesia was famous for its political hierarchies in which clothing played a significant part, being used to gesture respect, dominance or submission. Yet clothes, or chiefly insignia, did not simply symbolize political status, but were also believed to provide means of capturing and transmitting *mana*, the efficacy over life, health or death. In other words, clothes did not have the aloofness of symbols, but were held to be instrumental in *accomplishing* certain ends, of expanding a person's capacity for action.

Chiefs in Polynesia and certain parts of Melanesia were not simply expected to lead, but also to secure the fertility of the land and the health of the people. The materials from which chiefly dress was made, and/or the formality of patterns used to embellish the surface of their clothes, established an intimate, material connection between the chiefs and their gods, who were held to be the source of vegetation and growth (see Henry 1928). In central and eastern Polynesia many ritual sculptures were clothed, and major political and agrarian rites revolved around the removal and renewal of these clothes or wrappings (see Babadzan, Chapter 1 in this volume). Similar clothed sculptures have also been described in Western Polynesia (Hooper 2002) though it seems that the clothing of the chief in rites of installation assumed a more important role in the wake of missionary activity. 'A good chief is a good cloth, under whom the bananas will ripen and everything will be plentiful' as Hocart wrote with regards to Fiji (Hocart 1952).

Given that clothing seems to have contributed greatly to the respect of chiefly authority, it is hard to understand how chiefs could have been persuaded to forgo such capacities. Yet it is important to recognize that these complexes were not static. Instead, there was a tradition of usurpers trying to locate new external sources of agency and new kinds of ritual clothing (see Thomas 1995; and Addo in Chapter 6 of this volume). Research has established that pre-contact political rivalry between different island populations centred on attempts to wrest control of a given ritual complex, often involving clothing or body decorations or even gestures, from elsewhere (Harrison 1992, 1993). In Northern and Southern Vanuatu, where titles were not established by genealogical connection, status-grade alteration systems involved the acquisition of gestures and status-related styles of dress, permitting political rivalry on a smaller scale (Harrison 1993). If early on in the history of conversion some political rivals seem to have been attracted to European clothes because they offered access to new sources of agency, later usurpers seem to have wanted to reinforce their authority by finding clothes and images which would re-invoke beliefs in old capacities of agency (see Chapters 3, 4, and 6).

Missionary activity also threatened the balance of gender relations insofar as imposed Western notions of femininity circumscribed women's involvement in ritual and therefore their capacity for action (see Bolton, this volume, Chapter 5). Throughout the Pacific, ritual activity involved a gendered division of labour. The manufacture of ritual clothing allowed certain women to tap into sources of agency and an expanded time frame that extended their own capacity for action. Even today, Pacific women are likely to respond very sharply to suggestions that making barkcloth is merely craft by saying 'No! It is a sacred thing!' (personal communication, Suva, Fiji 1995).

Visual Analogy and Histories of Appropriation

A second theme concerns the changing nature of the nexus that was achieved between Pacific and European clothing. That is to say, we are concerned to investigate the nature of the connections that were made between foreign and indigenous clothes, for in many cases it seems that it was the discovery of *visual* relations between surface phenomena, what Gell refers to as the 'relations between relations', which would shape the nature of social interaction (Gell 1998). As in early accounts of contact, issues of interpretation and translation are at issue here. For in Central and Eastern Polynesia, where missionary activity brought about the collapse of barkcloth production, this did not contribute to the total cessation of the use of cloth and clothing in life-cycle rites. Instead it seems that relationship between indigenous and foreign Christian forms was discreetly made manifest in the ostensibly foreign-looking needlework (quilts, embroidery and appliqué) that women produced, through the choice and arrangement of motifs (see Chapter 4).

These composite forms are of interest because it has been very forcefully argued that the significance of cloth in the Pacific is that the authority of many Polynesian and Melanesian lineages – indeed, their distinctive identity as a people – lies in their control of certain vital cultural assets, such as chiefly insignia, religious rites, spells or other highly valued forms of clothing and pattern. Noting the efforts that people exert to withhold, or regain, these forms of tangible and intangible property from circuits of exchange, Weiner argued that this showed how cloth and cultural conservatism have been central to sustaining stable political hierarchies in the region (Weiner 1991). The value of this perspective is that it highlights the value that people attach to certain key ceremonial artefacts that link minds across the generations. However, the ways that cloth – and clothing practices – might be used to link minds cross-culturally, to bridge cultural difference, or to ally seemingly incompatible practices or patterns of thought, is never directly tackled as such.

Nevertheless, this is a pertinent question to address, for in the post-contact period, different cultural strands, including indigenous and introduced Christian religious practice, have given rise to a number of new composite clothing styles and practices, many of which have since become consolidated into established cultural forms. Christianity was accommodated and altered by means of a series of such mediating composite forms in many parts of Polynesia. In some instances European-style clothing was made from indigenous cloth, in other instances as in Tonga for example, body wraps made from matting, barkcloth or leaves were worn layered on top of Western-style garments. In Western Polynesia, where the indigenous production of barkcloth survived missionary and colonial activity, Christian icons and images of sovereignty and power such as the dove of peace, the design of a lace hem, the barrel of a musket, the British royal seal, and even Leonardo da Vinci's *Last Supper*, are either or printed or hung on top of lengths of barkcloth used in domestic displays (cf Toren 1999).

The overlay of imagery suggests that, rather than cloth and clothing being central to the transmission of a lineage's immutable identity, they are, so to speak, 'promiscuous', providing vehicles for associative thinking, thereby allowing people to achieve new and unprecedented combinations of both domestic and European religious forms. More important, they show how external forms such as clothing, surface decoration and detail may serve to articulate seemingly incompatible belief systems or cultural strands.

Several chapters in this book express criticism of studies of appropriation which suggest that novel things are simply slotted in to pre-existing social categories or contexts, and reject the implication that indigenous cultures typically deploy conservative strategies which serve to maintain a pre-existing social order rather than producing a new one (see, for example, Thomas, Chapter 3). As Thomas argues, the view that objects are merely passive, relative to a context of thought that is determinant, seems ill-suited to Pacific beliefs regarding the way that chiefly insignia and other forms of clothing may be invested with *mana*, or other capacities for action. By demonstrating analogical connections similar capacities could be invested in foreign cloth and clothes (see Küchler, Chapter 4). Thus, although the adoption of new clothing, which conformed to new ideals of modesty, was often seen as proof of conversion (Jolly 1991), we cannot assume that Pacific Islanders understood the adoption of European-style clothing in the same way as the missionaries did.

The question of visual analogy is pertinent to reassessing context-based models of appropriation. For a defining feature of many post-missionary clothing styles and related representational imagery is that they exhibit a characteristic 'doubleness' or parallelism, which emerges from the overlay of foreign and indigenous components of fabric, clothing or imagery. Both the layering clothes and the overlay of distinctive clothing-related practices or imagery, described in Chapters 1, 4, 6 and 7, suggest that European clothing was not subsumed within an overarching interpretative framework but that it was added to a pre-existing system of clothes, thereby making manifest a larger reality comprised of distinct levels or layers.

A question raised by some of the chapters is whether composite clothing forms and clothing-related practices have helped to accommodate and synthesize seemingly incompatible belief systems and religious practices, or whether they have helped to achieve a working coexistence of these incompatibilities. Some such 'working coexistence' may be found in Samoa, where different occasions, such as going to church or attending the village council, require men to show respect by either covering or uncovering their torsos (see Tcherkézoff, Chapter 2).

Chapters 3, 4 and 7 in this book indicate that Pacific Islanders' interpretation of foreign Christian clothes or Euro-American imagery has been driven by discovering visual or material correspondences that are particularly telling, or revelatory, because they make novel connections between substantially different practices of belief and usage. What these findings suggest is that tracing analogies is not confined to metaphor or to other figures of speech. Instead, many of the most innovative and surprising analogies are discovered through an optically driven, visual or material process that involves the overlay of imagery. Thus, our findings point to an inversion of accepted models of appropriation, for we suggest that the articulation of apparently superficial forms such as clothing, fabric or motifs may provoke new kinds of association which can help to shift, or turn, the contexts of people's thought.

Visual analogy, however, is concerned with establishing degrees, or proportions, of similarity between ostensibly dissimilar forms, and therefore it should be distinguished from the dissolution of difference through the achievement of a higher synthesis, or the hardening of oppositions into fixed dualities (see Stafford 1999). It therefore should be seen as occupying a range within a broader spectrum of possibilities. Nor should the effects of analogies be taken for granted, for of course it does not follow that old analogies continue to startle and amaze, just as the English language is littered with anachronistic figures of speech. Our point is rather that the need to articulate resemblance between indigenous and foreign forms may explain why styles of pattern, and the layering of clothes, played such an important part in the appropriation of Christianity – and produced such a startling diversity of clothing and imagery.

A second question is whether these techniques of analogy were provoked by contact with Europeans, and whether they are without precedent in the Pacific. It is intriguing to note that a combinatory, and revelatory, approach to expression is a recurrent feature of body art and ritual art in the Pacific. This suggests that the process of tracing material and visual analogies was not merely a post-contact phenomenon, but that pre-existing practices of revelation were extended to embrace novel European impositions. Readers familiar with Marilyn Strathern's work will know that the layering of male and female imagery is characteristic of much Melanesian art. She has shown that Melanesian body art and ceremonial exchange focuses on the revelation of gendered relations. Through the images presented at exchange, both things and people are revealed to be connected to their antecedents – whether to kin, or to different states of being, or to different, gendered sources of creativity. By means of such imagery, reality is presented as a multidimensional entity. Therefore, although a strict division of labour according to gender remains a characteristic feature of ritual activity throughout the Pacific, her work has shown us that we should be wary of seeing things like barkcloth, netbags and quilts, or clubs and spears, as unambiguously female or male objects (cf. Mackenzie 1991). Instead, objects do not have fixed identities, but are capable of revealing differently gendered attributes in different contexts as they are assembled or combined in different ways. Many of these observations also hold true for Polynesia, where female gifts may be assembled to form composite images that credit male ancestral creativity, though typically women's contributions are partially concealed, hidden within a more publicly ostentatious male form (Colchester 1999).

Clothing and the Body

It has previously been suggested that the relationship between cloth, ancestrality and renewal was made manifest through the *discourse* surrounding the manufacture of indigenous cloth in the Pacific (Weiner and Schneider 1989: 3). Yet the abridged and translated chapters of Alain Babadzan's book *Les Dépouilles des Dieux*, (lit. 'The Moulting of the Gods), which provides our first case study, shows that, during the period of contact, Tahitian ceremonies involving clothing created dress-related *images* that consecrated the objects involved by enabling people to perceive the connection between ancestrality and renewal.

Like many sculptures in the ancient world Tahitian cult images were dressed in clothing; or rather, they were dressed in shrouds – wrappings of barkcloth and feathers that were bound in place with sinnet rope. Babadzan's analysis of the ceremonies involving the renewal of these shrouds sheds light on the place of clothing in conversion because it shows how attitudes to clothing and agency may be implicated in deeply rooted beliefs regarding world-embracing or world-rejecting conceptions of resurrection, or renewal.

The subject of Babadzan's chapter are the clothed effigies from Tahiti, called staff-gods, or *to'o*, which were observed by early voyagers and members of the London Missionary Society (LMS) prior to the mass conversion of Tahiti in 1820. These effigies played a central part in the cult of the god 'Oro, which is believed to have spread from the island of Raiatea to Tahiti in the early to mid-eighteenth century, and to have contributed to the differentiation of chiefly lineages and to the consolidation of the Pomare chiefs' sovereignty (see Thomas 1995).

Central to the cult were the ceremonies called *pa'iatua* ('the wrapping of the gods') that involved the ritualized removal and renewal of the god's old coverings. Babadzan particularly draws attention to the removal and exchange of sacred red feathers that were taken from either the core of the principal effigy or its outer wrappings, and were distributed to the lesser effigies (that were gathered together for the ceremony) in exchange for new ones. The Boraboran chronicler Teuira Henry has shown that these sacred feathers were used to make new lappets for the highest-ranking chiefly insignia, the red-feather girdles called *maro ura* which were worn by the Pomare chiefs, thus establishing their intimate connection with the gods (Henry 1928).

The remaking of the *to'o* established an intimate connection not merely with the gods but also with original acts of creation. Babadzan draws attention to the analogy between funerary practices that required the periodic renewal of the deceased's wrappings and the *pa'iatua* rite. His surprising conclusion is that the god is displayed as a corpse, which rots, and produces bodily remains or moultings, and which is subsequently restored so as to reappear before the people, ever the same. As he argues, the presentation of the god as a corpse who after a given period of time, sheds layers of cloth-skin and feathers provides the key to understanding how these 'moultings' are rendered *tapu* (consecrated). Indeed, the presentation of the god as a corpse is only paradoxical from a European perspective, as it recalls the original act of creation in Polynesia. In Maohi creation mythology, plants and plant life are attributed to the transmutation of an original god's moultings of feathers and skin.

Chapter 2 approaches the relationship between clothing and the body by looking at practices of divestment in Tahiti from an entirely different angle, considering the relationship between clothing and nakedness. Serge Tcherkézoff's case study focuses upon early eyewitness accounts of contact between Europeans and Pacific Islanders that describe how young Tahitian women, who came to visit the voyagers on the beach, stripped themselves provocatively and offered their clothing to Cook, Bligh and the notorious mutineers of *The Bounty*. The puzzle he wishes to investigate is this: were early voyagers to the Pacific right to interpret these ceremonies of divestment as stripping, or did undressing represent something different to Europeans and Tahitians? This leads him to address the broader issue of whether nakedness is universally experienced and perceived. In answer, he argues that the reason that European voyagers interpreted such gestures as a form of provocation was also due to deeply entrenched attitudes to morality and dress, stemming from the opposition between clothing and nudity in Judaeo-Christian mythology.[1]

In interpreting the Tahitian perspective, Tcherkézoff demonstrates that both the perception and self-perception of nudity are dependent upon a sense of clothing, which is subject to cultural variation. Rather than focusing upon the place of clothing in the visual conventions of ceremonial performance, he develops his analysis of the Polynesian sense of clothing and nakedness through describing its place in ceremonial custom and manners. He describes several situations where the removal of clothing from the torso was required to gesture respect in the Pacific. Even the exposure of young girls' bodies in their entirety (which would seem to reveal the limits of the cultural variation of gestures with clothing) could, he argues, given the weight and significance attributed to clothing in Polynesian evocations of creativity, reveal a different attitude to sexuality and not mere coquettishness.

Chapters 3 and 4 move on to the question of conversion by examining how a distinctively Tahitian interpretation of Christianity was conveyed to Samoa and the Cook Islands through the medium of clothing. In Chapter 3, Nicholas Thomas describes how Tahitian missionaries, who were originally deposited in Samoa in the 1830s (several years prior to being joined by British members of the London Missionary Society), initially faced considerable resistance to their attempts to impose foreign ideas of modesty in Samoa, and were mocked by Samoans' deliberate gestures of self-exposure and provocation.

The puzzle Thomas wants to solve is this: how could Tahitians have persuaded Samoans to suddenly accept foreign notions of modesty by adopting foreign barkcloth ponchos called *tiputa*? In order to solve this problem, Thomas argues, one needs to find out what European clothes represented from a Pacific Islander perspective. Since in Polynesian ritual practice the quality and abundance of clothing was perceived as a means of securing health, efficacy and empowerment, it is possible to speculate that Samoans may have been attracted to Christianity by evidence of an effective external source of agency.

His argument pivots on a citation from the missionary John Williams, who noted that Samoans were 'impressed by the strength and the superiority of the Europeans with their ships and their full dress'. Yet, as Thomas points out, although this would seem to suggest that Samoans' perceptions of clothes were influenced by their cultural experience, we should be wary of assuming that Samoans simply slotted European clothes into pre-existing social practices. Instead he urges us to consider how clothing may be regarded as a kind of technology that 'recreated certain contexts anew'. Henceforth, Samoan codes of dress would become more heterogeneous, a matter of polarities, with indigenous clothing achieving its fullest expression at ceremonial occasions, and Christian clothing achieving its fullest expression in 'Sunday best', and a range of heterogeneous practices and codes of conduct and dress coming into play in between.

The story of the conversion of Samoa through the use of barkcloth ponchos is an example of the way in which a new and surprising cultural synthesis may emerge quite suddenly, being triggered by a single occasion, or by an unusual coincidence or a surprising set of events. Yet, there are other examples where cultural syntheses or correspondences emerge gradually, as links between European and Pacific clothing are perceived over time. The links may be the discovery of individuals (as appears to have been the case in Samoa), or they may be the result of a series of discoveries made by different people, some of which are then gradually taken up and spread across a region.

It is this second pattern that seems to be more appropriate to understanding the role of clothing in the history of conversion in the Cook Islands. As Susanne Küchler argues in Chapter 4, the process of converting the Cook Islands was not a singular event but rather an extended process that was effected and later consolidated by a *series* of mediatory forms of clothing – including Tahitian and Cook Island ponchos, European clothes, European-style clothing made from bark-cloth – which culminated in the emergence of appliqué quilts known as *tivaevae* or *tifaifai* (in the Cooks and Tahiti respectively).

Quilting (which is first mentioned in the travel literature *c.* 1850) was probably introduced to Hawaii by the wives of evangelists from New England along with other forms of needlework, and seems to have reached the Cook Islands via Tahiti considerably later, around the turn of the century. It may seem odd to have a chapter on quilts in a book about clothing. Yet *tivaevae* may, in fact, be regarded as fulfilling Polynesian conceptions of clothes. They are only prominently displayed (as a backdrop, or as a heap of cloth wealth) at 'traditional' occasions such as hair-cutting ceremonies that mark the child's coming of age, or marriage and burial rites where they are used to wrap the body, in conformity with the traditional use of *tapa*.

Outwardly, *tivaevae* would appear to involve a foreign visual idiom. The brilliantly coloured figurative images of foreign and indigenous flowers on so-called 'bird quilts' (*tivaevae manu*) seem very different to the abstract designs on Polynesian barkcloth. Yet, as Küchler shows, *tivaevae* are composite objects that are linked by a series of technical and visual scheme transfers – the use of layering, and of superimposition and complex rotational symmetry, which 'locks motifs into an intricate play of resemblance and difference' creating a dazzling effect of arrested movement – to the pre-existing ritual complexes of clothing in the region. Küchler suggests that today floral quilted 'clothing' offered as gifts that will ultimately be used as shrouds 'are deemed effective because they created visual resemblance and thus connected practices and modes of worship which hitherto may have been thought of as distinct and different'.

Clothing and Agency

So far, the case studies have indicated how Pacific Islanders invested cloth and clothing with their beliefs regarding the mediation of divine or ancestral agency. Chapters 5 and 6 argue, conversely, that a more contemporary perspective on the adoption of foreign clothes in the Pacific suggests that at a given point European attitudes to dress *did* have a profound impact, and affected local definitions of personhood. Both of these chapters describe cases where the adoption of European dress meant that people's capacity for action was curtailed in certain respects. By implication, one may infer how these changes would have had a knock-on effect for power relations more generally – just as one relates differently to someone carrying a loaded or unloaded gun.

In Vanuatu, introduced cloth and clothing, together with foreign attitudes to domesticity and femininity, changed the pre-existing system of social distinctions that was manifested through dress, and had a profound effect upon gender relations. Although gender had been central to social differentiation prior to the arrival of the mission, by far the most significant elaboration of body adornment had formerly related to inherited or achieved status. Hitherto, clothing and adornment marked the acquisition of both men's and women's ritual knowledge in a mass of different localized ritual systems. With the arrival of the mission these ways were challenged. For in Vanuatu, as in many other parts of the Pacific, dressmaking and other domestic chores prevented women from participating in status-alteration systems in many parts of the archipelago.

These changes are all the more significant today since homemade mission dresses, together with attendant notions of femininity, have started to be naturalized as 'customary practice', which is itself coming to be seen as vital to ni-Vanuatu national identity. Since the achieving of independence by Vanuatu in 1980, there has been an ongoing debate about the need to consolidate the nation through encouraging all ni-Vanuatu women to wear tent-like Mother Hubbard mission frocks. As a result, women living in urban areas, for example, who have begun to wear divided skirts to work, have become the victims of public censure. The debate about divided skirts, Bolton argues in Chapter 5, shows how dress continues to feature prominently in arguments about women's capacity for action.

In the Kingdom of Tonga, it would be much harder for such debates to take place because both Church and State, together with rites of reproduction, have achieved a far greater degree of consolidation through the layering of European-tailored and indigenous clothes. Yet European and Tongan clothes were not always worn together. Initially the adoption of foreign clothes and the rejection of aspects of indigenous clothing helped a faction of the Tongan nobility to establish a new monarchy. The appropriation of European ritual trappings of monarchy (combined with the imposition of sumptuary laws intended to boost the consumption of European clothing and to suppress barkcloth production) contributed to the consolidation of power in the hands of the first Tongan monarch, who was supported by the British Protectorate and legitimated by a modern constitution in 1875. It seems that by adopting a new religion and by tapping into foreign sources of agency (conveyed through the use of both European and Samoan ritual clothing) and at the same time briefly suppressing the indigenous production of Tongan barkcloth, which had formerly been associated with that of a rival Tongan lineage (the Tu'i Tonga's line), King George Tupou I managed to create a centralized monarchy (Gailey 1983; Kaeppler 2001: 222).

However, during the course of the twentieth century, the Tongan Christian State re-embraced and reasserted its cosmological authority through extending the use of waist mats. Whereas in many parts of the Pacific indigenous clothes were elevated into ceremonial garb that can only be worn on specific occasions, in Tonga, certain forms of Samoan ceremonial dress, such as waist-mats and waist ornaments became part of the everyday dress of civil servants and other Tongans, pervading everyday life. Moreover, barkcloth production has revived with a vengeance. Tonga is now the largest exporter of barkcloth in the region, *ngatu* (Tongan-style barkcloth) is exported to Fiji and Samoa, as well as to the kingdom's diaspora in Australia, New Zealand and the United States. Today *ngatu* is a composite artefact – a combination of Tongan and European imagery. Old abstract designs made from bound sennit, that can be seen in the late eighteenth-century samples held in museum collections, were gradually replaced by figurative motifs, which have been supplanted in turn by images of the Tongan Royal Seal, the principal cathedral and the approach to the Palace which is lined with Norfolk Pines (see Kooijman 1972: 330–40; Herda 2001: 153). According to Addo, the layering of foreign-derived and indigenous clothes, as well the ongoing outpouring of Tongan-style barkcloth, has helped to foster a code of conduct based on respect and duty that is believed to sustain 'the bounty of the crown'.

Over a third of people born in Tonga now migrate overseas to join substantial diaspora communities abroad. Here, the presence of Tongan corporate cultures based upon a pervasive culture of loyalty naturally contradicts the nineteenth-century assumption that the state is based on national unity and loyalty to territory (Spoonley 2001). Yet out-migration has also had an impact on clothing practices in Tonga. Addo describes how the import of British and American second-hand clothing for sale in the Tongatapu flea market is encouraging the emergence of 'youth styles' in the home islands. These youth styles are almost as exotic or unusual as 'Sunday best' was in the nineteenth century, for they remain confined to a tiny chink in time – Saturday morning, which is one of the few occasions when wearing culturally accepted clothing or school uniforms is not enforced.

Clothing in the Diaspora

In Auckland it is of course contemporary Pacific interpretations of nineteenth-century mission clothing which seems exotic, a quaint anachronism in the midst of modern life.Today, old-fashioned clothing, together with an old fashioned formality of bearing has started to be challenged by younger people from the Pacific community, whose work has begun to achieve public recognition and support. The final two chapters of this book address the emergence of a Pacific, dress-related youth culture, which indicates a profound shift in the nature and control of cultural forms in the Pacific Diaspora.

The reunion, in the suburbs of Auckland, of Pacific populations who diverged between 2000 and 800 years ago has been conducted in adverse circumstances of unemployment and a decline of welfare provision. And it is on the street where inter-Polynesian relations have often been strained, that most contemporary fashion is emerging. Although the social issues are local, much of this new street wear has been drawn from transnational networks. Second or third-generation New Zealanders of Samoan extraction have started to develop stronger connections with other members of the Samoan diaspora living in Los Angeles, and elsewhere, than with their homelands (Spoonley 2001). It is these connections that have led to the appropriation of hip-hop, as well as to genres of T-shirt graphics from Hawaii and the United States.

T-shirt art being produced in the suburbs of Auckland is of interest, as is all art on the frontier and in transition. For although T-shirts are the archetypal garment of modern American teenage rebellion, Samoan designers have used T-shirt graphics to voice distinctively Pacific criticisms of modern consumer culture. In fact the designs contain an admirable comic force, which springs from the contrast between the blandness of commercial iconography and a Pacific inlay, taken from ancestral ceremonies. But this contrast has a serious aspect because it highlights the essential conflict faced by Pacific youth in the diaspora, who are torn between the advantages and limitations offered by their own traditions or by foreign consumer culture.

Clothing the Pacific concludes with Chapter 8, which is a visual essay by Rosanna Raymond documenting her activities as a stylist and as a promoter of Pacific youth style and fashion, as well as her work with a group of artists, fashion activists and performers called The Pacific Sisters. The heterogeneous character of their work indicates the difficulty of slotting their work with clothing into pre-existing categories.

As one of the primary movers behind the organization of the fashion show at 'Pasifika', the annual event celebrating contemporary Pacific culture in New Zealand, Raymond has been a leading figure in the recent development of Pacific fashion. While insisting that Pacific clothing must be seen as being relevant to the present, and not confined to the world of museums and cultural festivals, she is also deeply critical of European-derived fashion aesthetics and the anxiety about personal appearance that they provoke. In order to develop her own Pacific clothing style – and to promote her own sense of 'girl power' – she has rejected mission clothing and has chosen to work with traditional Pacific materials such as coconut husks and barkcloth which she combines with jeans or videotape. One of the main tenets of The Pacific Sisters' ethos is that both traditional and modern clothing materials need to have their qualities presented through performance.

In a moving section of her chapter she describes one such performance staged by The Pacific Sisters. Dressed in a body stocking, Raymond respectfully 'exposes' herself before the crowd assembled in front of Government House in Apia, thereby revisiting some of the classic encounter stories that took place nearly two and a half centuries before. Hers is a candid account of a new kind of encounter that is taking place between Islanders and the descendants of Pacific migrants, which shows that the attempts to use clothing and appearance to change the terms of exchange are no less charged, and no less hazardous, than before.

Note

1. Here it may be noted in parenthesis that there is an interesting disparity between the verbal and visual descriptions of these encounters. For, in spite of their commitment to ancient Hebraic ideas of clothing and nakedness, Christian European visual culture had its origins in Mediterranean Classical traditions, which were devoted to the celebration of nakedness; and this classical ideal

may be strongly detected in the eighteenth-century drawings and prints (cf. Bernard Smith 1993).

References

Bayly, C.A. (1983), 'The Origins of Swadeshi (Home Industry): Cloth and Indian Society, 1700–1930', in Appadurai Arjun (1983), *The Social Life of Things: Commodities in Cultural Perspective*. Cambridge: Cambridge University Press.

Cohn, Bernard S. (1989), 'Cloth, Clothes, and Colonialism: India in the Nineteenth Century', in A. Weiner and J. Schneider (eds), *Cloth and Human Experience*. Washington DC: Smithsonian Institution Press.

Colchester, Chloë (1999), 'Barkcloth and Endogamous Reproduction in Natewa, Fiji Islands', University of London: Unpublished PhD Thesis.

Comaroff, Jean (1996), 'The Empire's Old Clothes', in D. Howes (ed), *Cross-cultural Consumption: Global Markets, Local Realities*. London: Routledge.

Eves, Richard (1996), 'Colonialism, Corporeality and Character: Methodist Missions and the Refashioning of Bodies in the Pacific', *History and Anthropology,* 10(1) 85–138.

Gailey, Christine Ward (1987), *From Kinship to Kingship: Gender, Hierarchy and State Formation in the Tongan Islands*. Austin: University of Texas Press.

Gunson, Neil (1978), *Messengers of Grace: Evangelical Missionaries in the South Seas*. Melbourne: Oxford University Press.

Harrison, Simon (1992), 'Ritual as Intellectual Property', *Man* (ns) 27(2).

—— (1993), 'The Commerce of Cultures in Melanesia', *Man* (ns) 28(1): 139–158.

Henry, Teuira (1928), *Ancient Tahiti*. Bernice P. Bishop Museum Bulletin 48. Honolulu: Bishop Museum.

Herda, Phyllis (2001), 'The Changing Texture of Textiles in Tonga', *Journal of the Polynesian Society* 108(2), 149–167, Auckland: University of Auckland.

Henderson, G.C. (1931), *The Journal of Thomas Williams, Missionary in Fiji 1840–1853*. Sydney: Angus and Robertson.

Hocart, Arthur Maurice (1952), *The Northern States of Fiji*. London: Royal Anthropological Institute.

Hollander, Anne (1993), *Seeing Through Clothes*. Berkeley: University of California Press.

Hooper, Stephen (2002), 'Memorial Images of Eastern Fiji: Materials, Metaphors and Meanings in A. Herle, N. Stanley, K. Stevenson and R.L. Welsch (eds) *Pacific Art: Persistence, Change and Meaning*. Honolulu: University of Hawaii Press.

Jolly, Margaret (1991), 'To Save the Girls for Brighter and Better Lives: Presbyterian Missionaries and Women in the South of Vanuatu 1848–1870.' *Journal of Pacific History* 26: 27–48.

Kaeppler, Adrienne (2001), '*Kie Hingoa*, Mats of Power, Rank, Prestige and History', *Journal of the Polynesian Society* 108(2), Auckland: University of Auckland.

Koestler, Arthur (1989 [1964]), *The Act of Creation*. London: Penguin Arkana.

Kooijman, Simon (1972), *Tapa in Polynesia*. Bernice P. Bishop Museum Bulletin 234. Honolulu.

Leota Ete, Jaki, Raymond, Rosanna and Kihara, Shigiyuki (2002), *Concerning the Politics of the Body: Pacific Fashions in New Zealand*. Wellington: Te Papa Museum ND.

Lévi-Strauss, Claude (1966), 'Introduction à l'Oeuvre de Marcel Mauss'. In Marcel Mauss, *Sociologie et Anthropologie*. Paris: Presses Universitaires de France.

Mackenzie, Maureen A. (1991), *Androgynous Objects, String Bags and Gender in New Guinea*. Melbourne: Harwood Academic Publishers.

O'Hanlon, Michael (1989), *Reading the Skin: Adornment, Display and Society Among the Wahgi*. London: British Museum Publications.

Parker, Roszika (1983), *The Subversive Stitch: Embroidery and the Making of the Feminine*. London: Women's Press.

Phillips, Ruth, B. (1998), *Trading Identities: The Souvenir in Native North American Art from the Northeast, 1700–1900*. Seattle: University of Washington Press.

Rutherford, N. (1996), *Shirley Baker and the King of Tonga*. Auckland: Pasifika Press.

Smith, Bernard (1992), *Imagining the Pacific in the Wake of the Cook Voyages*. Melbourne: Melbourne University Press.

Spoonley, P. (2001), 'Transnational Pacific Communities: Transforming the Politics of Place and Identity', in C. Macpherson, P. Spoonley, and M. Anae (eds), *Tangata o te Moana Nui: the Evolving Identities of Pacific Peoples in Aotearoa/New Zealand*. Palmerston North: Dunmore Press.

Stafford, Barbara (1999), *Visual Analogy: Consciousness as the Art of Connecting*. Cambridge MA: MIT Press.

Stevenson, Robert Louis (1979), *Dr Jekyll and Mr Hyde and Other Stories*. London: Penguin.

Strathern, Andrew and Strathern, Marilyn (1971) *Self Decoration in New Guinea*. London: Duckworth.

Strathern, Marilyn (1990), 'Artefacts of History: Events and the Interpretation of Images', in Jukka Siikala (ed.), *Culture and history in the Pacific*. Helsinki: Finnish Anthropological Society.

Thomas, Nicholas (1995), *Oceanic Art*. London: Thames & Hudson.

—— (1999), *Possessions Indigenous Art/Colonial Culture*. London: Thames & Hudson.

—— and Diane Losche (eds) (1999), *Double Vision: Art Histories and Colonial Histories in the Pacific*. Cambridge: Cambridge University Press.

Toren, Christina (1999), *Mind Materiality and History*. London: Routledge.

Weiner, Annette and Schneider, Jane (1989), *Cloth and Human Experience*, Washington: Smithsonian Institution Press.

—— (1992) *Inalienable Possessions: The Paradox of Keeping While Giving*. University of California Press.

Part I
Clothing the Body

–1–

The Gods Stripped Bare

Alain Babadzan

> The Indian fetish (I use the term advisedly to describe this lumpen and crudely fashioned block) as I was saying, the Indian fetish is in keeping with the artistic instinct of the people who made it. This instinct is non-existent, and as a result these objects bear no resemblance to a work of art, or to any living creature whatsoever.
>
> Edmond de Bovis (1855)

This chapter presents an anthropological analysis of the ritual symbolism of religious effigies from Tahiti and the Society Islands that are known as *to'o*. At the time when Europeans first made contact with these islands, toward the end of the eighteenth century, these objects played a central part in Tahitian religion, where they represented, the god 'Oro, the principal deity of the local pantheon.

Tahitian religion is without doubt one of the most poorly understood religions in Polynesia. All that we know is derived from a few sketchy eyewitness accounts made by voyagers and British missionaries; moreover, the latter's accounts are extensively marked by the prejudices of the period as well as by that of their profession. Analysing material that features such lacunas is a delicate exercise that relies in part upon drawing comparisons with other, better-known, Polynesian religious systems.[1]

When Europeans invaded Tahiti, soon to be followed by missionaries from the London Missionary Society in 1797, Tahitian religion had evolved into a cult system in which a principal deity presided over other subordinate gods, at the very same time as the political system was transforming itself into a system of sacred kingship. However, the mass conversion of Tahitians in 1820 would soon bring a halt to these internal changes, since it entailed the disappearance of traditional religious life and of the ceremonies that are described below. The effigies themselves are the only material evidence that remains. The methodological gamble that is attempted here, as in the larger work from which this text is taken,[2] is to make these dumb witnesses speak, by treating them as a path of privileged access that can lead us toward some understanding of what is at stake in ritual expression.

Although they are less well known by the museum-going public than either wooden or stone statues, *to'o* from Tahiti nevertheless represented principal deities in the local pantheon. During the period of contact and the decades thereafter, the Tahitian political system revolved around the possession of the effigy of 'Oro, and rival districts fought bitterly over them. For, by presiding over ceremonies of the investiture of chiefs, *to'o* attested to the paramount chief's genealogical relations with the principal deity.

To'o were central to the worship of 'Oro, however, and indeed to Tahitian religion more generally, because of a ceremony called *pa'iatua* that involved the renewal of the sacred cords and feathers of which the effigy was made. This chapter will outline the morphological properties of these objects, and analyse their symbolism and usage in the *pa'iatua* rite.

The *To'o*

To'o have practically no anthropomorphic features. They are composite objects, comprised of a long piece of wood, or *'aito*, of varying length (ranging between the size of a ruler to the height of a man) that is shaped like a staff or a club. The stick is entirely invisible because it is tightly bound with layers of plaited sennit cord. The bindings are made of plaited coconut fibre and may include many layers of *tapa* (barkcloth) wrappings. The whole thing is covered in different-coloured feathers, but mainly sacred red feathers (*'ura*) that are either arranged around the *to'o*'s exterior or in between the object's wooden armature and its wrappings. In sum, the object resembles a parcel or a mummy. One end of the *to'o* is larger than the other and bears roughly delineated facial features and rudimentary limbs woven from sennit cords (see Figure 1.1).

To'o are what were called 'feathered gods' by the first European visitors to the islands. A sense of their contempt for these things – de Bovis (1978 [1855]) speaks of 'swaddled blockheads' – emerges from their accounts. However, although European travellers felt that these objects were unfit to represent even pagan deities, it is clear that the indigenous population had made them recognize that the largest *to'o* were indeed the effigies of their principal gods.

A great number of these images existed, each owned by a family, a lineage, a clan, a district, and even a whole island. The images were generally kept in a *marae*, or ceremonial ground, belonging to the social order concerned. De Bovis' account is relevant here:

> The idol, or rather the great idol of the *maraë* belonged in principle to the king; it was his god. Each king owned one, and the size of the idol corresponded to the rank of the owner. The idol of a royal *maraë* was a simple piece of wood, but which, once wrapped in precious indigenous cloth and covered and crowned with special feathers looked like

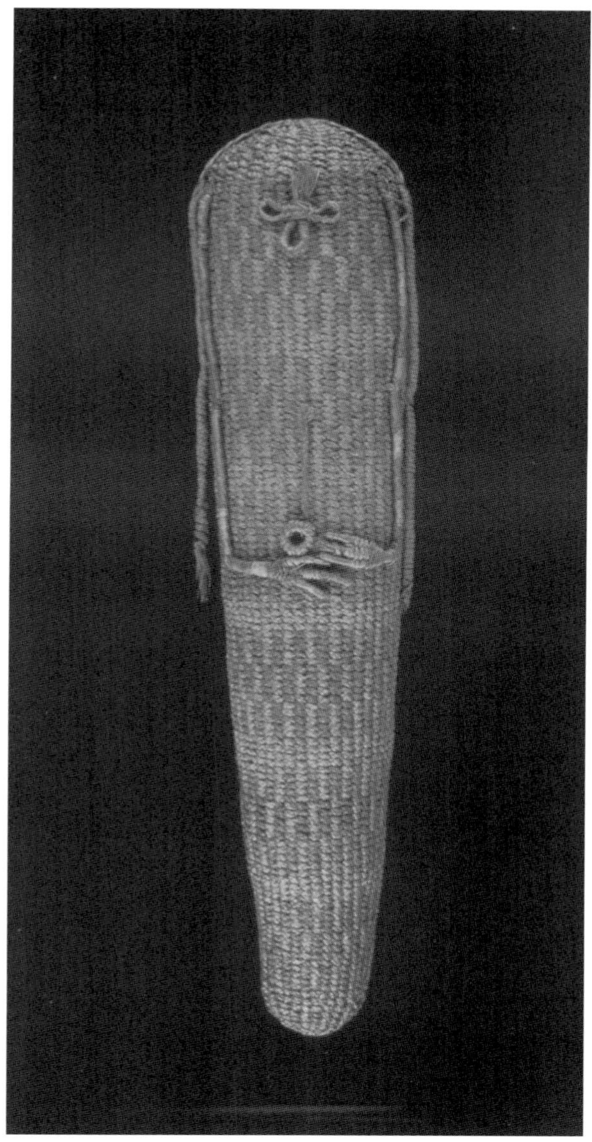

Figure 1.1 *To'o* figure (38 cm), Tahiti, © The British Museum (BM TAH 67).

a man wrapped up as a parcel. This 'parcel' could be more than two metres long [. . .] The idol belonging to a prince of secondary rank was shorter, even in his own *maraë*; being rarely four feet long. Those belonging to the nobles and the lesser chiefs were less than a metre and were rarely larger than two feet. Finally, the lower orders had pocket

> gods, which they kept in bamboo cases. They withdrew them to say their prayers, either at the edge of the *maraë*, or at home. (De Bovis 1978 [1855]: 53)

It is therefore probable that the majority of *to'o* were dedicated to particular gods, or to lineage or clan ancestors (and named after them), and that the hierarchy of their scale corresponded not only to the hierarchical ordering of the gods, but of the different social groups that held them. Rank determined the nature of men's relationship with their cult objects: each social unit possessed its own effigy, but the effigy was subordinate to others of greater importance and to the principal effigy of the 'national *marae*'. But as we shall see, not only matters of precedence were symbolized through the object's stylistic features.

All the *to'o* were reunited in the ritual of the *pa'iatua* where they were gathered around the principal *to'o*, the idol of the royal *marae*, the effigy of 'Oro. Nevertheless, it would be inaccurate to see *to'o* as being exclusively dedicated to the cult of 'Oro. For although it is beyond doubt that the ceremonies which were observed in Tahiti and in some of the Leeward Islands were cults in which the principal *to'o* represented 'Oro, there were nevertheless analogous ceremonies, using similar objects and an identical liturgy, that took place in neighbouring islands which were dedicated to other principal gods, not 'Oro.

According to Walsh and Biggs (1966), the Tahitian term *to'o* is derived from the proto-Polynesian *toko*, signifying pole, or staff. This meaning is given to the terms *to'o* or *toko* in most of the Polynesian languages though the words are sometimes translated as 'prop' or 'support'. Thus the name of the *to'o* describes both the form – a pole – and the object's function – that of a prop supporting the heavens. For *to'o* was also the term used to describe the pillars, or dividers, that kept the two worlds – the heavens and the earth – apart. In Polynesian mythologies these two worlds were conceived as the two sides of the original shell (Handy 1927: 121). In what follows we shall see how ritual places the *to'o* at the juncture between the human and the divine.

In Davies's Tahitian dictionary we find the following references: 'a length of wood forming the body of an idol, a pole for punting canoes', but also 'to impose a restriction'. *To'o* is also used to describe the man who leads a troupe of dancers, and the largest fruit in a bunch of bananas (Davies 1851). Let us note in passing that the term *to'o* also exists in Maori, where it likewise denotes similar-looking effigies in which the great gods of the pantheon became incarnate. These small objects were composed of sticks bound with cord, with a carved head protruding at one end (Handy 1927:124).

Davies' dictionary provides another reference, which highlights the important distinction between the staff of the *to'o* (which Davies curiously describes *as* the *to'o*) and the object's wrappings of cordage, feathers and *tapa*. According to him, the term *to'ounuhi* signifies 'the decayed *to'o* of a god taken out', which would

Figure 1.2 Tahitian mourner's dress, collected during Cook's second voyage, reproduced by kind permission of The British Museum (BM TAH78).

logically refer to the removal of a piece of spoiled wood from the effigy. The verb *unuhi*, according to him, denotes separation: to slip out; to retire or withdraw; to leave, like the soul after death; to extract, to draw from the scabbard like a sword or a spear, etc.; to faint, to fade away (Davies 1851).

This separation is also conceived as having certain affinities with death, which results in the separation of the soul (*varua*) from its corporeal envelope (*tino*). Words derived from the base term *unuhi* are specific on this point: *unuhiarei*: 'to be deceased or in the process of dying'; *unuhifarere*: 'to have departed, as in following death'; *unuhitauritia*: 'a sudden or instant death' (ibid).

Conversely, the *to'o* (in my understanding of the term, that is to say both the staff and its wrappings) is also called *urua* when the body of the *to'o* is wrapped up. It follows that the distinction between the dressed *to'o* (*urua*) from the undressed *to'o*, corresponds to the distinction between life and death: the verb *uru* and its derivatives (*urua* in the passive voice) is connected to the idea of spirit possession in most Polynesian languages (that of a priest or a sorcerer by a god, for example). The ritual of *pa'iatua* may therefore consist of the rite where the image becomes possessed, as the god inhabits its representation (see Figure 1.2).

A *to'o* without its wrappings is unthinkable: they are part and parcel of it. The loss of the wrappings only occurs in very particular situations: when the *to'o* is defiled by enemy warriors in the course of war (which will necessitate its reinvestment in new bindings and feathers at a *pa'iatua* rite); or when it is retired from ritual usage because of its decrepit physical condition (*to'ounuhi).* A *to'o* that had accidentally lost its wrappings would be perceived as an image lacking divine presence (*unuhi*), just as the spirit withdraws itself from the body after death.

Without its wrappings the *to'o* is just a piece of wood. Its wrappings are not simply an adjunct but a constitutive part of this object. There is, however, one particular instance where these wrappings are removed: the *pa'iatua* rite.

Pa'iatua: The Object on Stage

The *pa'iatua* ceremony is the Tahitian ritual with which we are most familiar, being practically the only rite to have been described. It was the principal Tahitian rite during the period of contact, and therefore merits analysis. The description of the rite is primarily provided by Teuira Henry's valuable rendition of the accounts given by 'Pomare II, Mahine' and the priests:

> The largest ceremony at the *marae* was the *pa'iatua* (the assembly and undressing of the gods), which took place at the national *marae* on certain occasions, such as the consecration of the sovereign, or his extended illness, or laying a foundation stone of a national *marae*, at prayers during a period of famine, and in the wake of a disaster. (Henry 1928: 157)

The opinion of de Moerenhout on the circumstances that called for the performance of the *pa'iatua* is somewhat different. According to him:

> A feast was celebrated every three months at the turn of each season. And it appeared that each feast was preceded by a ceremony whose purpose was hard to fathom, since the Indians did not provide one, saying only that it was the paa atoua, the renewal of the corpse's shell or the gods' coverings.' (Moerenhout 1837: I, 514–5)

This version is challenged by Oliver (1974: 112) who believes that Moerenhout confused the *pa'iatua* with certain other rites and has either exaggerated the importance, or indeed fabricated the existence, of a *mao'ohi* calendar divided into four seasons. Nevertheless, the *pa'iatua* was celebrated every three moons according to Ellis (Ellis 1829: II, 217).

The authors' translation of the word *pa'iatua* is not entirely correct. Literally, the term means 'the wrapping of the gods', from *pa'i*: wrapping, clothing and *atua*: god(s). As its name implies, the ceremony focuses on the wrapping of the gods, that is, on the ritualized removal of the gods' old coverings that are then replaced with new wrappings. This ceremony was so *tapu* (sacred, restricted) that, according to Henry, 'Only *tahu'a* [the priests] were permitted to witness the *pa'i-atua* and live' (Henry 1928:157). Here are the principal sequences.

Prior to the renewal of the effigy's wrappings, 'In preparing for the *pa'i-atua*, everything about the *marae* was renewed.' (Henry 1928: 157) This preliminary sequence, called the *vaere'a mara'e* consisted of the meticulous weeding of the site by the *ari'i* and people of highest rank. Grass and moss growing on the site were thrown in a ditch of rubbish along with the old *marae* ornaments, and 'they placed new strips of cloth and matting in the *unu* (carved boards), collecting all the old ones that the wind had spared and also the former coconut leaf *tapa'au* (images) from the priests' kneeling stones, which they threw into the pit' (Henry 1928: 159).

Once the *marae* was cleared and the decorations had been renewed, a nocturnal procession comprised of the priests and other effigies approached the *fare ia manaha*, the sacred platform on which the principal *to'o* was erected and where the ceremony was to be performed. This procession was led by someone Henry calls the 'high priest' who was the leader of the national *marae* priests as well as the guardian of its principal *to'o*. Other priests, bearing 'messenger or fetcher gods' (probably *ti'i*: the term *ti'i* means 'to fetch, to seek' in Tahitian) followed behind. These 'fetcher gods' were charged to call the gods to earth and to invite them to participate in the ceremony.

Once they had arrived in the *marae* the assistants were seated as the high priest undressed each of the fetcher gods in turn while singing the chant for 'sending forth the messengers'. The *ti'i* in question must therefore have also been wrapped in coverings of *tapa*, sennit cord and sacred feathers. It is possible that they were in fact *to'o*, but I am more inclined to think that they were *ti'i* considering that they were charged to seek the gods and that in her description of another part of the ceremony Henry specifically refers to *ti'i*.

Chanting and prayer continued all night, describing the dispatch of the messengers, their journey to the gods so as to convey them to the ceremony, followed by their return to earth to announce their arrival. We should note the importance attributed to this sequence, which requires the effigies' mediation and which emphasizes the necessity of the physical presence of the gods. For the gods did not always inhabit the effigies or the consecrated sites: their efficacy had to be captured through a series of operations (the imposition of *tapu*, the procedures of weeding and sending the messengers), each of which represented successive stages of the path that led from the humans to the gods. The many stages of the bidding ceremony had to be observed with respectful precision. Thus, the entire procedure served to emphasize the gulf that separated men from the gods, which could only be bridged by means of the most perilous procedures.

At dawn the high priest invites the assistants to fetch (*ti'i*) the gods: 'that we may get through the assembling of them before people come and die in their presence' (Henry 1928: 165). We must therefore move from the *marae* to the *fare ia manaha*. This building, located outside the ceremonial compound, was made to protect the mobile 'ark' (*fare atua*) of the *to'o*, the effigy of the tutelar god – that is, the god to whom the *marae* was dedicated and which greeted the gathering of effigies carried by the priests. The place probably served as the priests' quarters during the ceremony. Henry described it in the following manner:

> In the *fare ia manaha* the treasure and images of the *marae* were conserved. The leading tutelar god was represented by a wooden image called a *to'o* or by an image of reeds covered in feathers called *a hua manu*. The image was laid in a bed of *'ura* feathers made into *apa'a* which was placed within a little ark, set on a pedestal placed on a polished slab of stone in the corner of the house. Its head was turned towards the sea. Numerous smaller images of lesser gods that were attached to the person of the tutelar god were likewise wrapped in scented cloth and placed on shelves along the walls. On these same shelves were also placed the sacred cord of the god Tane, used together with the images for other purposes.' (Henry 1928: 154–5)

Here then are the gods gathered in their idol house, each intending to possess the effigy that is dedicated to him. A solemn procession will now take place from the *fare ia manaha* to the *marae* where a crucial sequence of the ceremony will occur.

The gathering of the priests and the bearers of the cult objects take their positions in the cortege according to strict rules of precedence. The high priest leads the way with the ark of the *to'o* followed by:

> [A]ll the fraternity , including those of social, ancestral and royal *marae* with their minor gods in their coverings; and as they advanced, they were joined by the doctors, canoe builders and fishermen, with their gods covered. Finally came the sorcerers with their fetchers in all their odd costumes placed upon a plank and carried upon a shoulder open to view.' (Henry 1928: 166)

Behind the *to'o* (encased in both its wrappings and its ark) came all the other simulacra, including, at the back of the procession, the effigies used by the sorcerers. Note that the hierarchy of the effigies is correlated strictly with that of their bearers, the representatives of various *marae*. Once the procession reached the *marae*, and the ark of the *to'o* had been placed in the *marae* court (*'ava'a*), the assistants found their place in the sacred enclosure or on the walls encircling the *marae*, according to their rank. At this point the primary sequence of the ritual took place. Here is Henry's account of it:

> When all were seated, the high priest opened the ark and took out the dreaded image, and as he uncovered it upon the mat, the others all uncovered theirs in unison . . . The minor gods then exposed, with their wrappers folded under them, remained in the hands of their owners, facing the *'ava'a* ready for presentation to the tutelar god . . . When the image of the tutelar god was revealed from the profusion of red and yellow feathers lying upon its many coverings on the mat within the *'ava'a* . . . Then followed the presentation of the minor gods by their owners in their proper turns, with offerings of new *'ura* amulets and loose feathers, which were given through the high priest to the tutelar god in exchange for some in his possession. This act was called *taritoara'a-atua* (the god's exchange) and was supposed to add new power from the greater god to the lesser ones. . . (F)inally the wrappings of all the images were changed for new ones brought for the occasion, upon which they were laid out exposed on the mat of the tutelary god, within the *'ava'a*. The former wrappers were kept for deposit in their own *marae*.
>
> Then were brought newly made, uninspired images of wood and stone, fully decked with feathers and sennit, to be consecrated by the high priest, who, as he received each one in turn in his hands, would address by name the god or goddess represented and say: "*Teie te to'o, teie te 'ura; te to'o 'ura fa'aau ia 'oe e te atua e! E u i ô, e mau i ô ta'u upu e.*" (Here is the image, here are the feathers; the image with feathers represent thee, O god! My invocation will enter over there; it will hold over there.) Thus inaugurated, they also exchanged feathers with the tutelary god, and were placed according to their rank in like manner with the others upon the mat. (Henry 1928: 166–8)

After several sacrifices and prayers the ceremony of unwrapping and exposing the gods drew to a close:

> While the minor idols were being wrapped up by their owners, the high priest in great awe covered and replaced the tutelar god in its ark, as it was supposed that no one could come into close contact with the image and live – hence the refusal of King Tû to allow Captain Cook and his companions into the ark containing the god 'Oro which they saw during the *pure-ari'i* (kings-prayer ceremony in North Tahiti). The discarded wrappings were carefully folded and placed in a cell for that purpose beneath a slab in the *`ava'a*, as they were too sacred to throw into the *tiri-a-pera* (Henry 1928: 168–9).

While the *to'o* will remain on the *marae* until the end of the ceremony, the other effigies are returned to the *fare ia manaha*. The *tapu* is raised, to the relief of the general population who have had to undergo strict sanctions punishable by death. Another long session of prayers takes place, involving animal sacrifice. This ceremony is also explicitly opened and closed, indicating that it is a distinct rite that is connected to the handling of the effigies. In sum, it is a means of bidding farewell to the gods, of enjoining them to return to their place in the universe, and of once again separating the dangerous co-mingling that the ritual had achieved.

Other sources provide more succinct descriptions of the ceremony. Moerenhout supplies the following description:

> The idols were withdrawn from their sanctuary (the shelter in which they were housed in the Marai) and were borne out in the open sun. They were stripped of their old coverings, and, after having been scrubbed and anointed with sacred oil, they were wrapped in new coverings and were replaced on the altar where they were offered prayers and sacrifices. (Moerenhout 1837: I, 515)

We should note that the wooden armature of the *to'o* undergoes specific treatments between being undressed and reclothed: exposure to the sun; cleaning; unction. Ellis's testimony adds more significant detail:

> Among the numerous ceremonies observed, the *paeatua* was one of the most conspicuous. On these occasions, the gods were all brought out of the temple, the sacred coverings removed, scented oils were applied to the images, and they were exposed to the sun. At these seasons, the parties who wished their emblems of deity to be impregnated with the essence of the gods, repaired to the ceremony with a number of red feathers, which they delivered to the officiating priest.
>
> The wooden idols being generally hollow, the feathers were deposited inside of the image, which was filled with them. Many idols, however, were solid pieces of wood, bound or covered with finely braided cinet, of the fibres of the coconut husk: to these the feathers were attached by small fibrous bands. In return for the feathers thus united with the god, the parties received two or three of the same kind, which had been deposited on a former festival in the inside of the wooden or inner fold of the cinet idol. These feathers were thought to possess all the properties of the images to which they had been attached, and a supernatural influence was supposed to be infused in them. They were carefully wound round with very fine cinet, the extremities alone being visible. When this was done, the new-made gods were placed before the larger images from which they had been taken; and, lest their detachment should induce the god to withhold his power, the priest addressed a prayer to the principal deities, requesting them to abode in the red feathers before him (Ellis 1829, II 205).

Another source appears to describe the central section of the *pa'iatua* ritual but makes no reference to any specific ritual context. It is taken from de Bovis' account of ceremonies in the *marae*.

> Whilst the high priest unwrapped the idol, the people outside the *marae* withdrew their idols from their boxes laying them respectfully on the soil or on a stone during the course of the prayers. If the *marae* in question were a royal enclosure, you would usually find it encircled by lesser *marae*, located at some distance, each belonging to princes or chiefs of lower rank. Here the goings on in the principal *marae* were aped with precision, in spite of the trees which obscured the view. I seem to remember that men were positioned so as to relay the words of the ceremony but I cannot be entirely sure.
>
> Once the orator had finished speaking (the speeches were generally fairly long) the idol was wrapped up anew and placed on the bearer's shoulders; then everybody put their gods back in their boxes. Depending upon their size the people carried them in their pockets or tucked under their arms, the scale of the idols corresponded to the rank of their owners. These portable gods were also displayed in people's homes when the owner wanted to make a prayer. When the principal idol had been carried away the ceremony drew to a close, unless the prince felt it necessary to make certain public political announcements. (De Bovis 1978: 60)

Thus de Bovis attests to the political hierarchy of images, while introducing the idea that these ceremonies could take place in many *marae*, not simply the national *marae*. Considerable emphasis was placed, however, on the simultaneous performance of identical ceremonies. This detail is significant, and I shall return to it later.

Ritual and the Object

Oliver was the first scholar to attempt an analysis of the *pa'iatua* in his overview of traditional Tahitian society. He presents two arguments. First, he points out that *to'o* needed to be periodically reconsecrated at the *pa'iatua*. The hypothesis is a little tautological, for even if this was the case, this does not explain why they require reconsecration in such a particular manner. His second argument is a functionalist one. He suggests that both verbal metaphor and ritual objects can be used to symbolize hierarchical social relations (Oliver 1974: 119).

Hierarchy is certainly a central theme of the *pa'iatua* rite but to see the exchange of feathers reductively, in terms of the interplay of social relations, is surely mistaken. The expressive nature of this ceremony begins where Oliver's analysis ends. For the *pa'iatua* calls into play not merely social relations, but the ideological principles underlying them, which are supposed to be of a metasocial nature, as if the ritual suggested that it was necessary to seek the principles governing hierarchy in the Netherworld. Oliver's analysis leaves many other questions unanswered.

Given that hierarchical relations must have been self-evident, why perform them in this manner? Why use these specific objects to symbolize social relations in this particular way? I shall approach the rite in a different way, by focusing upon the removal, distribution and renewal of the *to'o*'s wrappings.

The Removal of the Wrappings

If the wrappings are regarded as a veil or a screen, the removal of the *to'o*'s wrappings can be thought of as an act of exposure. The dialectic between seeing and veiling is reinforced by supernatural sanctions surrounding the revelation of the unveiled object: although something is suddenly revealed, one is forbidden to approach it, or to observe it closely.

If the undressing of the *to'o* really is an act of exposure, it follows that the function of the wrappings is not merely to cover, but to intercept sight. The wrappings exist to be removed, and conversely, to emphasize the process of covering up and concealing a *thing*.

The periodic revelation of the thing that is perceived to be a god further emphasizes the interplay between hiding and seeing. For however they perceive it, the thing is merely a rough piece of wood, not a carving. The refusal to reveal a representational carving, particularly of a human form, highlights the Tahitian tendency toward pure abstraction. The effect of unveiling is therefore to reveal the absence of a representational form. Polynesian creation chants also portray the god, or rather, the principle presiding over the creation of the universe and all things past and present, as an *absence*: for at the origin of all created things is the uncreated and at the origin of form is formlessness. Perhaps this is what the principal *to'o* reveals when it is undressed.

The Exchange of Feathers

Yet the ritual does not merely prompt such questions. The removal and exchange of feathers is also the means by which the principal god enters into physical contact with the assembled gathering of minor gods. Old red feathers – taken from either the core of the principal effigy or its outer wrappings, or both – are distributed to the lesser effigies in exchange for new ones. These are used in the *to'o*'s new wrappings. These new feathers will be distributed, in turn, after they have been in contact with the principal effigy for some time.

The exchange of feathers is manifestly unequal, for these objects only *appear* similar, but in fact are things of a different order. For the feathers presented to the high priest are natural things, while the distributed feathers are *mana*, objects that

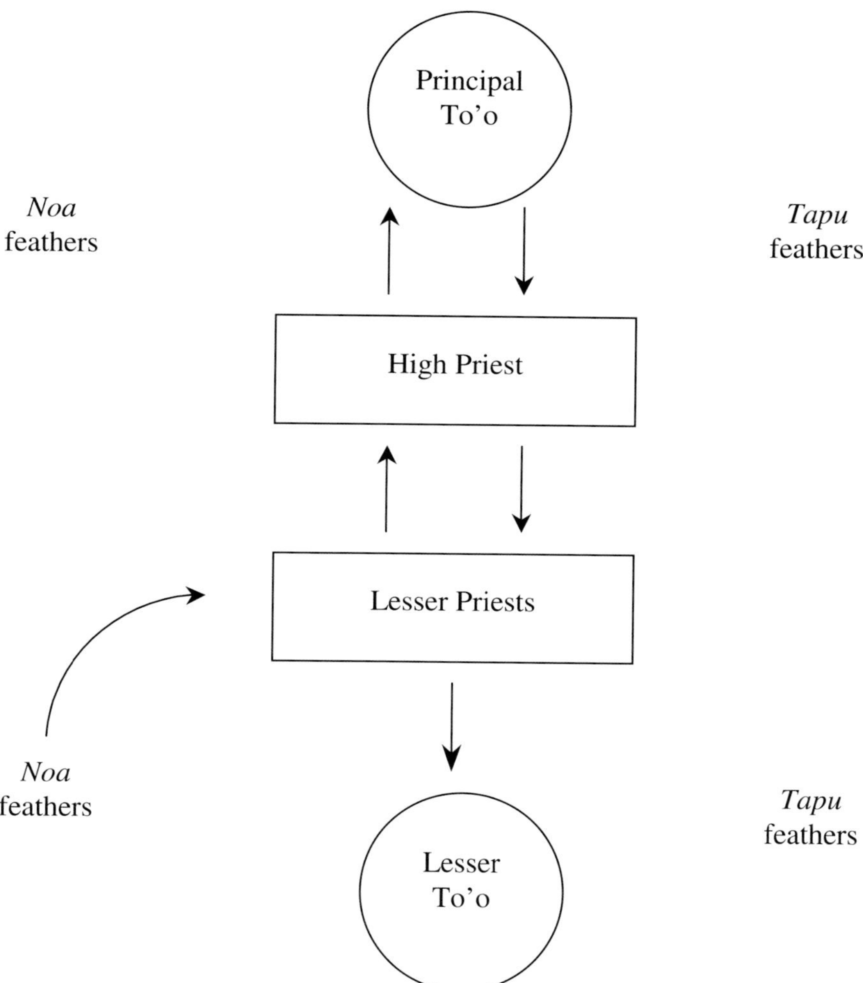

Figure 1.3 'The Exchange of Feathers', from Alain Babadzan, 1993, *Les Dépouilles des Dieux* reproduced by kind permission of the Éditions des Sciences de l'Homme.

have been consecrated by virtue of their contact with the *to'o* (see Figure 1.3). By coming into contact with the *to'o*, the feathers acquire a new quality. This change is not instantaneous, but the product of time: namely, the interval between each ritual ceremony when the object is withdrawn from display. Everything happens as if the contrast between the feathers' transience and the durability of the core were emphasized deliberately.

It is the time that the feathers spend in contact with the *to'o* that effects this transformation. What is the nature of this change? In contrast to the feathers presented by the priest that are *noa* (unrestricted), the feathers that are removed from the *to'o* have been rendered *tapu* (restricted, forbidden). The feathers of the principal *to'o* are no less than part of its body that are *tapu* by virtue of the *mana* of the effigy. It follows that they carry and transfer the objectified *mana* that they are supposed to have captured from the principal *to'o*.

The treatment of the feathers taken from the lesser *to'o* would seem to support the argument outlined above. For the faded feathers taken from the lesser effigies (and by extension from the principal effigy) are treated in a manner reserved for the most sacred things. The old feathers are kept in the *marae* (Henry 1928: 167) in a special ditch for putting 'rubbish' (that is, matter too sacred to be disposed of outside).

The transmission of feathers has an explicit aim: to carry and transfer the *mana* – or the primary god's substance – to the many lesser gods, providing physical proof of their connection. Thus the distribution of *mana* is clearly symbolized in such a fashion that it establishes a hierarchy of images.

Remains of the Dead and the Remains of the Gods

Once the exchange is over the high priest replaces the *to'o*'s coverings while the lesser priests do the same to their own *to'o*. This stage of the ceremony invites comparison with the *ari'i*'s funerary ceremonies. For although the renewal of the *to'o*'s wrappings would seem to be the logical sequel to the exchange of feathers, it also has some striking parallels with the treatment of corpses. A brief ethnographic note is necessary here. For although it appears that Polynesian funerary rites were very varied, all funerary rites involved wrapping the corpse in quantities of precious cloth that have been presented during the ceremony. According to the status of the deceased, these presents might include red feathers. I will simply supply some examples that are indispensable to my argument (see Figure 1.4).

Ellis describes the complex treatment of the corpses of people of high rank in Tahiti (Ellis 1853: I, 400–5).

> The practice of embalming appears to have been long familiar to them. . . Once the intestines brain etc. were removed, all moisture was extracted from the body, which was fixed in a sitting position during the day, and exposed to the sun, and when placed horizontally, at night was frequently turned over, that it might not remain long on the same side. The inside was then filled with cloth saturated with perfumed oils, which were also injected into other parts of the body, and carefully rubbed over the outside every day.

Figure 1.4 'Waheiadooa, Chief of Oheitepeha, lying in State', *c.* 1789 (etching by John Webber).

> This, together with the heat of the sun, and the dryness of the atmosphere, favoured the preservation of the body. (Ellis 1853: I, 402)

The corpse was likewise exposed:

> The corpse was usually clothed, except when visited by relatives or friends of the deceased. It was however for a long time carefully rubbed with aromatic oils each day. . . In some of the islands they dried the bodies and, wrapping them in numerous folds of cloth, suspended them also from the roofs of their dwelling-houses. (Ellis 1853: I, 404)

The analogy between the treatment of the corpse and the treatment of the *to'o* – which is likewise exposed to the sun, rubbed with scented oil before being recovered – is arresting. With reference to Mangareva, an island in the Gambier archipelago, Laval provides a description of the periodic renewal of the deceased's wrappings:

> After exposing the corpse to the air for five or six days (or at the very least three) of the funeral until decomposition had set in, they removed the outer skin of the body which came away easily. Then the corpse was wrapped in layers of papyrus, bound with coconut cords, without being embalmed. Instead of being anointed with the scented oil

> of the Paumotou, the mortal remains were dried in the air under a shelter. From time to time the corpse's wrappings were renewed. When the corpse was fully dried, he was taken within becoming the household's most treasured possession (Laval 1938: 21).

Laval supplies a further account of the initial funeral rites of a king. He tells us that, after the recitation of the royal genealogy:

> They removed the corpse's coverings in order to replace them. Not an attractive operation, given the corpse's state of decay. They changed its *maro* and belt. Though both things were sodden with pus the *taura-tao'i* in charge of the operation wound them about his head as one would a turban! Meanwhile the chiefs of the *rogorogo* made invocations to inaugurate the new belt. (Laval 1938: 352)

In Pukapuka (the Cook Islands) there is a striking resemblance between the parcel comprised of the corpse and its wrappings, and the *to'o* or 'bundle gods' of neighbouring islands:

> For internment the body was bundled in mats brought as death gifts; the other gifts were placed inside the bundle, and the whole secured with a large covering, such as the sail of the chief's canoe. Trussed with numerous traverse turns of sennit, the bundle was described by informants as "looking like a long cigar-shaped bundle (*sai*) of Samoan tobacco". (Beaglehole 1938: 302)

Finally in Tahiti:

> When any great personage such as a member of the Royal family or a chief among his subjects dies, the king and all the great folk comprised in that family assemble together. Each one carries a piece of new cloth to the deceased, and a plantain shoot. They all form into two lines and walk in a procession towards the deceased's house, preceded by two of his female relatives . . . As each mourner approaches the deceased in turn he places the piece of cloth he is carrying at the feet (of the corpse), and lays down the plantain sucker in front of the widow, who occupies a position near the deceased; and each one offers her some words of condolence (Corney 1915:262, cited in Oliver 1974: 490).

Moreover, Ellis describes an unusual mortuary rite, performed after the death of a chief, in which the use of plantain shoots recalls the presentation of feathers at the *pa'iatua* rite:

> In commencing the process of embalming, and placing the body on the bier, another priest was employed who was called the *tahua bure tiapapau*, literally 'corpse praying priest'. His office was singular; when the house for the dead had been erected, and the corpse placed upon the platform or bier, the priest ordered a hole to be dug in the earth

> floor, near the foot of the platform. Over this he prayed to the god, by whom it was supposed the spirit of the deceased had been required. The purport of his prayer was, that all the dead man's sins, and especially that for which his soul had been called to the *po*, might be deposited there, that they might not attach in any degree to the survivors, and the anger of the god might be appeased.
>
> The priest next addressed the corpse, usually saying . . . "With you let the guilt remain". The pillar or post of the corpse, as it was called, was then planted in a hole, perhaps designed as a personification of the deceased, to exist after his body had decayed – the earth was thrown over, as they supposed the guilt of the departed – and the hole filled up.
>
> At the conclusion of this part of the curious rite, the priest proceeded to the side of the corpse, and, taking a number of small slips of the *fa maia*, plantain leaf stalk, *fixed two or three pieces under each arm, placed a few in the breast*, and then, addressing the dead body, said, There are your family, there is your child, there is your wife, there is your father, there is your mother, Be satisfied yonder (that is, in the world of the spirits.) Look not towards those who are left in this world – the concluding parts of the ceremony were designed to impart contentment to the departed, and to prevent the spirit from repairing to his places of former resort. (Ellis 1853: I 402, emphasis added)

What should we retain from all this evidence, aside from the troubling analogy between the treatment of corpses and the treatment of *to'o* during the *pa'iatua* ceremony? In both cases we witness the treatment of a body, the body of a corpse or the body of a god. This body is conceived of in terms of its relation to a soul: the body is the vessel of the soul which quits the body (in the case of the corpse) or which returns periodically (in the case of the *to'o*). Both operations require the performance of certain procedures that are ritually sanctioned, and can only be undertaken by ritual specialists. In each case, emphasis is placed upon wrapping the body or the object with renewable and therefore perishable materials. The procedures are strictly analogous in both cases.

No doubt one could object that the liturgy differs in one important respect, insofar as the substance of the corpse is not distributed to the funerary participants. Certainly, the gift of feathers distinguishes one rite from the other. But it must also be remembered that the corpse will eventually produce highly valuable *relics*. Like the feathers, relics are the product of time – the skull is obtained during the second funerary rite, just as the feathers will be recovered during a subsequent ceremony. Once they are removed, both the feathers and the relics are carefully preserved. Each body part shares the same destiny, standing metonymically for the whole.

It is therefore quite legitimate to see the *to'o* as an inexhaustible source of relics. The feathers therefore have a twin function: at once they guarantee the efficacious transmission of *mana* and they are the god's relics. Nevertheless, the correlation between the two ceremonies carries one important consequence: if the *to'o* is treated like a corpse, and the feathers like relics, it follows that it is the divinity, and in certain cases, the paramount god, which is brought down to humanity. The incarnation of the god in the principal *to'o* paradoxically submits to the condition of the mortals a god, who is defined by the mythology as a pre-human and an immortal entity, insofar as the symbolism of the ritual is a reiteration of a funerary rite.

The ritual performance powerfully conveys the apparent contradiction that exists between the physical appearance of the object, and what it is supposed to personify and incarnate. These contradictions flow from the conflict between the object's role in representing the god on the one hand, and the treatment it undergoes which mimics the performance of funerary rites on the other. However, if the god is displayed as a corpse, it is a corpse unlike any other, for time works differently upon it. Of course it rots, and produces relics, but it is also restored and reappears before the people, ever the same. Its periodic appearance and disappearance constitutes an ongoing oscillating cycle. Thus, the *to'o* affirms the stability and continuity of an endless source of *mana*. Through ritual this source comes into contact with the affairs of men; it is captured.

Thus ritual effects a perilous contact: death is the sanction for any error, any transgression of *tapu*. The rite of the *pa'iatua* begins with the gathering of the gods and ends with their departure. Thus, the time of the rite corresponds to the moment of the god's physical presence in its effigy, when the mortals can gather around him and share his relics. But the ritual also brings together men and gods in another way. Being incarnated in an effigy that figures as a corpse, and that is treated as such, the divinity is also drawn toward the human realm, right to its very frontier: death. The god that men summon takes its place among them as a dead body wrapped in funerary clothing, thus having followed the path that normally leads men to ancestrality, in reverse (see Figure 1.5).

By becoming incarnate in human form, or rather ex-human form, the divinity approaches its creatures so much so that it assumes their form and perishable substance. At this stage, all the barriers between men and gods are abolished, save the one boundary between the world of the living (*ao*) and the world of the gods and the dead (*po*). This boundary also constitutes the point where the procedures by which the divinity has descended to humanity are reversed. As soon as the divinity assumes form, men beseech it to depart. It is at this point of inversion that men come into possession of the relics of the god, and ritually arrange the conditions of his re-departure, as they would do if he were a dead man.

In both operations, everything happens as if the contact between humanity and the divinity could only be achieved through the mediation of a ritual that occupies an interval in time and space. The object itself is a mediator, being neither human nor divine, neither concrete nor abstract, of neither the world of the living nor that of the dead. This mediation between the human and the divine is accomplished when the god and the object are both submitted to a process of metamorphosis. The

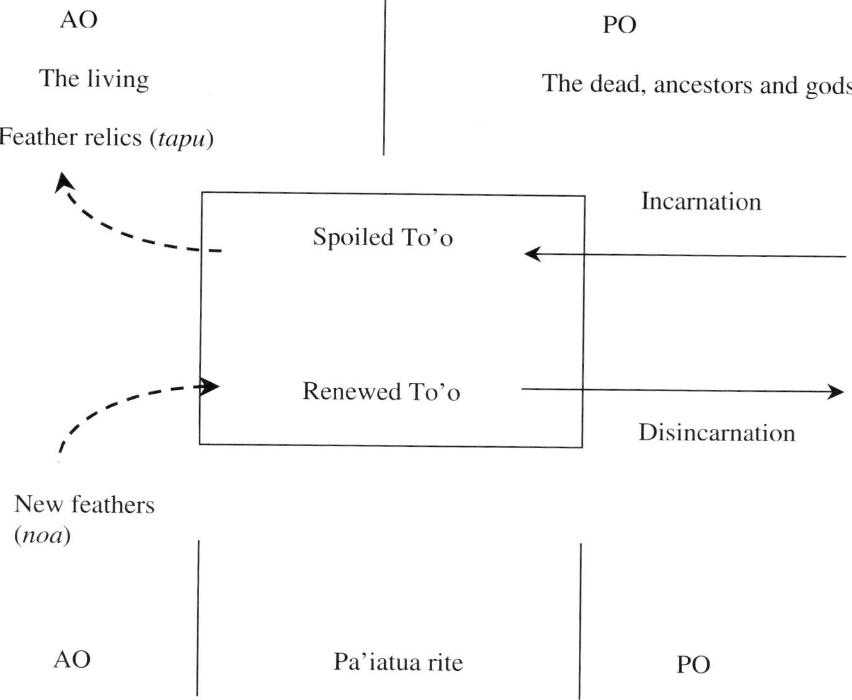

Figure 1.5 'The Dynamic of the *Pa'iatua* Rite and of the God's Circulation', from Alain Babadzan, 1993, *Les Dépouilles des Dieux* reproduced by kind permission of the Éditions des Sciences de l'Homme.

to'o's moulting is the effect of human ritual agency, and constitutes the point of inversion of the process, as well as the signal of the divinity's near departure.

What is the nature of this transformation? Tahitians used to mock the first missionaries when they came to pester them with their Christian theory of resurrection. One missionary thought to note two arguments presented to refute Christian dogma: 'They held that the dead might not return to life for two reasons: 1) though many have died none have revived, from which they infer that there is no resurrection; 2*) they are decomposed and therefore dirty, so they argue that it would be impossible*,' (Elder and Wilson, cited by Oliver 1974: 488, emphasis added).

Tahitians regarded the condition of the corporeal envelope as a condition of life – of the union between body and soul. The presence of the spirit depended upon the outward appearance of its receptacle. This held for the presence of a spirit in a god as well as for the soul in the body of a human. Once the corporeal receptacle began to rot, the spirit – rather than be annihilated – abandoned the corpse to follow its own journey.

In certain respects, funerary rites and the *pa'iatua* share a common objective: to deny the physical disappearance of the corpse and to use all possible means to secure the spirit's renewed habitation. Embalming, the exposure of corpses, the continuous renewal of the *to'o*'s coverings all play upon the common theme of degeneration and the final withdrawal of the spirit, which is likened to its final annihilation. Therefore, the renewal of the *to'o* may be seen as a form of *regeneration*, derived from the belief that the spirit would not inhabit a rotten body. The *to'o* only becomes the body of the god periodically, as each renewal of the coverings enables it to be reinvested with divine presence. Thus, the regular maintenance of the object is necessary to assure its repeated capture that results in the capture of *mana*.

But paradoxically, the renewal of the object also serves to assure that the divine presence will be kept at a distance. Indeed, the entire ceremony is performed as if it were in the power of man, and above all the priests, to gather and disperse the gods, to control and command them.

The *Pa'iatua* Rite and the Cult of 'Oro

We must now consider this rite in the context of the 'Oro cult, the cult of this 'dying god' being the central referent of the *pa'iatua*. All the written sources agree that this was the principal cult when Europeans discovered Tahiti. A few points must be raised here. Although not all *to'o* represented 'Oro they nevertheless featured in the ceremonies which were dedicated to him. All were subordinate to him; the smaller effigies derived their substance, their *mana*, from their relationship with him. Secondly, it should be pointed out that the renewal of coverings was in no way peculiar to Tahitian ritual nor to the cult of 'Oro. All Polynesia performed versions of these rites, particularly during the New Year festivals. The principal liturgical feature that distinguishes Tahitian ritual is the exchange of feathers between images.

Such political and historical variations notwithstanding, it is clear that we must study the 'Oro cult in order to deepen our understanding of the *pa'iatua* rite. For this was the dominant ritual complex in Tahiti during the period of contact. Indeed, the significance of the renewal and distribution of the *to'o*'s wrappings can only be appreciated through considering the myths relating to 'Oro. For in Tahiti this rite was specifically associated with the renewal of 'Oro, the god who fructifies and brings fertility, whose periodic return was associated with the return of the dead who bear abundance. The ongoing movement of the divinity between the world of the living and the world of the dead is clearly evoked in the ritual. The god is invited to inhabit his body and subsequently to leave it. Thus the ritual achieves firstly the renewal of 'Oro's body – a ceremonial act which evokes the changes that the presence of the god is supposed to have promoted on earth, i.e. the renewal of vegetation and alliances, and secondly, the transmission of divine *mana* which is symbolized through distributing 'Oro's remains to the lesser effigies.

As well as the analogy to funerary rites, the exchange of feathers refers to the mythological accounts of the god's gift of his substance to men. The red feathers were the major attribute of 'Oro. Tahitians attached the highest value to these sacred feathers, for according to certain myths of origin the gods were made of them. Teuira Henry writes, 'Red and yellow feathers were supposed to be the coverings of the gods in the beginning' (Henry 1928: 338 n13). The feathers of 'Oro's father, Ta'aroa, brought about the creation of the first plants, 'When Ta'aroa shook off his feathers, they became trees, plantain clusters, and verdure on the land.' (ibid.: 338)

In Polynesia, the mythic origin of plants is generally linked to the decomposition of a human corpse, or to the metamorphosis of certain parts of a god's body. For as she adds: 'When Ta'aroa shook off his feathers. . . they produced upon the earth; but after the sky was raised to its present position and mortality of human beings increased, many new plants sprang up from their bodies' (Henry 1928: 420).

The corruption and metamorphosis of corpses therefore lead to the creation of plants used for food, whereas Ta'aroa's feathers only produced wild plants. From the long list provided by Henry, I will mention three essential plants:

> The *uru* or bread tree (*Artocarpus incisa*) sprang from a man; the trunk was his body; the spreading branches were his limbs, and the leaves his hands; the fruit was his head, and within it was his tongue (the heart of the breadfruit).
>
> The *haari* or coconut (*Cocos nucifera*) sprang from the human head; the shell was the skull, the husk the hair, the ridges upon the shell were the cranium sutures, which meet at the bottom of the coconut. The veins of the skull are still traced all over the shell; the two small holes were the eyes; the big hole on the top of the coconut, from which sprouts the young plant, was the mouth; the tears became the water of the nut; and the brain became the *uto*, or spongy substance that grows and absorbs the water in the coconut and feeds the young sprout; the ribs became the leaves and the blood became the sap of the tree . . . Taro was produced from the feet of a man, and his lungs became its leaves. (ibid.: 420–1)

As the substance of 'Oro's body the red feathers of the *to'o* are not merely regarded as the symbols of vegetable growth, which recall Ta'aroa's feathers. As we have seen, they are regarded as relics, charged with *mana*, which are withdrawn from the fertile body of a corpse who returns periodically to earth. They symbolize the condition for fertility, being both the source and product of original creation or processes of growth, (*tupu*).

Like all relics, red feathers played an important role in securing individual protection.

> They value relics as much as some of us do, and put them to similar uses. They protect their owners from illness or enchantment . . . They provided help in times of need; for if they were faced with danger they would run to fetch them, believing that their presence might save them. When they were at sea and a storm was approaching they held them up to face the source of the storm and commanded it to recede either on account of these signs, or of the gods they represented. (Moerenhout 1837: I, 473–4)

This was why they were attached to the little fingers of the dying, to serve as a cure and a means of offering '*ura* feathers. For the dead were required to offer feathers to Ro'o-ma-Tane prior to being admitted to Rohutu-noa-noa. By themselves, feathers were not (had no) *mana*. They became (acquired) *mana* from being in contact with the *to'o*, through being offered to the gods, or metaphorically, through their departure and return from the world of the dead in the company of 'Oro. This imbalance in the exchange of feathers – between the *noa* fathers and the *tapu* feathers that are (charged with) *mana* – merits attention. *Each ceremony was a re-enactment of 'Oro's original gift of fertility and abundance.* It is an odd kind of 'gift' because the god is constrained – he is obliged to reciprocate by an initial offering.

In other versions of the myth, 'Oro descends to earth in search of a wife. Finally he is united with the beautiful Vairaumati. To his intense embarrassment she offers him gifts, for he has no earthly things to present in return. These gifts are evidently matrimonial prestations, made to seal the alliance between gods and mortals. 'Oro cannot remain empty handed. He is shamed. He is ashamed because he has made no gift to his companion. She has brought many things with her, but he, 'Oro, has nothing . . . He must offer his wife gifts that correspond to the ones he has received (Monchoisy 1888:177).

So 'Oro returns to *po* to find a return offering. His sister's children are changed into a boar and a sow, as are his two servants, whom his sisters had always regarded as brothers. 'Oro presents them to his wife with a bouquet of red feathers. In Moerenhout's version 'Oro's two brothers, Orotetefa and Ouretetefa, descend to earth in search of 'Oro and present themselves to the bride. 'One was changed into a sow, the other into an *ourou* or red feathers and on becoming themselves again, although the sow and the feathers remained, they approached the newly weds, bearing these gifts, (Moerenhout 1837: I, 487). In Ellis's version, the brothers were changed into a pig and a bunch of '*uru* (Ellis 1829: I, 314). The same night or the next night, according to the different versions, Vairaumati became pregnant, and the sow gave birth to five male piglets, the first-born being the 'sacred pig of the 'Arioi', named after 'Oro. According to the myth of 'Oro, red feathers and pigs are the two major symbols of fecundity, being the equivalent of the divinity. The matrimonial counter-prestation that 'Oro brings back from *po* is *his very substance*, his own flesh, the embodiment of fertility-cum-fecundity.

But the gift of fecundity is conceived of as a return gift. From the moment that 'Oro finds himself driven by his desire to unite himself with a mortal, he is made to submit to man's law, to the 'maussian' double obligation to receive and to give back in return. For, if 'Oro is literally summoned by the priests during the *pa'iatua*, it is because he is indebted to them. This debt derives from the prior gift of feathers during the previous ceremony. By offering ordinary *noa* feathers to the effigy of 'Oro, men oblige the god to make a return. As in the myth, 'Oro appears only to disappear once again into *po*. He will return with a pledge which symbolizes that earthly fecundity and new growth has been restored, symbolized by the feathers charged with *mana*.

Obliged to men, 'Oro is entirely under their control during the time of the ritual, trapped by the 'unequal reciprocity' similar to that which we encounter when looking at Polynesian first-fruit sacrifices. The logic of *do ut des* also applies to less ritualistic contexts, such as the one documented in Cook's Journal, 25 April 1774.

> When we were at Amsterdam (island of Tongatapu in Tonga) among other curiosities we collected some Parrot Feathers which were highly Valued by these people; When this came to be known in the isle all the Principal people of both Sex endeavour'd by every means in their power to Ingratiate themselves into our favour in order to obtain these Valuable Jewels by bring[ing] us Hogs and every other thing the Island produced, and generally for Tiyo (Friendship) but they always took care to let us know that Oroa (red Feathers) were to be part of the return we were to make. (Beaglehole 1961: 382–3)

The gift yields, it yields of necessity. The gift to the gods (and by extension to these demi-gods that were the first European navigators), necessitates a counter-gift, superior both in quality and quantity. The Tahitian language uses the term *'ara* to convey this. *'Ara* is to harass the gods, to coerce them with presents, in order to gain their support in war (Davies 1851: 31). This term can be found in other Polynesian languages where it denotes invocation, calling and the prayers that accompany sacrifice. Through the renewal of the *to'o*'s coverings where the god finds himself tightly bound by the priests, the god is coerced and fertility is brought under human control. As Valeri has noted with regard to the many instances where Hawaiian gods find themselves bound:

> There is more to wrapping than sacralisation, though. What is wrapped is also bound, constrained. Wrapping can thus represent man's control of the divine, his taming of it at the very moment it becomes divine in full, 'true' . . . The idea that wrapping involves control is also illustrated by the custom followed by noble women on certain ceremonial occasions, when they roll themselves up in skirts (pa'u) made of ten layers of cloth, each thirty metres long. (Valeri 1985: 301)

This last custom recalls the practice of greeting the members of this initiatic society devoted to the cult of 'Oro, the *'arioi*. Certain *'arioi* women would be wrapped up from head to foot by their hosts in vast yardages of *tapa*. After receiving this offering the chief of the *'arioi* would distribute the cloth among his companions (Henry 1928: 239). Let us note also that the ceremonies of royal investiture linked to the cult of 'Oro also involved wrapping the body of the *ari'i* in a sacred belt, the *maro 'ura*, made of feathers taken from 'Oro's effigy in the course of the *pa'iatua* rite (Henry 1928: 189–96).

If the *pai'atua* is indeed a ceremony in which mortals capture divine *mana* by obliging a return gift, if this exchange recalls the mythical sacrifice of 'Oro's body, then the *pa'iatua* may well be classed as a fertility rite. But such a formulation is possibly misleading. The 'Oro rite is not only a fertility rite. It is a means for the priests to renew their source of *mana*. For without *mana*, none of their activities could succeed (literally, in Polynesian terms: could *mana*), including the fertility rites they were charged to perform. For the primary objective of the rite was to renew all that grows and makes grow *(tupu),* in the broadest sense.

Of course, the renewal of vegetation provides a paradigm for the whole: it comes as no surprise to discover that the Tahitians performed the *pa'iatua* prior to the annual rituals, regulating the change of the seasons (Moerenhout 1837: I, 514–15; Ellis 1829: II, 217 'every three moons'). These had to be performed on a specific date. But the *pa'iatua* was also a moveable feast, that was staged 'for the consecration of a monarch, his extended illness, the laying of a foundation stone in the national *marae*, during periods of drought, and in the wake of disasters' (Henry 1928: 125). These were then not merely fertility rites, but rites for the restitution of order, and this was represented in these cultures as a regeneration, a mimesis of original creation. People turned to 'Oro, as a symbol of eternal renewal, in diverse situations: at the end of period of drought; to restore the conditions for life on earth; when investing new *ari'i*; to mark the end of an anarchic period of mourning; or when 'cloning' a new cult site, using a stone taken from the oldest *marae*.

It is surely a paradox that such an omnipotent figure – who is the origin of all re-production – should be evoked through funerary imagery. However, this contradiction is only apparent from a modern Western point of view. Many traditional cultures share this metaphysical foundation: believing that there is no point of rupture between growth and decomposition. In order to be the god of continuous renewal, 'Oro must trace the agrarian cycle, through a corresponding cycle of incarnation and dis-incarnation. And if 'Oro appears on earth as a (human) corpse, it is because this 'Polynesian Osiris', as Frazer perhaps would have said, can only be the emblem of fertility insofar as he is also the emblem of death, and is represented and handled as a dead body, for according to Tahitian mythology it is the decomposing substance of the dead that is the source of all vegetation.

Notes

1. A longer version of this chapter is published in *Les Dépouilles des Dieux, Essai sur la Religion Tahitienne à l'Epoque de la Découverte* pp 89–141. The original may be consulted for more extensive documentation and a wider range of photographs.
2. Such as Hawai'i after the work undertaken by Sahlins and Valeri.

References

Babadzan, Alain, (1993), *Les dépouilles des dieux: essai sur la religion tahitienne à l'époque de la découverte*. Paris: Editions de la Maison des Sciences de l'Homme.

Beaglehole, Ernest and Pearl Beaglehole, (1938), *Ethnology of Pukapuka*, Honolulu: Bernice P. Bishop Museum Bulletin 150.

Beaglehole, John, C. (ed.) (1961), *The Journals of Captain James Cook on His Voyages of Discovery, Vol 2*. Hakluyt Society, Cambridge: Cambridge University Press.

Bovis, Edmond de (1978 [1855]), *Etat de la société tahitienne à l'arrivée des Européens*, Papetee, Tahiti: Société des études océaniennes, Bulletin nº 4.

Corney, Bolton Glanville (ed) (1915), *The Quest and Occupation of Tahiti, Vol 2*, London: Cambridge University Press

Davies, John (1851), *A Tahitian and English Dictionary*. Tahiti: London Missionary Society's Press.

Ellis, William (1829), *Polynesian Researches*. London: H. Fischer.

—— (1853) *Polynesian Researches*. London H. Fischer.

Emory, Kenneth, P. (1947), *Tuamotuan Religious Structures and Ceremonies*. Honolulu: Bernice P. Bishop Museum Bulletin nº 116.

Handy, E.S. Craighill (1927), *Polynesian Religion*. Honolulu: Bernice P. Bishop Museum Bulletin nº 4.

Henry, Teuira (1928), *Ancient Tahiti*. Honolulu: Bernice P. Bishop Museum Bulletin nº 48.

Laval, Honoré (1938), *Mangareva: L'histoire ancienne d'un peuple Polynésian. Mémoires ethnographiques conservés aux Archives de la Congrégation des Sacré-Coeurs de Picpus*. Edited and annotated by A. Métraux and R. P. M. Desmedt, Paris: Braine-de-Comte.

Moerenhout, Jacques-Antoine (1837), *Voyage Aux Iles du Grand Océan*. Paris: Maisonneuve.

Monchoisy, Ormond (1888), *La Nouvelle Cythère*. Paris: G. Charpentier.

Oliver, Douglas L. (1974), *Ancient Tahitian Society*. Honolulu: University Press of Hawaii.

Valeri, Valerio (1985), *Kingship and Sacrifice: Ritual and Society in Ancient Hawaii*. Chicago: University of Chicago Press.

Walsh, David. S and Biggs, Bruce (1966), *Proto-Polynesian Word List 1*. Auckland: Te Reo Monographs.

–2–

On Cloth, Gifts and Nudity: Regarding Some European Misunderstandings During Early Encounters in Polynesia

Serge Tcherkézoff

In cross-cultural encounters it is the things one thinks one has recognized that often turn out to be most misleading. Analysts of encounters between Polynesians and Europeans will be familiar with the issues of power and religion that are involved here. Further studies have shown that differing conceptions of gender also need to be taken into account (Tcherkézoff 1993; Douaire-Marsaudon 1998; Suali'i-Sauni 2001). Recent studies have added that even sexuality can be a major source of misinterpretation (Anae et al. 2000; Tcherkézoff 2001a, 2001b). It is nonetheless a bit surprising to discover that one also needs to consider how a material item like cloth can give rise to serious misunderstandings.

From a European perspective, one's surprise stems from the fact that one is used to thinking of cloth as being subject to cultural variation only in terms of design or technique. The social functions of cloth seem to remain the same cross-culturally: cloth provides a supple material, it provides protection and, furthermore, depending upon its formal properties (the material, the colour, the way it is cut, etc.), it provides a marker of social status. Again, from a European perspective, cloth and clothing are conceptually opposed to nudity, since dressing is conceptually opposed to undressing. A body stripped of its clothing is said to be 'nude'. This basic opposition gives rise to all kinds of association that, given our deeply entrenched Judaeo-Christian tendency to see a direct link between nudity and sexuality, serve to oppose the clothed person who represents obedience to social rules with the unclothed person who represents 'savagery' and/or the open expression of sexual desire.

Given these rather limited notions it should not come as a surprise to discover that, from early contact to contemporary times, European reports and studies entirely misconstrued the significance that Polynesians afforded (and which in certain circumstances they continue to ascribe) to the social manipulation of cloth, to its presentation as a ceremonial gift of cloth or to simple acts of investiture and divestment. For by focusing upon its functional aspects of cloth (as form of protection), Europeans overlooked the fact that certain kinds of cloth could be objects of great value and, as such, sacred gifts. By focusing upon the design and the material of clothing as a sign of social status, Europeans overlooked the fact that dressing and undressing could be social acts whose significance owed little to either the kind of material or the style of clothing involved. Last but not least, the conceptual opposition between dressing and undressing trapped them into seeing nakedness as nudity and divestment as stripping in anticipation of sex.

We shall try to undo these misconstrued narratives with the study of some cases from Samoa and Tahiti, mostly taken from the period of first contact but also, touching upon contemporary examples. A study aiming at a pan-Polynesian comparison cannot limit itself to one side of Polynesia and must start with comparing cases at least from one Western and one Eastern island group; hence the choice of Samoa and Tahiti.

Cloth

Throughout Polynesia, 'cloth' was and is, in Western words, barkcloth (or *tapa*), made from beaten strips of bark, or woven material, made with dried strips of leaves or fibres (mats, called 'fine mats' in the literature, and cloaks, sometimes decorated or even covered with tiny feathers). In Eastern Polynesia, there were mostly cloaks, in Western Polynesia only fine mats. We shall consider the Western Polynesian fine mats, woven from dried and very fine strips of pandanus leaves, and the all-Polynesian *'tapa'*.

The term 'fine mats' used by early visitors to the Pacific is misleading. Although both fine mats and floor mats are made from varieties of pandanus, their uses are different. Fine mats are a kind of ceremonial dress that is wrapped around the body. Fine mats were once wrapped around sacred representations of the gods, such as sacred stones, or were spread on the floor to provide a seat of the gods.

The term '*tapa*' is originally derived from the Eastern Polynesian term *Kapa* but does not exist in Western Polynesia or, when found, it means only the border of a piece of cloth. But like the term taboo (derived from *tapu*) it became part of Europeans' Pacific vocabulary, and was used indiscriminately, irrespective of local usage. The term 'barkcloth', which was used only by English-speaking visitors, is another misleading translation that reduces *tapa* to 'cloth' or 'clothes'. This fails to convey how, throughout Polynesia, the bark (which was often painted) served to wrap people of rank as well as other ritual objects (see Babadzan, previous chapter, and 1993) or, in Western Polynesia, was placed on top of a pile of other ceremonial gifts, completing a prestation (as in Tikopia, Lau, Samoa, etc.).

Other forms of dress, such as leaves tied around the waist, were never presented as gifts, and although introduced cotton fabrics have come to be used either as a substitute for *tapa* in many parts of Eastern Polynesia (see Küchler in Chapter 4 of this volume) and in Uvea and Futuna, this is not the case in Samoa, where people make a clear-cut distinction between fine mats, *ie toga,* and imported fabrics and clothes. The variable patterns in the continuity and discontinuity of indigenous-cloth usage in Polynesia are arresting. Samoan families only use fine mats as gifts; *tapa* is no longer used. In neighbouring Tonga and Fiji however, both *tapa* and mats are used in abundance. In Eastern Polynesia, where *tapa* and feather cloaks were once the primary gift objects used in ritual exchange, their usage ceased in the nineteenth century (Babadzan, Küchler this volume; Valeri 1985).

In Samoa and elsewhere in Polynesia the only garments to have a purely functional role were leaf skirts. They protected the midriff and concealed it; this obligation predated missionary arrival and was not the result of Christian puritanism.[1] Leaf skirts do not dissolve in water while *tapa* disintegrates if it gets wet, a fact that explains the extraordinary demand for European fabrics since early contact. The functional leaf skirt was only worn outdoors, for in Samoa, formal dress is largely worn inside the house; in common with Polynesian tradition, the house interior is still largely regarded as a formal public space, not as a place of intimacy (Tcherkézoff 1997a). Once this formal dress worn inside was *tapa*; today it is a length of spotless, vibrantly coloured printed cotton or, for very formal occasions (Church or political meetings), a dark fabric without any printed patterns.

In fact, there are no Polynesian words meaning 'cloth', 'fabric' or 'garment'. In Samoa, the word fabric is denoted by the word *ie* (from the Samoan term for the kind of pandanus used for fine mats) followed by a secondary term. The word for clothes is *ofu*, which is also followed by a second, specifying term. This word conveys the idea of wrapping, and it can also be used to describe the wrapping of food for example. In this case the secondary term will specify whether the clothes are a pair of trousers or a shirt. What *tapa* and fine mats shared in common then, was not so much that they were kinds of cloth as that both of these materials were made from plants that were seen as being integral to the group's identity. Both pandanus and paper mulberry were/are grown close to the house, rather than further afield in the plantations. In Samoa, the bark of the mulberry was beaten and then printed with designs using carved wooden boards. Fine mats showed – and still show – how lineages became interwoven, while their feather borders were once an indication of the rank of the family. (Nowadays, they tend to be alike in all cases.) In what follows, the term 'cloth' will be restricted to the sacred cloths that could serve as a sacred gift or in ritual manipulation: *tapa* and fine mats, but not cotton fabrics or leaf and fibre skirts.

Ceremonial Gifts of Cloth, and Manipulation of Cloth as a Ritual Act

A number of different cultures, apart from Polynesian ones, have based the acquisition of power and prestige on the act of giving. Anyone who has given a great deal may at any point activate the network of connections made up of all those people who have been on the receiving end of a gift. By giving constantly one accumulates relationships.[2] In Polynesia, two broad categories of gifts were, and indeed remain, prominent: food and (sacred) cloth. Both items are ceremonially prepared and formally presented. Food is presented wrapped in leaves. Cloth is initially presented rolled up and is then spread out in front of the recipients (and then refolded or divided and cut up, as the case may be). It is important to note that cloth and food are presented in tandem; somehow each plays its own and necessary part. In what follows we shall only cover the part played by cloth.

It is mandatory to give cloth in the Pacific. Although the way in which cloth is presented may suggest it is a gift that the giver was in no way obliged to make, everyone present is well aware of the truth, which is clear to the outside observer as well. In contemporary Samoa, if a household does not make any contributions to ceremonies involving the extended family or village (for births, marriages, funerals, the consecration of a house or a church, the installation of a new family or village leader, etc.) this is taken as a sign of their withdrawal from the family or village circle. The threat is actually an eviction order. Here lies the answer to the apparent enigma of the obligation to give that puzzled Marcel Mauss, the founder of the French school of social and cultural anthropology, and which led him to publish his famous essay, *The Gift (Essai sur le Don)*, in 1925. In his essay Mauss showed that a common feature of these practices was the 'sacred' nature of the objects presented. Here the term sacredness should be interpreted in the Maussian-Durkheimian sense as the object that symbolizes the larger group, be it society as a whole or one of its sub-groups. Only cloth of this kind was, or is, an object of gift exchange in Polynesia. Fine mats or *tapa* are never owned by an individual (while previously leaf skirts and now printed fabric are); they always represent the identity of a group.

The first example discussed by Mauss in the opening chapter of *The Gift* relates to Samoa. Quoting several missionary sources, Mauss noted that gifts could be of two kinds in Samoa: food and household implements on the one hand, and 'emblazoned mats' (mats bearing the history and emblem of the clan or extended family, its device) on the other. Quite remarkably, Mauss immediately had the intuition that only the second kind of gifts, the mats, were relevant to what he was looking for, since those mats were symbols of a group (a family, clan, or other), whereas the objects in the other category seemed to tend to be attached to an individual. This enabled him to link the Samoan example to other instances in which the objects given had the same character of 'totality'; that is, in which they symbolized a social unit (such as the case of the Maori sacred gifts *taonga*, Tapsell 1997).

Samoan mats are clearly symbolic of a group (a family name or 'title') and never of an individual. Conversely, all of the other ceremonial goods, which are not in circulation for as long, or do not circulate at all (since they are only given once), do not carry the history of a group inscribed on them. They may include pigs, fish, some tools, or domestic materials. Nowadays, these gifts may include very specific tinned foods, as well as paper money. But an old mat is a known and a renowned object. Even if it is kept far from its place of origin, it retains the memory of the family that wove it and gave it away for the first time. It carries with it the genealogy of that family. Nothing of the sort may be said of a pig, a basket of fish or a banknote. Finally, a mat can be used to pay for anything and everything, including the ceremonial gifts required for a marriage, a funeral, etc., but also the gift given to the carpenter who built a house, the craftsman who made a boat. This is as true today in Samoa as it was yesterday.

As a fine mat carries the idea of the permanence and history of a whole social group, one should not be surprised that such mats retain the power to give life. Here again, we come back to Mauss who had stressed in *The Gift* that those specific objects of gift exchange were at the same time a 'property owned' by the givers' group and a general 'talisman', efficient for everyone because of 'magical' properties.

Indeed, in Samoa, one can accomplish miracles with mats of this sort. According to the legends, such miracles can be acts of curing, returning someone to life, victory at war, and so on. One very tangible miracle can still be observed today. Mats provide sanctuary. A person, representing a group that has committed a murder or a serious insult, can save his life by wrapping himself in a mat. To this ritual act are linked numerous legends about the first fine mat that saved the life of a Samoan held prisoner by Tongans. Until the 1950s, a mat or a length of *tapa* could be used to recover the soul, if a person had been lost at sea for example, thus allowing funeral ceremonies to take place. In such cases a fine mat or a *tapa* was spread out near the sea or on the place of battle. The first insect to crawl on it would be said to represent the will of the soul of the dead to come to a resting place. Some legends also mention bones that, wrapped in *tapa* or mats, have come back to life. Rituals have the same effect (according to accounts from the 1960s). If descendants are bothered too often by the soul of a dead person, they dig up the bones, wash them and wrap them up again in a ceremonial cloth. In the neighbouring Tokelau culture, early observers found that an altar for invoking a divinity took the form of an 'upright stone wrapped in fine mats' (Huntsman and Hooper 1996: 146). In Hawaii and Tahiti, *tapa*s wrapped around images of the gods played very much the same role (Valeri 1985; Babadzan Chapter 1, this volume and 1993).

Fine mats and *tapa* were, and are, used in Polynesian ritual as efficient objects, meaning that they may create or reveal the presence of the sacred in a given place. Elsewhere this function may be fulfilled by an animal: pigs in Melanesia; sacred cows in East Africa and India; copper objects on the west coast of North America, etc. In Polynesia, it was and is 'cloth'. A good summary is provided by an example from Lau (far Eastern Fiji, of Polynesian culture):

> In the Lau islands, the symbolic function of cloth as a conduit between men and the gods is important and more visible than in other Oceanic archipelagos [. . .] the investiture of a chief, for example is conceived of as a funerary rite. The man dies to be reborn as a god. In order to achieve this he is symbolically set apart behind a screen of *tapa* for four days, the time it takes for the spirits [gods and ancestors] which inhabit the *tapa* to take possession of him and cause his rebirth as a chief. The cloth that serves to capture the spirits is called ' the cloth of the earth'. [. . .] Thus in Fiji *tapa* is a path to be walked upon or a shelter held aloft by two rows of women with their arms raised; it protects the path of access to the status of becoming a chief. This path metaphorically served to convey the breath of the gods and the ancestors which came to meet the living: a roll of white *tapa*, placed in a temple (*bure kalou*) considered to be the spirit house, was the vessel or the receptacle of the spirits. The end of the cloth is left hanging. By taking hold of the end of the cloth, the priest whom visitors had come to consult could become possessed with a specific spirit (Bataille-Benguigui 1997: 181–4).

Cloth and Rites of Wrapping at Encounters

In early cross-cultural encounters what Europeans call 'cloth' played a prominent and instant role in the interaction between Europeans and Polynesians. Guns and metal tools were also important, and served to administer both physical and cultural shocks. Both sides perpetrated extremely violent acts: when Polynesians attempted to appropriate these guns and tools, Europeans responded by avenging what they perceived to be acts of theft. Many fights would ensue until, in the nineteenth century, guns and tools became common in the islands and objects of trade. In contrast to that situation and despite the considerable misunderstandings involved, cloth became instantly an instrument of peaceful interaction. By coincidence, covering the body in layers of cloth was a common sign of status. In the case of the Polynesians, these layers consisted of *tapa* and mats; in the case of the Europeans, the layers were the shirt, waistcoat, jacket and topcoat that distinguished the captain from his crew. This was a point of connection. The Polynesians recognized the captains, and the Europeans recognized the chiefs, whose bodies were sometimes entirely covered with mats and barkcloth, whereas their followers were only lightly dressed, and were often bare-chested. (We will discuss the logic behind this below.)

A further coincidence was that the Europeans had brought lengths of cloth to barter, together with other trinkets such as glass beads and mirrors, and also knives and axes. The fabric was often a vivid red or blue, since the Europeans' idea was to attract the native population by the colour and dazzle of their wares. In this respect, glass beads and coloured cloth served a common object. Of course, the Europeans did not realize that they had reached a civilization where the established practice for initiating contact between strangers was to make a presentation of cloth to wrap around the body of the visitor. For instance, in Samoan practice, when a traveller arrives from another village, territory or island, he must offer his 'service' (*tautua*) and present food, or today money. He presents himself as someone who is ready to serve the local chief. In return he is presented with a fine mat, or money, or elsewhere (as in Tonga) with a gift of *tapa*. Such reciprocity plays on two levels. For his part the host indicates that he considers the incoming stranger is 'superior' (*malo*) by presenting him with his most precious valuables. But the act of presenting cloth is also a means of enveloping and thereby incorporating the stranger. For as a stranger, the new arrival must be incorporated, and whatever sacred powers he possesses must be domesticated and subsumed.

As other studies have indicated (Sahlins 1985a, 1985b; Valeri 1985; Babadzan 1993) Polynesian ritual played upon the duality of the exterior world, that was wild, nocturnal but vital, since it provided the source of life; and the interior, domestic and diurnal world of light. Yet the existence of this diurnal world depended upon the degree to which one had domesticated the source of light and life. Precisely, the primary attribute of Polynesian cloth is that it enables people to capture, constrain and release the sacred through procedures of uncovering and recovering. These actions served to obscure the source of life and at the same time they manifested its effects. One cannot stare at the sun – just as in the past one could not stare at a sacred chief – for fear of burning ones eyes. But there had to be a means for this source of light to be made manifest on earth. This is why cloth is so often conceived by Polynesians as being 'white' and 'luminous' (in Samoan: *mea sina*).

In Polynesia, cloth enabled the invisible bodies of the gods to be made manifest; it manifested women's matrix, and it provided an analogue for skin. In different regions of the Pacific different permutations of this common symbolic system are accentuated. This is why the simple act of wrapping cloth round a stone or an idol or a person transformed them into gods, rendering them efficacious. Cloth safeguarded life: if a culprit was wrapped in fine mats he became untouchable, and if a person was lost at sea, fine mats could be used to bury him or her by proxy. The association between cloth and skin, and acts of dressing and undressing were features of a common symbolic complex. Here we should emphasize that from the Polynesian point of view the skin covers and obscures the principle of vitality that is carried in the blood. This principle of vitality is invisible by definition. 'Blood' flowing in the body (the Samoan term is *toto*), can never be seen. For, when a wound or women's menstruation makes blood visible, it acquires a different name, and carries negative connotations. Thus, the vital principle (*agaga*, *mauli*) is both invisible by definition and present by definition. Wrapped cloth as a cultural skin, covering the natural one, is by itself the evidence of this double and contradictory definition. In some way the use of cloth as an envelope or covering is to bring evidence that within the body there is indeed, luminous although invisible, a life principle of a sacred origin.

No doubt this is why these cloths are always presented either rolled up or wrapped around the body. The gift-givers arrive with the cloth wound around them, and sometimes with a mat rolled up under one arm. The cloth is spread out and shown, but above all, the cloth is used to envelop the receiver in turn. The receiver is enveloped, or else the cloth is spread out at his feet or unfurled over the pile of other gifts such as food or tools. Cloth gifts of this kind still occur today throughout Western Polynesia, including the Lau Islands in Eastern Fiji (Douaire-Marsaudon, 1997, Hooper 1982). In the past, the recipient of a gift might have been a god, objectified as a stick or a standing stone, or might have been a chief, or any visitor. The god, the foreign chief, the visitor would have been conceived by the local people as occupying the dominant position. In rites of welcome, gifts of cloth serve to take into account this superiority and to establish a relationship that is not based on violence but on respect. In other words, these rites facilitate the transformation of an external form of sacredness that it is dangerous to touch, and is taboo (*tapu, sa, ra'a, mo'a*), and render it touchable, *noa*.

In their initial encounters with Europeans, Polynesians' attempts to integrate new arrivals through such cloth presentations gave rise to dramatic misunderstandings. For the Europeans saw these rites as an act of exposure, as a display of nudity and as open invitation for sex. This was a shocking error. For in Polynesian custom the most respectful way to present cloth was to wind it around the body of a young girl who had yet to bear a child. She would have been initially presented wrapped in a great length (of *tapa* and or mats) and to present the offering she would have divested herself of these wrappings until she stood 'naked'. Whether they responded in reprobation or pleasure, the visitors were astounded.

Some Misunderstandings Concerning Nudity and Polynesian Women's Sexual Appetites

In nearly all the accounts of first contact the use of this term 'naked' is highly ambiguous. Was the girl really stark naked? Would she not have retained a waist-band of *tapa*, her *maro*? Rodriguez the Spaniard visited Tahiti in 1774, soon after Cook's second visit. He provides an eyewitness account of the festival staged before the chiefs prior to a battle against another district:

> Some women decked in quantities of native cloth presented themselves before the Chiefs in order to strip themselves and make an offering of the cloth to the said Chiefs, being left with only a *maro* on to cover their nakedness. They call this festival a *taurua*, and after it they prepare for a *paraparau*, which is like a *tertulia* or well ordered conversazione of which the main topic is the wars these natives engage in against those of Morea. (cited in Oliver 1974, III: 1237)

Thus the 'naked' girl retained her *maro*. Certain passages from Bougainville also indicate that the term 'naked' can in fact refer to a girl dressed in a 'waistband, *maro*':

> The inhabitants of Tahiti are often seen quite naked, having no other clothes than a sash, which covers their natural parts. However, the chief people among them generally wrap themselves in a great piece of cloth, which hangs down to their knees. This is likewise the only dress of the women; and they know how to place it so artfully, as to make this simple dress susceptible of coquetry. (Bougainville 1772: 250)

So we can see how a Polynesian dressed normally (i.e. wearing a *maro*) can turn into someone whose 'nakedness' indicates the first stirrings of sexual desire. In several other eyewitness accounts the observers do not even bother to specify whether the private parts are exposed or not. Descriptions of 'nakedness' have to be treated with some caution. For Europeans saw the *maro* as a form of underwear; thus, in their view the person was lacking clothing, was already 'undressed'. Moreover, we know that Europeans regarded bare-chested women as being naked and sexually provocative.

Travellers who passed by Tahiti after 1767 (the date of initial contact) reinforced this view, since it so happened that the inhabitants wore a kind of poncho (*tiputa*). It was made from a rectangular piece of *tapa*, with a hole made for the head, and it hung down to the hips. This piece of clothing did not have any ritual significance, but simply provided protection from the cold, as many of the inhabitants were living in the mountainous interior at the time. But at ceremonies of welcome both men and women would remove the poncho as a gesture of respect. For the most part the visitors failed to understand these gestures. They thought they saw the women stripping in front of them. When Europeans saw dancers performing in a *maro* or a loincloth, they perceived them to be 'naked'; once they saw them as naked, they perceived them to be 'lascivious'. Bougainville's companion, the Prince of Nassau, regarded all female clothing as 'a refined obstacle to pleasure' [*une parure importune pour le plaisir*] and particularly appreciated seeing naked girls in Tahiti.

On 'Shaking the Hips in a Rotary Motion'

Furthermore, when the visitors saw these 'naked' bodies shake their hips while performing various dances they believed the Tahitians to be possessed with irrepressible sexual desire. In fact, Polynesian dances are often composed of rapid, staccato movements of the hips. Such movements lifted the dancers' loincloths, adding to the visitors' impression that they were witnessing an act of exposure (these dancers, male and female, would have typically occupied the front row). These early visitors did not realize that the female dancers in the front row had to be virgins or at least girls who had never borne a child. Sometimes the finale required these girls to strip off (with all the ambiguity this implies: stark naked or left with a *maro*?) and present cloth offerings to their guests. To the European mind these various 'observations' of 'nudity' and 'shaking the hips' led to an inescapable conclusion: the dance's evocation of sexual activity was at best a fertility rite, or at worst intended to provoke both the spectators' and the dancers' lust, 'as it might be expected', wrote Hawkesworth, 'of a people whose customs glorified sexual activity'.[3] (Words which summarize the European stereotypical account of Tahitian culture that developed after the visits of Wallis, Bougainville and Cook, 1767–1769.)

The interpretation of Tahitian culture as a generalized sex cult was based upon the erroneous belief that 'unmarried women' were living a life of 'free-love' lie. This belief itself was based on a few occasions where, in the very first moments of contact, chiefs had ordered some teenage girls to come forth 'naked' and made clear signs to the newcomers that they expected them to have sex with those girls. After 1775 the sex cult interpretation became widely established in salons throughout Europe, though the mass of documentary evidence attesting to this can hardly be treated here. Let us simply say that Europeans justified their account by claiming that all young Tahitians were educated in a custom based on a 'sex cult'. In fact, it would appear that Tahitian chiefs had aimed to get some girls pregnant as a means of capturing the mystical power of these new arrivals, whom they assumed to be partially divine.[4] Trapped by their preconceptions regarding the sex-cult society, Europeans could scarcely have other than a sexual interpretation of the movement of the girls' hips in dance festivals. But this conclusion involved another error, for it overlooked the fact that all Polynesian choreography was – and indeed remains – based upon a dualist conception of the body.

In their descriptions of Polynesian dances, all the eighteenth-century travellers noted the particular movement of the hips – a rapid oscillation from left to right – with wonder. Forster, the naturalist who accompanied Cook on his second voyage, noted the movement of the hips: 'But beside this, they shake their hips in a rotatory motion, both when they are standing and when they are leaning prostrate on their knees and elbows, with a velocity which excited our astonishment' (cited in Oliver

1974, I: 332–3). The velocity 'excited our astonishment', since Europeans never shook this part of their body at that time. At that point in time European hips were only meant to tremble during (lawful) intercourse. What other function could this part of the body possibly have? What else could women's motion of the hips possibly symbolize? Forster continues: 'The exercise of the common dramatic dances is very violent, the motion of the hands elegant, that of the feet not to be seen, that of the hips somewhat strange, and according to our notions indelicate' (Forster, cited in Oliver 1974: 332–3). Forster's admission of cultural relativism – 'according to our notions' – was highly unusual for the time. But this remark confirms, if indeed it is necessary to do so, that the movement of the hips was perceived by all European visitors as being not merely indelicate, but licentious.[5]

The Dual Body

What a misunderstanding! For as it happens, a dualist conception of the body is characteristic of Polynesian dance. While the upper portion of the body tells the story, the lower portion of the body marks the beat to the accompaniment of the tambourine players (and percussionists) and a small group of flute players and/or singers who supply the story's melody. All this is consistent with the dual organization of domestic and ceremonial space, in reference to an old Sky/Earth cosmology, and indeed can be substantiated by any detailed observation of current dance practice, such as that at Pacific Art Festivals, for example. Two leading authorities on Polynesian art confirm this.

> Missionaries considered Polynesian dancing lascivious, when in fact the hip motions to which they objected so strongly were often little more than a time-keeping element . . . In Polynesian dance . . . small steps, and the hip movements that derive from them, keep the rhythm; it is the arms that give meaning to the performance. Polynesians considered the European form of dancing, in which bodies of men and women actually touched in public, as lascivious. (Kaeppler 1997: 112)

Sandra Silve, who teaches traditional Hawaiian hula in Paris recently remarked:

> Certain movements in Hawaiian dance are like the sign language used by people who are deaf and dumb. Each gesture corresponds to the expression of a word. The dancers' primary concern was to relate history and they concentrated on the movements of their arms and chest; the movement of the feet and of the lower part of the body, particularly the shaking of the hips, supplied the basic rhythm. (Silve 1997: 18)[6]

Thus we can see that the movement of the dancers' hips had nothing to do with sexual provocation. Yet this discussion has revealed how important it is to consider whether the duality of the body played a part in acts of investiture and divestment.

Concerning the Divestment of the Upper Part of the Body in Indigenous Contexts

Polynesians attributed specific meaning to the divestment of the torso. Let us consider Tahiti between 1767 and 1789. We have already noted that the act of enveloping the other's body was a means of signalling the other's superiority that would be typically made to a visitor or a chief at formal occasions. Thus, when an inferior presented himself before his superior, he had to make a sign of humility, and cloth provided the medium to do so. If, as was the case in Tahiti, the new arrival, or incomer, wore a piece of clothing on his torso he was expected to remove it when passing before his superior. Cook, Banks and Parkinson noted something of the sort in 1773, though they never advanced a systematic explanation of this practice. Yet it is important to recognize that during the period of contact, the spatial registration of hierarchical relations was marked throughout Polynesia. For example, when Samoan fishermen passed in front of the house of a high chief they had to abase themselves, even if this involved lowering themselves from their canoe and swimming beside it. Even today, it is impossible to stand when one's superior is seated. So if one is obliged to leave a gathering one does so in a crouching position, while sustaining a deep bow. Then again, if someone makes use of a parasol for protection against the sun, he or she must either lower it or close it when passing in front of a superior.[7]

Descriptions of these practices occur in the eyewitness accounts of the initial contacts made between Europeans and Polynesians. During Cook's initial visit to Tahiti in 1769, Parkinson, the official draftsman of the expedition, noted in his journal:

> Our tent was nearly filled with people; and soon after, Amoa, who is chief of several districts on the other side of the island, also came to us, and brought with him a hog. As soon as he appeared, the natives uncloathed themselves to the waist . . . On the 6th of July, in the evening, a young woman came to the entrance of the fort, whom we found to be a daughter of Oamo. The natives complimented her on her arrival, by uncovering their shoulders. (Parkinson 1784: 32, 35)

This observation is confirmed by Cook (Beaglehole 1955, I: 104). The rules of divestment were next noted by Forster in 1773. The case astonished him for it involved a father divesting in front of his son. But the son had been installed in his father's place as paramount chief (cited by Oliver 1974, III: 1184). On 27 September 1789, during Morrison's visit to Tahiti:

> On the 27th, having appointed that We Should meet at Opparee, and make our presents to the Young King, We marched in a body under Arms to Oparee, taking with us the

> Toobouai Images and several other presents of red Feathers, Friendly Island and Toobouai Cloth, Matting and War Weapons Iron work &c. . . . when we march'd to his House in procession each attended by a friend to remove the Taheite Cloth which we had on, all of Whom Strip'd as they entered the Sacred Ground, the men to the Waist, and the Weomen uncovering their Shoulders and tucking their cloths up under their arm, and our Taheite Cloaths were removed. (Morrison 1935: 77–78)[8]

These accounts reveal that the act of divesting the upper part of the body was an established gesture of respect. Rank was also made manifest by the number of layers of *tapa* that were wrapped around the body in ceremonial contexts. While noting that the way Tahitians wore *tapa* was varied, Parkinson detected a constant feature, namely that 'persons of distinction among them wrap a number of pieces of cloth about them' (Parkinson 1784: 338). We should note that the dancers were laden with *tapa*, far more than was strictly necessary either for reasons of modesty or for a festive occasion. During the same visit Banks noted: 'On their hips rested a quantity of cloth pleated very full which reached almost up to their arms and fell down below into long peticoats [sic] reaching below their feet' (Cited in Oliver 1974, I: 338).

Later Banks adds that the hips were covered in 'folds of cloth'. Another account by Radiguet, a young officer writing in the Marquesas, notes that the mass of *tapa* wound around the young dancing girls on the clearing seemed to trap their bodies in a 'block of marble' (cited in Scemla 1994: 838–46). Parkinson's drawings from Cook's first voyage, together with Webber's drawings from the third, are eloquent: the mass of *tapa* enlarges the bodies of the dancers almost four or five times (see Oliver 1974, I: 333 as well as Figures 2.1 and 2.2).

Concerning the Exposure of the Lower Body in Indigenous Contexts

Divesting the lower part of the body either could involve uncovering the lower portion of the body while the upper part remain covered, or could involve lifting the loincloth (*maro*) in a deliberate act of exposure. I shall be brief because the historical factual accounts of this practice are few. Leaving to one side the occasions where priests stripped themselves naked before assuming different garb as they entered the interior of the temple, or the instances where young women divested themselves to make a public gift of *tapa*, one might assume that the act of baring one's buttocks and private parts in an ostentatious manner was intended to be provocative. For we must recall Morrison's remarks (see note 1) regarding the care that people took to cover this part of their bodies in ordinary contexts, such as fishing in the lagoon (Morrison 1935: 225 cited in Oliver 1974, I: 153).

Contemporary observation from Samoa would appear to confirm this. Gestures of exposure are recognized, they have a specific name and, whether a man or a

Figure 2.1 Sketches of Tahitian dancing girls (Raiatea, August 1769) – Sydney Parkinson. Reproduced by kind permission of the British Library (BL add. Ms 23921 f.38b).

woman is involved, they are regarded as provocative. If somebody exposes him- or herself in a non-ceremonial context it will cause a row. Only adult men or old women do it during festivities, making the crowd roar with laughter. It is a form of clowning that emerges when two teams face each other. The local team of dancers may do it to provoke a response from the visiting team of dancers. Such rituals of clowning, of marking the inversion of respect, were also noted in Tahiti, though in this instance it was the representation of a god that was being so dishonoured (Oliver 1974, III: 1307–8).

The provocation was not intended to be gross because Polynesians did not equate sex and evil (or sin and filth). It was intended to convey an impression of domination, physical force, a form of rape; in other words, it was an assertion of masculine authority, though in certain instances married women may convey this too (Tcherkézoff 2001a). The provocation was also scatological. Baring the buttocks was also a form of domination. 'Eat shit!' is a popular insult in contemporary Samoa. In Tikopia the officiant attested to his humility and inferiority in front of the god by saying 'I eat your excrement' (Firth 1967: 210, 226; Monberg 1991: 268–70).

Concerning the Divestment of the Upper Part of the Body in Early Encounters and its Subsequent Adaptations

Let us go back to the quotation from Morrison,

Figure 2.2 'A young woman of Otaheite, bringing a Present' (1777) – John Webber. Reproduced by kind permission of the British Library (BL add. Ms. 15513 f.17).

Having made known our business to Areepaeea – who told us that we must not approach the Young King as he was yet Sacred, unless we Strip'd the Clothing off from our Head & Shoulders, which we refused telling him that it was not Customary to remove any part of our Dress except our hats and if we were under arms it was not our Country's manner to remove our hat even to the King. However that we might not seem to be deficient in point of Good Manners each was provided with a piece of Taheite Cloth to put over their Shoulders and take off in the Young King's presence (Morrison 1935: 77–78).

Morrison refused because he wanted to sustain respect for English manners, which prohibited one from removing one's shirt on formal occasions while prescribing the removal of hats. Nevertheless, as he notes, English manners of the time decreed that one retained one's hat if one carried arms. Therefore, since the English bore muskets, they could not doff their hats in the king's presence. According to his code of conduct, removing one's shirt at a formal occasion was deemed disrespectful, and it would therefore have shown a lack of patriotism to do so in the Pacific. This presented a conundrum, but a compromise was soon reached, though whether this was in response to a suggestion from their Tahitian friend or to their own initiative it is hard to tell. The crew would wear a length of *tapa* over their shirts and in this way they could show their respect to the new king by removing it in his presence while retaining their shirts – thus satisfying both codes of dress (Morrison 1935: 78).

Such ancient dress prescriptions have persisted, although they have been adapted in response to changing circumstances. For the missionary view was of course consistent with European notions of dress. To be dressed in a loincloth (*maro*) or a grass skirt made of leaves was to be regarded as naked, licentious, even evil. They begged men to be decently dressed in a shirt for church services just as they forced women to wear dresses which extended from the neck to the floor. For if European etiquette demanded that men remove their hats, torsos had to be covered in the presence of God. So how did Polynesians manage to reconcile this with their own code of dress?

In contemporary Samoa, Sunday is comprised of two consecutive occasions: after the church service there may be a gathering (*fono*) of the chiefs and village elders. When in the house men wear nothing but a *lavalava* (a Samoan sarong made from an island print); to change for church, men put on a white shirt and sometimes a jacket and a sarong made of material in a single colour. When they go on to the *fono* they remove their shirt and jacket and sit bare-chested, out of respect to the founding ancestors whose names they bear, or else the lesser chiefs remove their shirts as a sign of respect while the paramount retains his.[9]

The Whole Body in Early Encounters: Male Gifts of Cloth

Such demonstrations of respect were also made to Europeans. But in their initial encounters, Polynesians wanted to achieve the cosmological incorporation of the new arrivals. Acts of divestment were a prelude to the act of enveloping the new arrivals in cloth. It seems that on various occasions Polynesian chiefs wrapped the ship's captains in barkcloth they had removed from their own bodies. Probably, the dual distinction between upper and lower part of the body was not pertinent here. The cloth, given in enormous quantities, wrapped the whole body. A Tahitian chief gave in succession his upper and lower garments, his poncho (*tiputa*) and his sarong (*pareu*) (see below). The female dancers were covered with cloth before offering it. But another distinction seems to take place: the gender of the donor becomes important. For though the chief divested himself of cloth, it appears he was not stripped naked. Unfortunately, the descriptions are vague, for it is evident that the European visitors were more interested in female nudity. Yet when women presented cloth, they do specify that the bottom of the body was uncovered too. It thus seems that an additional dimension was operative when the giver was female.

Let us examine first the case of the male donor. In 1768, the first Tahitian (his name was Ahutoru, it later emerged) to climb aboard Bougainville's ship presented a plantain bough to the tallest officer he could see. Then, according to Vivès the ship's surgeon:

> He wanted to swap his three ponchos [*tiputa*] or white cloths that enveloped him [*ses trois ponches ou nappes blanches*] for a European shirt. Mr Lafontaine, one of our officers of about the same height, dressed him in a shirt, trousers, jacket and hat. He indicated his thanks and embraced him. He came back to Lafontaine, caressed him and embraced him and wrapped him in the loincloths [*pagnes*] he had been wearing. In return Mr Lafontaine gave him a shirt, trousers and a jacket which we had much difficulty to put on him, so large were his shoulders.' (Vivès, ed. Taillemite 1997: 237)

In 1841, the first captain to stay on the atoll of Fakaofo (part of the Tokelau archipelago next to Samoa), whose inhabitants had already experienced violent encounters with Europeans at sea and gunfire on their shores, was enveloped by a chief who seemed overcome by fear: 'The King . . . pointed at the sun, howled, hugged me again, and again, moaned, howled, pointed to the sun, put a mat around my waist, and secured it with a cord of human hair' (Huntsman and Hooper 1996: 143,146).

Female Gifts of Cloth in Early Encounters

In 1789 some of the crew of *The Bounty*, commanded by Captain Bligh, mutinied after their stay in Tahiti (1788–1789). The ship was on its way back to England when the mutineers forced the vessel to return to Tahiti. Thus it was that Morrison returned to Tahiti and lived there for more than a year, and compiled his famous journal. Once Bligh had returned to England, a punitive exhibition was mounted under the command of Captain Edwards. Hamilton, the ship's surgeon, relays the story of their arrival in Tahiti: 'The king, the two queens and retinue, came on board to pay us a formal visit, preceded by a band of music. The ladies each had about sixty or seventy yards of Otaheitee cloth wrapt round them and were so bulky and unwieldy with it, they were obliged to be hoisted on board like horn cattle' (Edwards and Hamilton 1915: 107). If the narrator was not exaggerating about the 'sixty or seventy yards', it is not surprising to read that the women had to be heaved aboard with ropes like bales from one of the wharves on the Thames. The followers brought with them food of many different kinds 'as a present for the captain'. Hamilton continues: 'As soon as they were on board, the Captain debarassoit [*sic*, i.e. relieved] the ladies, by rolling their linen round his middle; an indispensable ceremony here in receiving a present of cloth' (ibid.).

Previous visitors had also remarked upon this important ceremony. The following episode is described in Cook's Journal, as well as that of the naturalist Joseph Banks and the ship's artist, Parkinson. It was 12 May 1769. One morning a double-hulled canoe approached the English fortifications on the beach. Once again Banks was aboard the longboat anchored near the shore, busy 'bartering with the Indians'. The Tahitians he was exchanging with indicated that he should go to meet the group of people who had just arrived. Banks disembarked from the longboat. The group had already disembarked and were ten yards away. The Tahitians formed a line. They ceased to approach and signalled to Banks to do likewise. One man in the group carried several boughs. He approached Banks with two boughs, one of a young plantain and another one. Tupia, a Tahitian who had become an assistant for the English, 'acted as my representative', Banks noted: he received the boughs and placed them in the long boat. He repeated this action six times. With each gift, the gift giver said a few words 'that we could not understand'. When this was finished, another man approached, holding a great bundle of cloth in his arms. He unfurled it and started to spread three pieces of cloth upon the ground. A woman from the group (Cook speaks of a 'young woman') stood at the fore:

> Banks: 12 May 1769: The woman 'stepd upon [the cloths] and quickly unveiling all her charms gave me a most convenient opportunity of admiring them, by turning herself gradually round'. (Beaglehole 1962: 275)

> Cook: 12 May 1769: Step'd upon the Cloth and with as much Innocency as one could possibly conceve, expose'd herself entirely naked from the waist downwards, in this manner she turn'd her Self once or twice round, I am not certain which, then step'd of (sic) the Cloth and drop'd down her clothes. (Beaglehole 1955: 93)

Banks and Cook indicate that this was repeated for each set of pieces of cloth. There were nine pieces of cloth in all. The woman 'once more displayed her naked beauties'. After the final lot of cloths, she 'immediately approached me', and the man following behind her gathered up the cloths and she 'immediately gave me to understand that this present was destined for me'. Banks indicates that he took both ladies by the hand and took them to visit the encampment (Beaglehole 1962: 275). Cook indicates that the two women embraced Banks (Beaglehole 1955: 93). In this case, it does seem that the female giver was 'entirely naked from the waist downwards', thus without even a *maro*. Parkinson brings confirmation: 'exposed herself quite naked'.

But Parkinson adds a crucial indication: the whole thing started with the clothes that *the young woman was wearing*: 'A woman passed along the next, having a great many clothes upon her, which she took off, and, spreading them upon the ground, turned round, and exposed herself quite naked; more garments being handed to her, by the company, she spread them also upon the ground' (Parkinson 1984 [1784]: 27). This detail might explain what may seem strange in Cook's formulation: naked 'from the waist downwards' and 'dropped down her clothes' after stepping and turning on the pieces of cloth spread on the ground. One might think that the young woman lifted up her poncho and then dropped it again at the end, which would then raise the question of a deliberate stripping of only the lower part of the body. But, more probably, Cook (whose style of writing, in his notes, is always very hesitant), wanted to remark that *even* the part usually not shown ('from the waist downwards') was 'entirely naked'; and the 'dropping of clothes' would refer to the various stages when the woman took off her clothes and/or dropped the additional pieces of cloth that were handed to her by her company.

A little later, Bligh's ship, The *Bounty*, returns to Tahiti, albeit in the hands of the mutineers. In 1790 Morrison witnessed a ceremonial dance performed before Captain Cook's portrait (which had been painted by Webber and presented to the Tahitians in 1777).

> On the 1st of February our attention was drawn from our Work by a Heiva which according to Custom was performd in our Neighbourhood before the Chief of the District, to see which all the inhabitants of the District were Assembled.
>
> Everything being ready Captain Cook's picture was brought (by an Old Man who has the Charge of it) and placed in front, and the Cloth with which it was covered being removed, evry person present paid the Homage of striping off their Upper Garments, the Men bareing their bodys to the Waist, Poeno not excepted, and the Weomen uncovering their Shoulders. The Master of the Ceremonies then made the Oodoo (or usual offering) making a long speech to the picture, acknowledging Captain Cook to be Chief of Maatavye and placing a Young Plantain tree with a sucking pig tyed to it before the Picture.
>
> The Speech running to this purpose – 'Hail, all hail Cook, Chief of Air Earth & Water, we acknowledge you Chief from the Beach to the Mountains, over Men, Trees and Cattle over the Birds of the Air and Fishes of the Sea &c.&c.'
>
> After which they proceeded to perform their dance, which was done by two young woemen Neatly and elegantly dressd in fine Cloth, and two Men, the whole was conducted with much regularity and exactness, beating drums & playing flutes to which they kept true time for near four Hours.
>
> On a signal being given the Woemen Slip'd off their Dresses and retired, and the whole of the Cloth and Matting which was spread to perform on, was rolld up to the

> Picture and the old man took posession of it for the use of Captain Cook. (Morrison 1935: 85-6)

Morrison's narrative is interesting because he distinguishes the moment when all the assistants uncovered only their shoulders and chest as a gesture of respect in front of a superior, from the moment when the women finished their dance and removed '[all?] their clothes' to present it. Thus, offerings of cloth (*tapa*) were received by Cook when he was alive, then twenty years later by his portrait, and also on his behalf by the Tahitian chief Poino himself, as Morrison relates in another passage of his journal.

It is important to realize that the presentation of offerings of cloth by naked female dancers was not a recent innovation that emerged during the period of contact. One cannot assume that it was occasioned by European demand. There is nothing to suggest that the new arrivals requested *tapa*, for they did not know what to do with it. During the very first encounter, in 1767, Wallis did not even want to take the *tapa* that the Tahitians had left for him on the beach (the initial encounter took place at some distance). Banks quickly rid himself of these unending gifts. In any case there are enough sources, such as Rodriguez and, later, Wilson, which indicate that the practice was already well established between Polynesians. We have already drawn attention to the observation made by Rodriguez the Spaniard soon after Cook's second visit: 'Some women decked in quantities of native cloth presented themselves before the Chiefs in order to strip themselves and make an offering of the cloth to the said Chiefs' (cited in Oliver 1974, III: 1237). Twenty years later this practice is still observable. Wilson, the captain of the first ship of missionaries to arrive at Tahiti (1797), relates: 'Any number of women may perform at once; but as the dress is very expensive, seldom more than two or four dance; and when this is done before the chief, the dresses are presented to him after the *heiva* is finished; and these contain thirty or forty yards of cloth, from one to four yards wide' (Wilson 1799, cited in Oliver 1974, I: 338).

Wilson conveys how the young girls could be laden with *tapa* during the dance. It seems that this way of offering was peculiar to young women or rather young girls. Cook specifically mentions young girls in his notes on dances, though later accounts which mention nudity or sexual provocation of 'young girls' or 'young women' seems to have been changed to 'women' out of considerations of decency, prior to their publication. Such offerings were made at the end of a dance and (according to both the sources of Cook's voyages as well as missionary sources on Samoa) the 'women' in the front row were unmarried, and therefore ostensibly virgins.

Conclusion

These interpretations give rise to a question. It is possible that the young women bearing cloth remained clothed in a *maro*, and were only naked from the European point of view. In which case, all these accounts simply document the respectful presentation of cloth before a superior, as a means of enveloping and incorporating this superior. Then again it is possible that these accounts describe how the young girls'/women's bodies were deliberately stripped naked, in which case we should regard them as being linked to more specifically sexual displays, which are recorded as having occurred in the first instances of contact. In this case they recall Samoan myths, which describe how young women presented themselves naked before the first rays of the sun so as to be divinely impregnated. It would seem that this mythical logic was transposed on the scene of the encounters with the first Europeans, through the formal presentation of cloth and of naked young female bodies. We have insisted on the Tahitian case. But similar scenes were observed in early encounters in Samoa. For example, in 1832, the first missionary to arrive in Samoa met with a young beachcomber, formerly a surgeon, who told him how he was received on his arrival:

> When he first went on shore among them, the females gathered around him in great numbers, and some took their mats off before him, exposing their persons as much as possible to his view. Perceiving him bashful, the whole of women, old and young, did the same and began dancing in that state before him desiring him not to be bashful or angry as it was Faa Samoa, or Samoa fashion. (Moyle 1984: 232)

Thus it is probable that these sexual displays were not evidence of any 'sexual hospitality' offered to male voyagers in search of rest and pleasure, but rather, evidence of the attempt to capture through impregnation, real or metaphorical, apparently superhuman powers. To capture these powers is to incorporate these new arrivals. In Polynesian civilization, to incorporate was and, in some cases, still is to envelop. *Both cloth and the young girls/women were intended to envelop the new arrivals.* The young girl who has yet to bear a child does not strip herself of offerings of cloth as an act of provocation and domination, so much as in an appeal to harness cosmological fecundity. The very same scenes of stripping and offering cloth that were performed before Europeans also took place at dances before the gods, and at dances before visiting neighbouring chiefs when the young girls/women were being offered in marriage.

Perhaps young girls/women were the most effective means of incorporating what was fearful and foreign. In Polynesian mythology there is a wealth of material that evokes connections between sacred cloths, birth, the sacredness of the first-born and young girls' bodies which I cannot begin to go into here. The mention of the female gifts of cloth brings to an end our present study on the importance of cloth in Polynesia at the time of contact. But this analysis leads also to another dimension that needs to be dealt with if one is to appreciate the full story of the first encounters between Polynesians and Europeans.[10]

Notes

1. The notes of the first eyewitnesses, such as Morrison in Tahiti (at the end of 1780s), show that this trait existed prior to the arrival of the missionaries. 'The Single Young Men also had dances wherein they shew many indecent Gestures which would be reproachable among themselves at any other time but at the dance, it being deem'd shameful for either Sex to expose themselves Naked even to each other and they are more remarkable for hiding their Nakedness in Bathing than many Europeans, always supplying the place of Cloaths with leaves at going and coming out of the Water' (cited in Oliver: 1974, I: 153).
2. For a more extended discussion of the Samoan case outlined in *The Gift* see Tcherkézoff 1997b; for examples of mythical and ritual uses of the fine mat in Samoa see Tcherkézoff 2002a.
3. 'It cannot be supposed that, among these people, chastity is held in much estimation. It might be expected that sisters and daughters would be offered to strangers' (Hawkesworth 1773, II: 206–7). Hawkesworth was the official writer chosen by the Admiralty to document Cook's voyages. His rendering of both Cook's and Banks's notes reveals his bias toward making sexual allusions and condemning Tahitian morals.
4. This is similar to Sahlins' argument regarding Hawaii (1985a). On the Polynesian interpretation of Europeans as non-humans, see Tcherkézoff 2002b. Looking at several accounts of first contact in Polynesia, it seems that the girls chosen to make these presentations were always of a very young age, apparently virgins, or at least never having borne child, thus ready for capturing through impregnation the powers of the Europeans, since it was regarded in Polynesia that the first-born might have a particularly sacred essence.
5. In order to imagine the visitor's amazement it may be worth considering the introduction of the twist or the hula-hoop to Europe in the 1960s. Both dances involved keeping rhythm with frenetic hip movements. But the older generation could not help themselves from reading more into it, and being shocked.
6. Thanks to Pascale Bonnemère who brought this reference to my attention.
7. The range of Samoan attitudes of humility has been evoked in discussions on the 'nurture/nature' determinism in human behaviour (see Tcherkézoff 2001a).

As it is clear here, these gestures of lowering were part of a whole Polynesian cultural system involving the conceptions of the cosmos and of the body.

8. Morrison was one of the first visitors to stay in Tahiti for a significant time. He was the only one of the mutineers from the *Bounty* to have made an account of his stay on Tahiti once he had returned to London.
9. Those who are tattooed divest themselves; the others sometimes retain their shirts to express their shame for not being tattooed, in which case they undo the buttons of their shirts to expose their chest and stomach (the tattooing runs from the base of the back to the thighs); a chief is shamed not to have a tattoo; although tattooing has for some time become a personal and individual choice, it is still the case that men who want to become the chiefs (*matai*) of their families frequently choose to be tattooed.
10. In his book on Polynesian tattooing, Alfred Gell has already commented on the scene of offering cloth to Cook and Banks and has evoked an hypothesis linking cloth and female fecundity (Gell 1993: 140).

References

Anae, Melani, Nite, Fuamatu, Ieti, Lima, Mariner, Kirk, Park, Kirk and Tamasailau Suaali'i-Sauni (2000), *Tiute ma Matafaioi a nisi Tane Samoa i le Faiga o Aiga.* [*The Roles and Responsibilities of Some Samoan Men in Reproduction.*] Auckland: University of Auckland Pacific Health Research Centre, Department of Maori and Pacific Health.

Babadzan, Alain (1993), *Les dépouilles des dieux: essai sur la religion tahitienne à l'époque de la découverte*, Paris: Editions de la Maison des Sciences de l'Homme.

Bataille-Benguigui, Marie-Claire (1997), 'Le tapa, vêtement des hommes, symbole de statut et véhicule du divin', in Annick Notter (ed.), *La découverte du paradis. Océanie: curieux, navigateurs et savants.* Paris: Somogy Editions d'Art/Association des conservateurs des musées du Nord-Pas-de-Calais.

Beaglehole, John C. (1955–1974), *The Journals of James Cook.* The Hakluyt Society, Cambridge: Cambridge Cambridge University Press.

—— (1962), *The Endeavour Journal of Joseph Banks 1768–1771.* Sydney: Angus and Robertson.

Bougainville, Louis-Antoine de (1772), *A Voyage Round the World, Performed by Order of His Most Christian Majesty, in the Years 1766, 1767, 1768 and 1769*, Trans. J. R. Forster. London: J. Nourse and T. Davies [original: *Voyage autour du monde par la frégate La Boudeuse et la flûte l'Etoile.* Paris: Saillant et Nyon, 1771].

Douaire-Marsaudon, Françoise (1997), 'Nourritures et richesses: les objets cérémoniels du don comme signe d'identité à Tonga et à Wallis', in S. Tcherkézoff et F. Douaire-Marsaudon (eds), *Le Pacifique-sud aujourd'hui: identités et transformations culturelles*, Paris: Editions du CNRS, coll. Ethnologie.

—— (1998), *Les premiers fruits. Parenté, identité sexuelle et pouvoirs en Polynésie occidentale (Tonga, Wallis et Futuna)*. Paris: Editions Editions/du CNRS de la Maison des Sciences de l'Homme (Chemins de l'ethnologie).

Edwards, Edward and Hamilton, George (1915), *Voyage of H.M.S. 'Pandora' Despatched to Arrest the Mutineers of the 'Bounty' in the South Seas, 1790–91: Being the Narratives of Captain Edward Edwards*, R. N., The Commander, and George Hamilton, The Surgeon, with an Introduction and Notes by Basil Thomson. London: F. Edwards.

Firth, Raymond (1967), *The Work of the Gods in Tikopia*. London School of Economics, Monographs on Social Anthropology, 1–2, London: The Athlone Press.

Gell, Alfred (1993), *Wrapping in Images: Tattooing in Polynesia*. Oxford: Clarendon Press.

Hawkesworth, John (1773), *An Account of the Voyages Undertaken by Order of Her Present Majesty for Making Discoveries in the Southern Hemisphere and Successively Performed by Commodore Byron, Captain Wallis, Captain Carteret and Captain Cook, in the Dolphin, drawn up from the Journals*, London: W. Stratham.

Hooper, Steven (1982), 'A Study of Valuables in the Chiefdom of Lau, Fiji', PhD thesis, Department of Anthropology, Cambridge University.

Huntsman, Judith and Hooper, Anthony (1996), *Tokelau: A Historical Ethnography*. Auckland: Auckland University Press.

Kaeppler, Adrienne L. (1997), 'Polynesia and Melanesia', in Adrienne L. Kaeppler, Christian Kaufmann and Douglas Newton (eds), *Oceanic Art*. New York: Harry N. Abrams [original: *L'art océanien,* Paris, Editions Citadelles & Mazenod 1993].

—— (1999), 'Kie Hingoa: Mats of Power, Rank, Prestige and History', *Journal of the Polynesian Society* 108(2): 168–232.

Mauss, Marcel (1925), *Essai sur le don. Forme et raison de l'échange dans les sociétés archaïques*. Paris: L'Annee Sociologique.

Monberg, Torn (1991), *Bellona Islands: Beliefs and Rituals*, Pacific Islands Monographs Series, 9, Honolulu: University of Hawaii Press.

Morrison, James (1935), *The Journal of James Morrison, Boatswain's Mate of the Bounty, Describing the Mutiny and Subsequent Misfortunes of the Mutineers together with an Account of the Island of Tahiti*. Owen Rutter (ed.), London: Golden Cockerel.

Moyle, Richard (1984), *The Samoan Journals of John Williams, 1830 and 1832*. Canberra: Australian National University Press.

Oliver, Douglas (1974), *Ancient Tahitian Society*. 3 vols. Honolulu: University of Hawaii Press.

Parkinson, Sydney (1984), *A Journal of a Voyage to the South Seas*. London: Caliban Books [facsimile of the 1784 edn: 1773].

Sahlins, Marshall (1985a), *Islands of History*. Chicago: The University of Chicago Press.

—— (1985b), 'Hierarchy and Humanity in Polynesia', in J. Huntsman and A. Hooper (eds), *Transformations of Polynesian Culture*. Auckland: The Polynesian Society.

Scemla, Jean-Jo (1994), *Le voyage en Polynésie*. Paris: Lafont.

Silve, Sandra (1997), Interview, *Le Monde*, 2–3 Novembre 1997: 18.

Suali'i-Sauni, Tamasailau (2001), 'Samoans and Gender: Some Reflections on Male, Female and Fa'afafine Gender Identities', in C. Macpherson, P. Spoonley, M. Anae (eds), *Tangata O Te Moana Nui: The Evolving Identities of Pacific Peoples in Aotearoa/New Zealand*. Palmerston North: Dunmore Press.

Tapsell, Paul (1997), 'The Flight of Pareraututu: an Investigation of Taonga from a Tribal Perspective', *Journal of the Polynesian Society* 106(4): 323–74.

Tcherkézoff, Serge (1993), 'The Illusion of Dualism in Samoa: "Brothers-and-sisters" are not "Men-and-women"', in T. Del Valle (ed.), *Gendered Anthropology*. London: Routledge & Kegan Paul.

—— (1997a), 'Culture, nation, société: changements secondaires et bouleversements possibles au Samoa Occidental. Vers un modèle pour l'étude des dynamiques culturelles (deux parties)', in S. Tcherkézoff and F. Douaire-Marsaudon (eds), *Le Pacifique-sud aujourd'hui: identités et transformations culturelles*. Paris, Editions du CNRS, coll. Ethnologie.

—— (1997b), 'Le *mana*, le fait "total" et l'"esprit" dans la chose donnée. Marcel Mauss, les "cadeaux à Samoa" et la méthode comparative en Polynésie', *Anthropologie et Sociétés* 21(2–3): 193–223.

—— (2001a), *Le mythe occidental de la sexualité polynésienne: Margaret Mead, Derek Freeman et 'Samoa'*. Paris: Presses Universitaires de France.

—— (2001b), 'Is Anthropology About Individual Agency or Culture? Or why "Old Derek" is Doubly Wrong', *Journal of the Polynesian Society* 110(1): 59–78.

—— (2002a), 'Subjects and Objects in Samoa: Ceremonial Mats have a "Soul"', in Bernard Juillerat and Monique Jeudy-Ballini (eds), *People and Things: Social Mediations in Oceania*. Durham NC: Carolina Academic Press.

—— (2002b), 'L'humain et le divin: quand les Polynésiens ont découvert les explorateurs européens au XVIIIe siècle', *Ethnologies comparées* 5 (http://alor.univ-montp3.fr/cerce/revue.htm)

Valeri, Valerio (1985), *Kingship and Sacrifice: Ritual and Society in Ancient Hawaii*. Chicago: The University of Chicago Press.

Vivès (1977), Log-book (1768) and Journal re-written after return (1774), in E. Taillemite (ed.), *Bougainville et ses compagnons*, 2 vols. Paris: Imprimerie Nationale.

Part II
Clothing and the Appropriation of Christianity

–3–

The Case of the Misplaced Ponchos: Speculations Concerning the History of Cloth in Polynesia

Nicholas Thomas

Introduction

Social anthropology, Marilyn Strathern suggests in a 1990 article, has continually reduced material artefacts to the relations or meanings in which they are embedded; our interpretations treat the object as no more than an illustration of things that are external to it (1990: 38). She pointed toward a kind of analysis that would engage with what the artefact itself revealed, raising the question of what effects were peculiar to its artefactual form and presentation. This chapter is in this spirit, in the sense that it looks at particular objects and asks what they make manifest. While the examples Strathern has discussed, drawn from Melanesian ceremonial exchange, focus upon the revelation of relations and collectivities, I draw attention here to the revelation of change, empowerment, and conversion to Christianity in nineteenth-century Polynesia.

This chapter, in other words, is concerned with the ways in which major social and cultural transformations may be implicated in material substitutions. Thanks to Arjun Appadurai's justly celebrated edited collection (1986), we are familiar with the proposition that things have 'social lives'. That volume drew attention to the ways in which passive objects are successively recontextualized; here, I am interested in a complementary issue, that is, the ways in which things actively constitute new social contexts. It is well understood that technological innovations such as printing presses and railways enable novel social forms. What I am concerned to investigate is whether this is true, and in what senses, for more quotidian objects; for things such as clothes, which we understand as artefacts or consumer goods rather than as machines or apparatuses. With this question in mind, I explore the history of indigenous textiles in nineteenth-century Polynesia, and consider how adapted and introduced types of cloth perhaps worked as a technology that made religious change – that is, conversion to Christianity – visible as a feature of people's behaviour and domestic life.

Having made those general theoretical statements, I need to explain why I have succumbed to the temptation to give this chapter a frivolous title. One reason is that it is important to acknowledge from the start that, at an empirical level, it is an incomplete and speculative study, one that ventures arguments concerning the interplay between objects and cultural transformations on the basis of the most limited information about *tiputa*, eastern Polynesian garments resembling ponchos, that were adapted by western Polynesians as Christianity was introduced. This is in fact a mystery story in which these objects are all at once the clues, the suspects and the stars. But there is perhaps a deeper affinity between this inquiry and the popular fictions of the mystery genre, which are so often focused around enigmatic, coveted or missing objects. The scholar who tries to build a historical or anthropological inquiry around artefacts in museum collections, or artefacts that appear in old illustrations or photographs, can be in a situation very similar to that of the investigator in a crime story. There is frequently a highly unsatisfactory contrast between the sheer physicality and tangibility of the object before one, and the paucity of whatever story one can tell about it. For Sherlock Holmes, the artefact may be replete with clues of all kinds; but just as often it is a missing or valuable object on which people's passions and aspirations are focused. Objects like the diamond, the Moonstone, in Wilkie Collins' novel of that title (1868), often seen as one of the founding works of the mystery genre, have obscure, highly-charged, cross-cultural histories, involving colonial wars, theft, migration, and esoteric forms of superstition and spirituality. It could be suggested that, in this literature, material culture has a dangerous potentiality that it has never acquired in social theory.

The objects I am going to discuss in this chapter certainly have confusing cross-cultural histories, if not especially threatening ones. More generally, it might be suggested that the poorly-documented character of most ethnological artefacts in museum collections requires a methodologically innovative approach that might be inspired by the centrality of the object in the mystery story. We could work toward a theoretical framework that is empowered by what we have – the artefact itself – rather than disempowered by what we lack – the contextual information.

The problem, of course, is that the artefact is never just a thing 'in itself': artefacts and technologies alike are more than physical forms and machines: they cannot be dissociated from the bodies of knowledge, practices, and values, through which they are animated and given what Appadurai calls 'social life'. However deliberately we choose to engage with the materiality of things, it will never be possible to invent a rigorous or pure study based on deductions from forms. We will always be led away from the artefact, and then perhaps back to it, in a succession of movements and speculations around implicit effects and meanings. We may attempt to establish how an artefact actively 'texts' its context, but we can often only hazard such interpretations by initially situating it within a given context. If this is unsatisfactory, these interpretive operations could be seen to reflect the uncertainties of the practices they attempt to describe: we have been taught by Pierre Bourdieu (1977) and others that we study not rules or behaviours but strategies that are prone to fail, and where these depend on the uses of objects to make effects visible, they may fail precisely because an object's meanings are only weakly or partially inscribed in it. Social life is surely a succession of gambles on the bad chance that things will be received in the spirit in which they were given.

Barkcloth in Polynesia

Barkcloth, or *tapa*, is one of the material forms and – to adopt the term of an old-fashioned comparative ethnology – one of the cultural traits that manifest the affinities of peoples across Oceania.[1] It was produced all the way from insular south-east Asia to Hawaii and Rapanui (or Easter Island). Though there were significant *tapa* traditions around coastal New Guinea, and even in the non-Austronesian interior, as well as in parts of the Solomon Islands and in southern Vanuatu, Pacific barkcloth is associated above all with Polynesia, where its production and use were pervasive. The cloth, beaten from soaked strips of the bark of various ficus and paper mulberry trees, was nearly everywhere made by women, though it does not necessarily follow that it was defined as 'women's wealth'. Much was undecorated, but much also was stained, rubbed, stencilled, stamped, or painted. Decoration often featured elaborate, optically dynamic non-figurative designs, some of which consisted of dense geometric motifs, and others of more open patterns and free-hand elements. The material was used in garments, in various artefacts, and in rituals associated with hierarchy and reproductive exchange such as marriage. There were generally various types and grades, ranging from heavy waterproofed clothes for common wear, to very fine white tissue, often compared by early writers to muslin, which was monopolized by members of the elite. Though typically made and circulated simply in the form of sheets of cloth that were wrapped around the body, bundled, or extended in long strips, tapa was also sometimes used in figurative constructions, presumed to represent ancestral deities, notably in the Cook Islands, the Marquesas, and Rapanui (Figures 3.1, 3.2).

The ritual significance of barkcloth related to identifications with the skin, which can be seen as 'natural' associations, insofar as the bark is the skin of the tree. Such identifications are certainly attested to by fragments of Tahitian folklore, such as the report that the *avaro* tree 'was the shadow of the god A-varo . . . Persons approaching it irreverently were supposed soon to become afflicted with blotches over the skin, resembling the spots on the bark of the tree' (Henry, 1928: 382). What is more systematically fundamental, though, is the functional affinity between skin and cloth; both wrapped the body, containing contagious sacredness

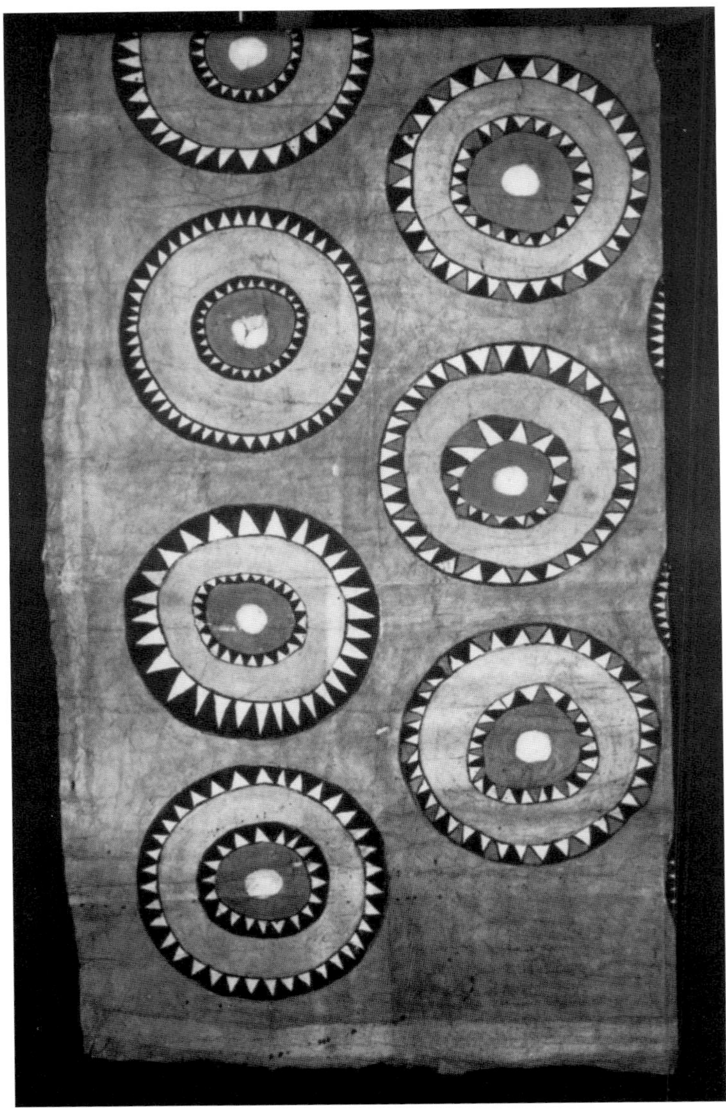

Figure 3.1 Decorated tapa (Peabody Essex Museum E3172)

(*tapu*); additional wrappings were frequently required under conditions of peculiar ritual intensity or exposure, such as childbirth, blood-letting rituals, and death (see Gell 1993). Barkcloth certainly also marked the often dangerous sacredness of a person or site. Mortuary places, the bodies of high-ranking people, and particular sacred artefacts, such as carvings of gods, were all consequently wrapped in *tapa*

Figure 3.2 Barkcloth figure, Rapanui (Easter Island). Painted barkcloth on wooden frame, height 41 cm. Reproduced by permission of the Peabody Museum, Cambridge, Massachussetts.

(Figure 3.2). Had an eighteenth-century Tahitian priest been transported through time and space to encounter one of Christo's wrapped landscapes or buildings, he would not have found the work difficult to interpret.

In Fiji, Tonga and Samoa, barkcloth making has never been abandoned. *Tapa* is still widely produced for huge presentations around events such as marriages, funerals, and high-chiefly celebrations; it also features in contexts such as national and Church diplomacy; through familial connections it is exported in considerable quantities for use among the Polynesian diasporas in New Zealand, the United States, and Australia; and it is also sold to tourists. In central and eastern Polynesia, that is in the Cook Islands, the Societies, the Marquesas, and Hawaii, *tapa* production on the other hand ceased at some point in the nineteenth century, perhaps as early as the 1820s or 1830s in Tahiti, and later in the nineteenth century in most island groups.

Even in those parts of western Polynesia where *tapa* is still extensively produced, its use as clothing has been long abandoned, except in exceptional ceremonial contexts and in cultural performances of various kinds. Hence it is partly misleading to speak of persistence in the west and abandonment in the east, since in both places a more diverse pattern of shifts has actually taken place, involving continuity in some domains, discontinuity in others, and new spheres of circulation, such as tourist markets.

Misplaced and Migrant Ponchos

This history of the changing uses of indigenous and introduced textiles is intimately linked with the history of conversion to Christianity in the Pacific. Missionaries everywhere encouraged girls and women to participate in sewing classes and to produce garments which conformed to their standards of modesty, particularly for the purposes of attending church. There is now an extensive literature on the ways evangelism was not limited to changing religious beliefs, but entailed at the same time a far wider conversion of 'social habits' of work, residence, conjugality, and gender roles (Jolly and Macintyre 1989; Jolly 1991; Thomas 1992; Eves 1996). Christianity brought not only new forms of worship and new beliefs; missionaries attempted at least to impose new ideas of work, a new calendar, and a new sense of the body. Sewing was important not only in itself, but because its discipline entailed the new way of being in the world that the missionaries sought to render pervasive. Yet we cannot suppose that the Pacific Islander women who took up sewing understood the practice in the same way as the missionaries did, nor that they were necessarily transformed in the way that the missionaries desired. The values of these new habits, modes of dress and forms of worship for Samoans, Tahitians and others, have to be investigated; merely because we know what was being offered, we cannot assume what was received.

The most important Protestant mission in Oceania was, of course, the London Missionary Society, which began work in Tahiti in 1797 and extended its efforts westward from there to the Cook islands, Samoa, Niue and elsewhere in the first decades of the nineteenth century (for the fullest review see Gunson, 1978). In all these places progress was initially slow, but indigenous chiefly elites as well as individual converts were gradually brought over to the cause; the great majority of Tahitians were nominally Christian by the 1820s, and by 1850 Christianity also was well established through most of western Polynesia. The popular demonization of missionaries has obscured the point that evangelization was effected, to a very substantial degree, not by white missionaries, but by Polynesian teachers and catechists. Though they were not, until much later, fully ordained ministers, Tahitians, and later Cook Islanders and Samoans, were frequently landed by missionary ships and left to deal with hostile situations as best they could, generally without the trade goods and other resources that gave the white missionaries some nebulous measure of prestige. Even when a mission was led by a white missionary and his wife, they were often accompanied by several Polynesian families, upon whom much of the fraught business of cultural negotiation and intervention presumably fell.

Not only was Tahiti the first base of London Missionary Society activity in the Pacific, it also happened to be one of very few places in which there was any type of upper-body clothing (Figure 3.3). Throughout Oceania, indigenous dress consisted of loin-cloths, waist-wraps, belts, and skirts of various kinds; although flax and feather capes were made by Maori and Hawaiians, the chest was generally routinely uncovered, except in Tahiti, where early observers such as Cook and George Forster described garments like ponchos, consisting simply of long rectangular pieces of cloth, bearing a slit or hole through which the head was inserted.

> Their cloathing are either of Cloth or matting or several differen[t] sorts . . . the dress of both men and women are much the same which is a peice of Cloth or Matting wraped two or three times round their waist . . . another peice or sometimes two or three, about 2 yards or 2½ yards long with a hole in the middle thro which they put their heads, this hangs over their shoulders down behind and before and is tied round their waist with a long peice of thin Cloth and being open at the sides gives free liberty to their arms. (Cook, July 1769; in Beaglehole 1955: 125–6)[2]

Although these were worn by both women and men, they were not so ubiquitous as to be remarked on by many observers, and the only early illustration of a *tiputa* being worn is of a chief (Figure 3.4). There is no definite information suggesting that *tiputa* were worn only by persons of high status, but people of lower relative status were generally required to bare their chests in the presence of those more sacred, and it may accordingly be assumed that only those of high status routinely wore garments of this kind. A type of poncho was also worn in the pre-contact or at least the early-contact period in the Cook Islands; extant examples are often described as the dresses of high-born individuals, and are elaborately perforated

Figure 3.3 Tahitian *tiputa* (poncho), c. 1815. (Powerhouse Museum, Australia 86/395).

with small diamond-shaped cuts, motifs associated in Cook Islands carving with sacred ceremonial adzes and the presences of deities (see Figure 4.2, p. 101). Kooijman points out that this does not mean that commoners did not wear *tiputa;* theirs, if they existed, were probably more basic and undecorated, and never attracted the interest of collectors (1972: 67).

At the time of the Cook voyages, Tahitian barkcloths in general were either undecorated, stained, or decorated in a minimal way, with circular motifs, stamped

Figure 3.4 'Téffaaora', a chief of Borabora, Society Islands – Ambroise Tardieu after Lejeune and Chazal Reproduced by Permission of the National Library of Australia.

in red or black with the end of a cut bamboo. By 1792, however, a new style emerged, involving direct printing with leaves and ferns: 'they imprint sprigs and leaves on the cloth by wetting them with this (juice, and impressing them on the cloth according to their fancy' (Wilson 1799: 371; D'Alleva 1995). Reasonably enough, Kooijman suggests that this was stimulated by printed trade cloth that was presumably introduced during the Cook voyages or subsequently. Some examples feature just a few leaves (Figure 3.4); others combine stamped ferns with painted botanical motifs within a clearly defined diamond-shaped area.

Figure 3.5 Niuean barkcloth *tiputa* (poncho). Reproduced by permission of the Peabody Essex Museum (PEM E14609)

If Tahitian ponchos undergo local changes in the late eighteenth and early nineteenth centuries, the question of what *tiputa* are and where they are from becomes, soon afterward, a great deal more complicated. There are many examples in museums that are decorated not with these stamped botanical motifs, but with designs that are unmistakably western Polynesian; some of these are accordingly attributed to Samoa, Niue or the Cook Islands, though others are said to be Tahitian, and even provenanced to collectors who visited Tahiti but not western Polynesia (Figure 3.5). If most of these pieces have simply been misprovenanced, it is possible that some are more anomalous, acquired in Tahiti but plainly bearing western Polynesian patterns. If the particular origins and histories of many specific *tiputa* remain obscure the larger picture is clear: the Tahitian teachers who constituted the missionary vanguard in Samoa somehow managed to get the Samoans to adopt garments of this type, and that from the early 1830s to the 1860s, or perhaps later, they were made and worn by Christian Samoans, Niueans and possibly Tongans. In the Cook Islands, older autochthonous poncho types were partially replaced by neotraditional varieties associated with Tahitian missionary influence (Buck 1944: 431–4). As imported cloth became more widely available, it came to be locally preferred, and by the time islanders were being extensively photographed, nearly everybody was wearing European garments, except on occasions when 'traditional dress' was required. The journals of the enterprising John Williams, notable for their ethnographic acuity as well as their evangelical and imperialistic zeal, enable us to make some sense of the question of precisely why a change of dress might have constituted an issue, during the early phases of the conversion process in Samoa.

Thanks to Bougainville and many writers since, Tahiti has the reputation of being an 'island of love', while Samoa, after Derek Freeman's demolition of Margaret Mead, is taken in contrast to have been a pretty repressed place. Going on the experiences of the Tahitian teachers deposited on Upolo by Williams in 1830, these images might be reversed: the Tahitians preached restraint while the Samoans paraded their sexual licence. The important point is not that the Tahitians were reputedly shocked by Samoan sexuality, nor that exhibitionism and orgiastic ceremonies loom large in C. Williams' account of heathen Samoan mores; it is rather that Tahitian teachers and Samoans alike evidently understood their differences in terms of the exposure and the display of the body, and played upon those differences, in their missionary efforts and reactive mockery, respectively. When Williams returned to Samoa in 1832, he enquired of the Tahitian teachers whether 'they had not taught them [the Samoans] to make their nice white Tahitian cloth' (incidentally thereby indicating that the barkcloth appealed to the missionaries because of its plain and chaste associations, associations that are hardly likely to have been present in the Tahitians' minds).

> They said they themselves had made a great deal for the Chiefs but they could not get the women to learn. They were so intolerably lazy. They liked the cloth very well to put round their middles but they could not induce them to cover their persons of which they are exceedingly proud especially their breasts which are generally very large. They are continually wishing the teachers wives to lay aside their garments & 'faasamoa' do as the Samoa ladies do, gird a shaggy mat round their loins as low down as they can tuck up the corner in order to expose the whole front & side of the left thigh anoint themselves beautifully with scented oil, tinge themselves with turmeric put a string of blue beads round their neck & then faariaria [make a display] walk about to show themselves. You will have, they say, all the *Manaia* the handsome young men of the town loving you then. (Moyle, 1984: 117)

Williams elsewhere reported that a young European whom he considered 'respectable' had initially been troubled by women removing their mats and exposing their genitals; his shy response prompted others to do the same and dance before him, 'desiring him not to be bashful or angry it was Faa Samoa or Samoa fashion' (1984: 232). It appears, in other words, as though Samoans, and Samoan women in particular, were responding assertively to Tahitian and European foreigners alike, insistently displaying their bodies, insisting on the pleasure of self-decoration, and on the value of these practices as Samoan practices. Even in 1832, however, this was not a sustained or consistent line of resistance. Williams had learned even as he was approaching Upolo and Savai'i the second time that many of the people had turned to Christianity. This would seem an extraordinary development, if one understood Christianity as a European system that perforce had to be imposed by some powerful force of white missionaries; yet it is plain that Williams happened to bring the Tahitian teachers at a highly fortuitous moment, when a high chief and priest had recently been assassinated, when the chief Malietoa, with whom Williams in effect formed an alliance, was in the ascendancy (Moyle 1984: 10–11). The Samoan enthusiasm for Christianity at this moment thus seems to have had little to do with the concerns of the London Missionary Society, and Williams himself well understood that a plethora of motivations were at play, not least the fairly obvious interest in the acquisition of European wealth in various forms. Here again, though, we need to do more than merely note that islanders wanted guns or cloth, but ask what guns and cloth represented to them, and what guns and cloth enabled them to do.

It is notable that in Samoa, unlike in neighbouring Tonga, and unlike in Tahiti and the Cook Islands, barkcloth was not routinely used in ordinary garments. Dress consisted instead of several kinds of simple leaf skirts, and in a variety of grades of mats. The latter may have been held in place by barkcloth belts, but sheets of barkcloth themselves were not worn, except in exceptional ritual circumstances. The bride, for instance, wore a large piece of white barkcloth underneath her fine mats, and this piece was stained with blood when she was ritually deflowered. The strong associations that barkcloth generally had with sanctity, and with ritually marked or dangerous states, elsewhere in Polynesia, can only have been intensified in Samoa, because it had fewer quotidian uses, though it is important to acknowledge that *tapa* was also used in household screens and in a few other situations, which were presumably not marked by peculiar sacredness.

It is striking that, if Williams' reports are to be credited, Samoan chiefs discoursing upon the merits of Christianity seem to have suggested that the religion was true because English people were visibly strong, and were visibly equipped with fine things, including, especially, clothes. He reported that one said 'Only look at the English people. They have noble ships while we have only canoes. They have strong beautiful clothes of various colours while we have only ti leaves. They have sharp knives while we have only a bamboo to cut with' (Moyle 1984: 237). Earlier, the chief Fauea, crucial as a go-between, had argued 'And you can see . . . that their God is superior to ours. They are clothed from the head down to the feet and we are naked' (1984: 68). Although Williams probably embellished these quotations (as he certainly did in his published account of the Pacific missions, 1838: 572–4), it is unlikely that they were simply concocted.[3] The suggestion that some spiritual condition is 'proven' by the efficacy and the well-being of the people concerned is very much in conformity with Polynesian rhetoric and ways of thinking. It is, at any rate, interesting that well-being should be identified not only with obvious technical advantage (the superiority of metal tools) but with an abundance of clothing, and with the full covering of the body.

It is hard to understand why a few fairly powerless Tahitians, or even one personally forceful Englishman, should have succeeded in imposing a Tahitian style of dress upon Samoans, whose political autonomy was in no sense compromised or threatened at this very early moment in contact history, and who clearly took pride in their own modes of comportment. But although Williams noted that some Samoan women sought to convert the Tahitian teachers' wives to the Samoan way rather than expressing any interest in changing themselves, some others, however, opted for cloth. Williams noted not only that 'Some few Samoans who have embraced Christianity have taken to wear cloth entirely' but also that 'On Sabbath days . . . the Teachers have succeeded in inducing the whole congregation men & women to attend properly clothed & decently covered' (Moyle 1984: 231). 'Cloth' means barkcloth and not mats, and 'decent covering' means that the women, or perhaps both men and women, were covering their breasts. Williams does not specifically mention *tiputa,* but these are presumably the upper body garments he has in mind. There is one early Samoan poncho in the Australian Museum which is supposed to have been collected by him, and even if this identification is spurious, Samoan *tiputa* were certainly being made by 1839, when the American explorer Wilkes noted that Samoans were wearing barkcloth 'wrappers' 'and the *tiputa,* a kind of poncho, of the same material, after the fashion of the Tahitians' (Wilkes, 1845, II: 141).

There are references in the missionary literature on Polynesia to converts wearing *tapa* ribbons to distinguish themselves from their pagan neighbours, but the point I want to make about these objects is that they were much more than mere markers of identities. To be sure, *tapa* clothes did indicate that a person was a Christian rather than a pagan Samoan, but I believe that the interpretative strategy of regarding things essentially as expressions of cultural, subcultural, religious or political identities depends on too static and literal an approach to their meanings (Figure 3.6). We also need to go beyond another fairly obvious statement about these Samoan *tiputa,* that defines them as 'local appropriations' of a more pervasive form. Again, it is certainly true that these are Samoan variations upon a regional

Figure 3.6 'Ancient *tapa* [barkcloth] dress of forty years ago: worn by a trader's wife', photo by Beatrice Grimshaw, *In the Strange South Seas* (London: Hutchinson 1907), probably taken in Niue.

type, but it would be misleading if we suggested that 'localization' was a Samoan project that motivated their production; it may rather have been an aspect of their practice that had other motivations. Anthropological rhetoric at present tends to treat the global as something insidious that locals have an interest in assimilating or incorporating, but the critical metanarrative of plural appropriations is ours rather than theirs; their investments may be in strategies that neither collude with nor resist global relations.

In this case, I suggest that the strategies used these material forms as a kind of technology, toward a new way of being in the world. Williams understood this; he was less interested in a badge or flag that declared a person's Christianity than in a technique of dress that altered the being of the convert, that manifested an inner redemption, or at least the scope for one. If it is unlikely that the Tahitian teachers shared this theology, they had in all likelihood adopted the notion of personal modesty, and saw the wearing of new garments as a means to that end. The Samoans, too, would surely not have adopted these clothes had they not themselves regarded them as a technique of conversion; but what conversion meant to them, in 1832, is by no means easy to measure or define. We can be sure that their ideas of self-transformation differed from those of Williams and the Tahitian Christians, and the most suggestive evidence lies perhaps in Fauea's observations on the strength and superiority of Christian people, with their ships and their full dress; this indicates broadly that the fully dressed body was an empowered body. We may infer, also, that the power of that body was conferred by *tapa* wrapping, by some kind of transmission of the sanctity that otherwise inhered in the use of *tapa* in more special ritual contexts. At any rate, if Samoans were transforming themselves, to some extent at the instigation of foreigners, they were also effecting a shift that was internal to Samoan culture and material culture. How far they were binding the values that cloth possessed in collective ritual uses in new forms that embraced the particular person, is something that at this stage I can only guess about.

If *tiputa* started out, in Samoa, by bearing a Samoan strategy of empowerment, these artefacts also entailed certain Christian values of individual self-presentation. The idea that a set of garments constituted one's 'Sunday best' implied both a new temporal order and a new spatial orientation, that made out of the church not only a space of worship, but a theatre in which people might display their persons in a novel way. Of course, it is impossible to know what was actually going on in the heads of the Samoans who began wearing cloth, but to some degree these transformations were implicated in their practices, in what they did and in the objects they deployed, rather than in what they thought or said. We may be missing the point if we seek discursive expressions of embodied habits and orientations.

Conclusion

I have previously argued that novel things can be assimilated to existing categories (Thomas, 1991). I was concerned to demonstrate that indigenous peoples possessed the power to redefine introduced objects, but perhaps that implied that their strategies were conservative, in the sense that they attempted to preserve a prior order rather than create a novel one. Here I seek to move beyond the constraints of an either/or approach. The value of *tiputa,* I suggest, inhered in their doubleness; they were things that mobilized certain precedents, certain prior values that cloth possessed, on the one hand, but possessed novelty and distinctiveness on the other.

Tiputa were more than just Christian clothes; they were more than clothes that covered the body and effected a new modesty. They were also wrappings that were understood by Samoans, initially at least, to empower their bearers. And they were also Sunday best; they gave a new Christian calendar visibility and practical meaning; they were not part of a repressive missionary law, as much as a productive effort, to teach people that their sense of self-worth and pride might be invested in their self-presentation on Sundays, on the path to the church. These artefacts were not just expressions of a new context, but technologies that created that context anew.

This way of seeing things perhaps also helps us move beyond the long-standing dilemma of historical anthropology in Oceania, which has lurched between emphasis on continuity and discontinuity, between affirmation of the enduring resilience of local cultures and critique of the effects of colonial history. Artefacts such as *tiputa* are neither inventions of tradition nor wholly unprecedented forms. They are at once implicated in the material history of Polynesian societies and departures from that history. Their fertile relation to prior and other forms of cloth is perhaps like the productivity of a metaphor. Metaphors must have affinities with the terms to which they are applied, but one chooses a metaphor, not for those affinities, but for its particular differences, because one wants to turn or twist meanings in a new direction. Those who have studied the cultural history of the Pacific may have neglected the interests in turning and twisting. More often than we have acknowledged, the indigenous peoples of the region have been concerned not to 'contextualize' things, but to use things to change contexts.

Notes

1. See Kooijman (1972) for a fine survey of Polynesian tapa traditions, albeit one that perforce leaves many questions unresolved. Other surveys include Neich and Pendergrast (1997) and Thomas (1995: ch. 6). There is no comparable review of Melanesian or island south-east Asian barkcloth.
2. About five barkcloth *tiputa* and one woven-fibre garment of similar form are among the Polynesian artefacts collected on the Cook voyages (D'Alleva 1997, II: 490–2).

3. Caroline Ralston (1985: 310–11) suggests that both these quotations refer to the same speech, in the course of an argument against the view that Polynesian millennial movements were motivated primarily by an extraordinary desire for European property. However, the Polynesian interest in guns, cloth, iron, ships and so on, is extraordinarily widely attested to, and does not mark a Polynesian thirst for 'Western goods' as such but rather an interest in the indigenous forms of prestige and power that possession and deployment of those goods at once enabled and marked. See Thomas (1991: ch. 3), and for further comment on the Williams passage, Smith (1998: 5–6).

References

Appadurai, Arjun, ed. (1986), *The Social Life of Things: Commodities in Cultural Perspective.* Cambridge: Cambridge University Press.

Beaglehole, J. C., ed. (1955), *The Journals of Captain James Cook. Volume* 1: *The Voyage of the Endeavour.* Cambridge: Cambridge University Press/Hakluyt Society.

Bourdieu, Pierre (1977), *Outline of* a *Theory of Practice.* Cambridge: Cambridge University Press.

Buck, Peter H. (1944), *Arts and Crafts of the Cook Islands.* Honolulu: Bernice P. Bishop Museum Bulletin 179.

Collins, Wilkie (1868), *The Moonstone.* Reprint, Oxford: Oxford University Press.

D'Alleva, Anne (1995), 'Continuity and Change in Decorated Barkcloth from Bligh's Second Breadfruit Voyage, 1791–1793', *Pacific Arts* 13–14: 29–42.

—— (1997), 'Shaping the Body Politic: Gender, Status and Power in the Art of Eighteenth-Century Tahiti and the Society Islands', unpublished PhD dissertation, Columbia University.

Eves, Richard (1996), 'Colonialism, Corporeality and Character: Methodist Missions and the Refashioning of Bodies in the Pacific', *History and Anthropology* 10: 85–138.

Gell, Alfred (1993), *Wrapping in Images: Tattooing in Polynesia.* Oxford: Oxford University Press.

Gunson, Neil (1978), *Messengers of Grace: Evangelical Missionaries in the South Seas.* Melbourne: Oxford University Press.

Henry, Teuira (1928), *Ancient Tahiti.* Honolulu: Bernice P. Bishop Museum Bulletin 48.

Jolly, Margaret 1991), '"To Save the Girls for Brighter and Better Lives": Presbyterian Missions and Women in the South of Vanuatu, 1848–1870') *Journal of Pacific History* 26: 27–48.

—— and Martha Macintyre, eds (1989), *Family and Gender in the Pacific: Domestic Contradictions and the Colonial Impact.* Cambridge: Cambridge University Press.

Kooijman, Simon (1972), *Tapa in Polynesia.* Bernice P. Bishop Museum Bulletin 234. Honolulu: Bishop Museum.

Moyle, Richard, ed. (1984), *The Samoan Journals of John Williams, 1830 and* 1832. Canberra: Australian National University Press.

Neich, Roger, and Mick Pendergrast (1997), *Pacific Tapa.* Auckland: David Bateman (also published as *7raditional Tapa Textiles of the Pacific,* London: Thames and Hudson.

Ralston, Caroline (1985), 'Early Nineteenth Century Polynesian Millennial Cults and the Case of Hawaii', *Journal of the Polynesian Society* 94: 307–31.

Smith, Vanessa (1998) *Literary Culture in the Pacific.* Cambridge: Cambridge University Press.

Strathern, Marilyn (1990), 'Artefacts of History: Events and the Interpretation of Images', in Jukka Siikala (ed.) *Culture and History in the Pacific.* Helsinki: Finnish Anthropological Society.

Thomas, Nicholas (1991), *Entangled Objects: Exchange, Material Culture and Colonialism in the Pacific.* Cambridge, MA: Harvard University Press.

—— (1992), 'Colonial Conversions: Difference, Hierarchy and History in Early 'Twentieth-Century Evangelical Propaganda', *Comparative Studies in Society and History* 34: 366–89.

—— (1995), *Oceanic Art.* London: Thames and Hudson.

Wilkes, Charles (1845), *Narrative of the United States Exploring Expedition.* Philadelphia: Lea and Blanchard.

Williams, John (1838), *A Narrative of Missionary Enterprises in the South Sea Islands.* London: John Snow.

Wilson, William (1799), *A Missionary Voyage in the Southern Pacific Ocean.* London: T. Chapman.

–4–

The Poncho and the Quilt: Material Christianity in the Cook Islands

Susanne Küchler

Large and elaborate appliqué and piecework quilts known variously as *tivaevae, tifaifai,* and *kapa lau* have been produced by women in the Cook Islands, the Hawaiian Islands, the Society Islands, and elsewhere in eastern Polynesia since the late nineteenth and early twentieth centuries. Quilting was restricted to eastern Polynesia where *tivaevae* (the Cook Island term used throughout this chapter) were at once substituted for barkcloth and used in ways which were unprecedented, yet keenly invested in the novel contexts of Christian domesticity (Shaw 1996; Hammond 1986; Pogglioli 1988; Rongokea 1992; Robertson 1989). While *tivaevae* retain some of barkcloth's former associations with high rank and sanctity, their novel uses as home decoration, as treasured possession and mode of timekeeping exemplify the way in which cloth came to mediate the constitution of new social relations and contexts.

Polynesian quilts share a tenuous relation with the Euro-American quilt in that they are generally the size of a double bed and are overtly associated with the nineteenth-century connotations of Victorian patchwork (the term *tivaevae* is taken from *vaivai*, 'to patch or to mend'). Pieces of both new and used cloth are patched together, but not in an additive manner as we would expect from Euro-American practice. Rather, Polynesian quilting involves the superimposition of layers of cloth, in a manner similar to barkcloth production in this part of the Pacific. In eastern Polynesia, a process of fermentation served to affix separate layers of barkcloth in a manner that enabled the production of long, thick trails of cloth. It is as if the availability of cloth, and of cotton thread and sewing, released the potential of a technology that was, as we will see, inseparable from ways of knowing and of being.

Visually and conceptually, eastern Polynesian quilts resemble each other. They are recognizable by their complex symmetry and intricate geometric patterns. These patterns are most abstract in Hawaii, most geometric in Tahiti and most representational in the Cook Islands. In Tahitian and Cook Island *tivaevae*, the three-dimensionality of the pattern is enhanced by the use of vibrant, usually clashing colours. Cook Island quilts are further distinguished by rich multicoloured

Figure 4.1 Wedding ceremony

embroidery adding to the three-dimensional appearance of the usually floral pattern which tends to be arranged in rotational symmetry. Women usually quilt collaboratively, often in Church-based associations. To present a quilt as a gift to one's relatives is seen as a necessary part of life-cycle ceremonies, from the first haircutting of boys and the twenty-first birthday of girls to the wedding and the funeral when *tivaevae* are wrapped around and piled on top of the deceased person inside the grave (Figure 4.1). A mother may stitch on average 15 *tivaevae* for each of her children, usually presented to them upon marriage but sometimes simply when they leave the parental home. Hidden piled up in wooden chests, quilts are on display inside the house merely once a year.

The emergence of quilting in Eastern Polynesia appears to have coincided with the London Missionary Society's conquest of the Pacific in the nineteenth century. For it was sewing and the dressing of body and home with embroidered cloth that expressed Victorian Protestant convictions about how to inculcate a rational mind into 'hot' and 'tempered' bodies common to children, women and savages (Park 1998; Parker 1984). Yet, what may have started out as Victoriana quickly became an object that enabled a translation of Western ideals of attachment into a quint-essentially Polynesian form of property. New concepts of person and of social relations, emerging from rapidly changing contexts of rank and sanctity, became tangible in the quilt. Rather than serving as an instrument of discipline, sewing fostered an empowering sense of control over a resource of material and spiritual importance, access to which allowed women to achieve the highest-ranking positions in a previously male-dominated hierarchy.

Christianity, however, thus not only brought into relation indigenous and European communities, but also involved the heightened interaction between different Polynesian communities. In fact, unique to Polynesia is the conversion of Polynesians by Polynesians. Conversion was a process in which mediatory objects preceding quilting, such as a form of upper-body garment known as the 'poncho' or *tiputa,* appeared to have played a primary role (Thomas, Chapter 3 of this volume). Quilting, therefore, was not a singular and unique testament of the arrival of Christianity, but was just one of a number of material translations which brought into relief the efficacy of cloth.

The speed by which Christianity came to be adopted as a mode of being and thinking was particularly pronounced in the Cook Islands. Here, I suggest that it was a series of cloth-based mediatory objects that enabled Christianity to be fitted into an existing body politic at whose centre stood strikingly performative images utilizing both layering and binding. It was the visual analogy of clothing, worn by early explorers and missionaries, with the bound and layered imagery that was found to be effective in establishing connections with the gods, which prompted conversion.

Conversion in eastern Polynesia was thus not a singular event, but a process punctuated by cloth things that translated indigenous knowledge technology into new media, and made it effective in relation to new resources. These objects, whether Western-style clothing made of barkcloth or cloth quilts composed of layers of cloth and bound thread, were deemed effective because they created visual resemblance and thus connected what hitherto may have been thought of as distinct and different. From this perspective it is clear that when cloth became widely available through trade in this part of the Pacific it assumed an agency that was already invested in the materiality and texture of bound and layered things. It was for this reason that the making of composites, through patchwork, cut-out and appliqué, was accepted as uniquely efficacious in ways which could never have been predicted by those who introduced sewing as a useful and disciplining pastime.

Cloth Things and the Body-Politic in Eastern Polynesia

Cook Island *tivaevae* are perhaps the most complex of Polynesian quilts. There are several distinct, named types of quilts, each being composed of up to four layers composed of pieces of cloth and cotton thread. Yet it is not just the visual and conceptual complexity of the quilt that suggests the Cook Islands as a suitable starting point for a discussion of the Polynesian quilt. It is also the Cook Islands' geographical and political position on the edge of the old and the new world, which allows one to observe quilts in action, paving new connections along which people and ideas move back and forth. Located within a small triangle of the Pacific defined by Fiji, Samoa and French Polynesia, Cook Islanders share close ties with Tahiti and with New Zealand, Sydney, and Los Angeles, where three-quarters of its expatriate population live today. Like the foreign flowers that decorate Cook Island quilts prosperity is found elsewhere, reaching the Cooks along the paths stitched into the quilts. Young men and women living far away will cherish the *tivaevae* given to them by their mothers and recall the place to which they will make many returns.

Geographically, the Cook Islands fall into two clusters: a northern group of seven coral atolls, and a much larger southern group of eight islands, most of them upraised coral formations. It is mostly in these southern islands that quilting is found today. Culturally, Cook Islanders belong to Polynesia, yet with the exception of Manihiki and Rakahanga, no two islands had the same cultural origin. Pukapukans in the far north originated from Western Polynesia centuries ago, while most of the peoples of the other islands came from various parts of Eastern Polynesia. Tradition holds that the Maori-speaking population of the southern Cook Islands came from Tahiti and Samoa sometime in the thirteenth century, but that immigrants from the Marquesas already populated the islands. Rarotonga, today the main administrative centre of the Cook Islands, is also the location of the mythical departure of canoes to New Zealand.

The post-contact history of the Cook Islands is commonly divided into three periods (Gilson 1980). From 1823–1888 was the heyday of the London Missionary Society (LMS), which was founded in 1795 during the evangelical revival as a non-denominational body dedicated to spreading the Christian faith. Poor harbours and powerful mission influence on the chiefs discouraged merchants, slavers, recruiters and the alienation of land. While Tahiti, Tonga and Samoa were fast becoming centres of foreign commercial enterprise, the smaller and more isolated Cook Islands were much less influenced by the impact of commerce. It was not until the 1860s that foreign traders, planters and beachcombers settled in significant numbers, and not until 1881 that the resident merchants succeeded in obtaining a British Consulate. The establishment of the British Protectorate was delayed until 1888. The Islands were annexed to New Zealand in 1901, and achieved independence in 1965 while retaining New Zealand citizenship.

The recorded history of the Cook Islands is peppered by material-culture collections that document the importance of its connections with Tahiti. Early nineteenth-century artefact collections from the Cook Islands document the existence of the so-called poncho, which it shared with Tahiti. Then, as today, Tahiti was the spiritual centre of Cook Island chiefly structure and the driving force of the work of Missions in Eastern Polynesia. Yet, compared to the white and thin

Figure 4.2 Cook Island barkcloth poncho with a cutout design coloured with turmeric (Auckland Museum 10166).

barkcloth used for the poncho in Tahiti, Cook Islands examples of the poncho fall into at least two types. There is a lightweight version, whose entire surface is covered in regular and symmetrical cut-out designs, in the form of triangles and linear configurations. Other ponchos are double-sided, heavy and layered. A blackened layer of barkcloth, perforated with triangular shapes made using the 'snowflake' technique of folding and cutting is superimposed on top of another layer of cloth. This snowflake technique became synonymous with Tahitian quilting a century on. While the snowflake technique is also found in Cook Island quilts, here techniques of layering utilize the stitch in ways that are reminiscent of free-hand line drawings and incisions on mid-nineteenth-century Tahitian barkcloth. A complex traffic of ideas and images thus connected inter-island communities in recorded history in ways that reflect on pre-conversion religious activity in the area.

As well as producing barkcloth ponchos the southern Cook Islands also shared a ritual complex in common with Tahiti. This complex was fundamentally linked to burial practices and focused on the wrapping and unwrapping of composite figures. Known as 'god staffs', these figures were carved from wood and wrapped in layers of knotted sennit cord as well as barkcloth that was covered with hand-drawn geometric figures. While we know next to nothing about the use of the poncho, these so-called 'god staffs' were widely collected in the Cook Islands in the nineteenth century and were exquisitely drawn and described by Peter Buck (1944) in his *Arts and Crafts of the Cook Islands*. Yet it is Alain Babadzan's (1993) ethnography on the Tahitian wrapped figures called '*to'o*' which brings to life some of the more salient features of key ritual paraphernalia of astern Polynesia. A brief excursion into the performative qualities of the composite and wrapped figures should bring to light the salient significance attributed to the layer and the line in cloth-like things. God staffs are still produced today for tourist purposes, but their connection to ideas of binding and layering and thus to *tivaevae* is lost to most.

As the Tahitian *to'o* is well described in Chapter 1 of this volume, a very brief account will suffice. Babadzan describes the *to'o* as a composite object, in general made of a piece of hard wood, elongated in shape like a stick or club, of about several centimetres in length to 1.8 metres for the most important pieces. This stick remains completely invisible, because the wood is covered in a tight binding of sennit cordage called *'aha* like the Hawaiian sacred cord. The binding is made of plaits of cords from the fibres of the coconut tree and/or different layers of *tapa* wrappings. The whole thing is covered in feathers of different colours, but mainly of red feathers, that are placed either outside the *to'o*, or between the wooden frame of the object and its different layers of wrapping. The mummy-like object is decorated on the outside with roughly delineated facial features and woven limbs made out of sennit cordage.

While the *to'o* were thought of as a specific representation of the god *'Oro*, they did not all represent the same deity, nor exclusively the principal gods alone. A great number of images existed, each owned by a family, a bloodline, a clan, a district, and even a whole island. The images were ranked according to size. The correlation between the ranked polity of images and social rank was given regular and formal expression in a ritual called *pa'iatua* which, translated, means the 'gathering and undressing of the gods'. This ritual consisted of three stages, mirroring the three cycles which compose the agricultural calendar, each stage being defined in relation to the manipulation of the *to'o:* 1) the unwrapping of the *to'o*, effecting the death or departure of the gods; 2) the exchange of feathers as the 'sharing' of the remains of the gods; 3) the reassemblage or 'renewal' of the *to'o* invoking the return of the gods and the period of abundance.

A close relation existed between this last stage and the treatment of the corpse at funerary ceremonies that witnessed the presentation of precious fabrics used as a wrapping for the corpse. Babadzan also remarks on the similarity between the practice of the wrapping of *to'o* and funerary practices outside of Tahiti such as in the Cook Islands as well as with the Polynesian bundle gods, all consisting of the wrapping of corpses in matting given as funeral presents which then were tied into a parcel with numerous rounds of sennit cord. The rewrapping of the *to'o* was thus also considered responsible for the summoning of the god under a shape evoking that of the deceased covered in his funeral costume, thus 'travelling in reverse . . . the whole journey which normally leads men to ancestrality' (see Babadzan, Chapter 1).

Owning a *to'o*, an artefact that could be stripped and reclad in its cordage, was thus likened to owning access to the remains of the gods, while keeping them most of the time at a safe distance. As in Tahiti, '*unu*' (god staffs) were a central part of the Cook Island temple complex, known as *marae*. The *marae* in Mangaia still has its boundaries sharply defined by basalt rocks embedded in the ground, forming a low raised rectangular court. The names and sites of the *marae* are remembered on each island today. They are recognized by rectangular slabs of coral limestone set lengthways into the earth, thus creating a surface that is raised above the ground.

Buck describes carved posts, decorated with flowers for the ceremony, which were wrapped in special thick white barkcloth and stored in houses erected on the *marae* between ceremonies (Buck 1944: 3, 8–9). Yet most attention in the literature is given to the finely carved images of gods that are reproduced for the tourist trade today. Covered in sennit and bark cloth, they have a protruding upper end with more or less abstract facial appearance. God staffs (*unu*) were complemented by bundle gods, *tapa* and feather-bundles that most resemble the Tahitian *to'o*. Buck mentions such a figure collected by the LMS, now part of the British Museum collection, which has a cylindrical body, bound with thick, two-ply coir cord, wrapped with white *tapa* and, near the upper end, sets of four red feathers from wings or tail of the parrot bound together with single strand of fibre (ibid.: 401). Its feather cap is constructed like a chief's headdress with rosette-like feather holders made from a fibrous cord. (ibid.: 89). These feather-holders have an intriguing likeness to the embroidered flowers on today's *tivaevae*, as both are composed of intricately bound thread.

Collected by missionaries or burned upon their request, the bound and layered figures may have disappeared from view. Ideas of deposition and recollection, however, did not vanish together with the figures, but found a new articulation in a quite unsuspected and surprisingly overt manner, straight in the face of the mission. In the first hundred years of mission influence, we can detect the increasingly important role of composite cloth-things in putting to work a political economy of 'recollection' that began to usurp Christianity as a new resource of prosperity and prestige.

Between 1821, the arrival of the first Society island missionaries trained by John Williams on the island Aitutaki, and Williams' return to the island Rarotonga in 1827, most of the Cook Islands had converted to Christianity. The donning of upper-body garments by the missionaries, which in style were not dissimilar to the barkcloth poncho worn by the chiefly leaders (*ariki*), may have appeared to signal a democratization of prosperity (cf. Thomas Chapter 3). Yet perhaps equally important may have been the perception of Western clothing as 'layered' (*papa'a* means in Maori Cook Island 'four layers' or 'white man') and as 'bound' (*aha*). Since it was multi-layered, Western dress may have suggested a form of empowerment associated with the Cook Island version of the Tahitian *to'o*, guaranteeing a new form of control over the remains of the dead.

As Polynesians rather than Europeans conducted the conversion of the Cook Island population, the demonstrative capacities of clothing as instrument of rank and spiritual agency must have been uniquely convincing (Gilson 1980: 23). This is apparent in the annexing of cloth-wealth by an increasingly female chiefdom that dominated the political life on the Cook Islands in the century following conversion.

For the ten years after the establishment of Christianity in the 1830s, the islands were almost solely dependent upon ships owned or chartered by the missions (ibid.: 40). It was not uncommon for several years to go by in between successive visits of vessels. Anticipation of possible exchanges of sweet potatoes for calico led to food-crop surpluses, then as well as today. By 1840 the commercial relations between islanders and Europeans were firmly under the control of the chiefly *ariki* with centralization of trading and a general exclusion of foreign settlers. In the same year, the local spinning of cotton in Rarotonga had been completely superseded by barter with visiting ships for cotton cloth (ibid.: 41).

Cotton clothing was clearly widely available in the 1850s, at least in the more easily accessible island of Rarotonga, whose harbour allowed ships to offload their cargo even in adverse weather. No mention is made, however, of quilting, although women had become fully participating members of the new Church, and the missionary wives, who were themselves very active, held special classes which stressed the importance of women as 'homemakers' (ibid.: 35).

With the expansion of trade in the 1880s, mission influence declined. By the late 1870s the money economy, based on the weak Chilean dollar, was so well established that even the mission had to abandon its system of barter for local goods and services (ibid.: 48). By 1882, four of the five *ariki* in Rarotonga were women whom Gill describes as being of 'Christian Character'. In Gilson's description of current affairs of the time, this fact is given great importance as it allowed the Church to express hope to regain hold over the growing independence of the council of chiefs (ibid.: 50). But the hope of Gill and his successor that the female *ariki* would cooperate more closely with the mission was not realized, for economic prosperity and contacts with new ideas produced different reactions. As a sign of the worldliness of the chiefs, one of the female *ariki*, Makea Takau, travelled to Auckland in 1885, were she was received as the 'Queen of Rarotonga'. Her husband, Ngamaru, was paramount chief of Atiu, Mauke, and Mitiaro, the three smaller islands of the southern group. The news of Makea's treatment by New Zealand's Native Minister as the head of a foreign government travelled thus quickly to the outer islands. It was upon her return that, much against the wishes of the mission, western attitudes spread to all levels of society. Some men adopted uniforms and the female wardrobe was enlarged by parasols and by 'as many coloured frocks as the owner could accumulate' (ibid.: 51).

By the turn of the century voyages to Tahiti and other islands had become fashionable, bringing new fashions to the Cook Islands. Beatrice Grimshaw made the first cursory mention of Cook Island *tivaevae* in her 1907 travel narrative *In the Strange South Seas*. Although there are no records to this effect, it is quite possible that quilting in the Cooks was influenced by the experience of the travellers who must have returned from Tahiti, as they still do today, laden with gifts. Inhabitants of Atiu island, who still today own real estate in Tahiti and who have extensive kinship relations to what is known as an Atiuan community on Tahiti, still proudly possess distinctively Tahitian *tivaevae* reaching back to the 1940s.

In the absence of any description of *tivaevae*, a rather curious collection from the last years of the nineteenth century gives an indication of the importance assigned to manipulating cloth so that it appeared to be part Western-style clothing and part bound and layered wrap. The collection came into the possession of the Dominion Museum in Wellington, New Zealand in 1907, having been collected at some point in the last few years of the nineteenth century (Baessler 1899; Davidson 1997). It consisted of canoes from Manihiki, fishing gear as well as traps and spears, but also of a set of western style clothes, including trousers and shirts, made of barkcloth, which together with a mask or headdress were collected on the island of Mangaia (Figure 4.3). Striking are the hand-drawn lines covering the clothing, resembling stitches, but also the surface of bound sennit cordage that once clad the *to'o*-like figures. Together with the headdresses, which appear to have been introduced by Cook Islanders who had been to the Papuan Gulf as London Missionary Society teachers, these shirts and trousers appear to have been used for performances called '*eva*, which once were part of the mortuary cycle, but had by the late 1890s become popular, yet formally structured, 'history' plays (Davidson 1997: 176 see Figure 4.4). These garments are hand-sewn down the sides and have

Figure 4.3 Barkcloth suit and headdress (Auckland Museum 8353,8354,8355).

separate sleeves and thus appear to be more like a shirt than a poncho. They were probably only a cursory phenomenon made for performances, as Cook Island women clearly were able to sew Western-style dresses and trousers from cloth. And yet, they bring to the fore a conscious concern with the creation of mediatory objects that assumed the agency ascribed both to cloth and to the surfacing of things with layers of bound thread.

Figure 4.4 Cook Island performers wearing barkcloth costumes used in history plays called *'eva*, c. 1890 (Auckland Museum C23696).

In addition to these composite things, the collection contains three large, rectangular pieces of barkcloth of which one is bright yellow on both sides and measures 2920 x 1720 cm – the size of a latter-day *tivaevae* (Buck 1944: 72). The other two pieces are dark matt brown on one surface and have a shiny almost black appearance on the other surface. According to Buck (1944: 73) this form of decoration was achieved by soaking the cloth in the mud of the sago swamp, washing and drying it, and rubbing the other side with a mixture of grated turmeric and grated coconut. The sizes of these two pieces are again similar to the above (Davidson 1997: 170). Examples from the British Museum collection dating to the 1880s document this characteristic of coloration and size which are a distinctive trait of Cook Island barkcloth of the time (Buck 1944: 70–3). Buck refers in addition to the use of flowers, as well as of coconut cream, to perfume the cloth – a fact that will become significant when considering the use of floral imagery in *tivaevae*. It appears as if quilting enabled the realization of technical concerns, not just with layering and binding but also with capturing olfaction that alone was assumed capable of mediating the realm of the visible with the invisible.

The hand-drawn lines so clearly visible and distinctive on the surface of Cook Island barkcloth of the late nineteenth century can be found again in the *tivaevae*, but on its underside. When judging the quality of a piece of sewing, women flip over a corner to look at the stitching visible beneath which should traverse the cloth in regular and neat lines. These lines bind the layers of cloth. Because of the use of *ombré* (shaded) thread, the stitches resemble rich embroidery, which covers layers of cloth pieces that are cut and laid out to depict floral arrangements in almost microscopic clarity. The layering of cloth, once an important and yet invisible aspect of all composite and mediatory objects in Eastern Polynesia, emerges as the distinctive visual trait of Polynesian quilting in which colour, once so powerfully linked to olfaction and recollection, appears as synonymous with the intricate geometric pattern.

Concerns with layering, with olfaction and coloration as well as with the line, have become fundamental to the large *tivaevae* that began to utilize cloth in novel ways. In this way, quilts illuminate a kind of 'doubleness' characteristic of composite and mediatory objects – in that they visualize resemblance not just with Victorian preoccupations, through visual reference to embroidery and domesticity, but also with intrinsically Polynesian concerns. Rather than being profoundly 'new', quilts are thus no different to any previous composite object. Yet they have facilitated a heightened accentuation of a ritual work of re-collection embedded in matters of layering and binding that have become inseparable from matters of the Church. The hours of stitching required for the completion of the richly textured quilt, as well as the performance of covering and uncovering afforded by the quilt, have quietly allowed to put to work new corporeal regimes of time management and domesticity for rather unsuspected ends.

Women of Quiet Thoughts

Women's associations are formed around the often communal making of these large, rectangular bedspread-like quilts called *tivaevae* (Figure 4.5) Every village, district and island tends to have its own associations, but most women have additional ties to other associations which are tied to religious denominations. The most active in matters of *tivaevae* are the associations of the Cook Island Christian Church, the contemporary framework of the London Missionary Society.

Associations meet regularly for the sake of planning and executing the making of new *tivaevae* required by its members for the many occasions that demand a prestation of a quilt. *Tivaevae* are expected as gifts at the first haircut of a boy, a wedding or a funeral when the body is wrapped in layers of quilts. Yet *tivaevae* are also required for the annual village and church competition known as *tutaka* when new *tivaevae* made during the year are displayed and judged for completion and perfection. It is only at this time that *tivaevae* are put on show in houses where they are draped over beds and sofas accompanied by embroidered pillows, cushion

Figure 4.5 *Vaivai* (patch or mend) quilt by Ake Takaiti, *c.* 2001 Atiu Island (photograph author's by own).

covers and tablecloths. Yet associations also look after each other's households, securing a common living standard among neighbours by collecting money for those in need.

The presence of *tivaevae* in women's lives can be easily appreciated when reflecting on the number of quilts, in addition to tablecloths and embroidered cushion covers, which have to be completed over the course of one year. Even when women, particularly those who are in full-time employment, delegate the work of cutting and sewing to others, the urgency of completing at least two or three large 4m by 3m quilts pervades every household. Every afternoon, the passer-by can see women sitting inside their houses facing the door, their knees draped in cloth. Some may work day and night when a deadline is looming close in order to finish a quilt in time.

And yet, for the visitor to the islands, the quilts are invisible. Folded and stored in large wooden treasure boxes, women keep *tivaevae* for their daughters who may be living in Sydney or Auckland or until they are required for one of the many exchanges. Just occasionally they are sold for money, but this tends to be an illicit affair in which both the maker and the product remain hidden. An advertisement of a market stall selling *tivaevae* in Rarotonga, posted in the Cook Island Herald, reads: 'Colina has one of the best selections of vegetables, fruit, *tivaevae* bed spreads, pearl shells and pure pawpaw juice . . .'. On most days one would not realize that *tivaevae* are kept inside this stall, and even when asking, *tivaevae* are taken out one by one to be bartered over. As Elizabeth Arkana says about Hawaiian quilts: 'quilts contain much *mana*. If one should die and leave much spirit behind, it could be damaging and might never be able to achieve real rest.' (Arkana, 1986: 5). Most quilts that are for sale are sewn by machine, thus not demanding such an investment of time and thought in their making. The intense attachment of person and quilt means that quilts are separated only temporarily from the maker, being returned eventually at death. Hawaiian quilts were burned, while Cook Island quilts are buried with the dead in concrete tomb-like structures erected next to the entrance of houses.

On first examination, the motifs and patterns of the Cook Island *tivaevae,* like those of Tahiti and Hawaii, are hard to visualize. Although the designs are based on the flora of the islands, making reference to local flowers and plants as well as to specimen found in magazines or embroidery books or while visiting relatives abroad, they may at first be unrecognizable. This is at least partly because of the complex symmetrical arrangement of individual motifs, set within a myriad of overlapping colours through which the relation between background and foreground appears to shift and change the longer one stares at the pattern in trying to work out how it is done.

On the whole, Cook Island quilts share many of the formal qualities of other Polynesian quilts. Yet their composite and distinctively layered appearance enables one to detect a Cook Island version of a common floral theme that may as well be found in Tahitian quilts. Also, unlike Tahitian and Hawaiian quilts, Cook Island *tivaevae* do not have borders, but a complex rotational symmetry, which locks motifs into an intricate play of resemblance and difference. Intricately stitched embroidery heightens the three-dimensional, almost tactile 'look' of Cook Island quilts – striving toward an apparent realism in the depiction of flora and fauna that is underscored through the use of opposing as well as carefully graded colours. Both rotational symmetry and colouration create a dazzling effect of arrested movement.

There are three distinct types of *tivaevae* in the Cook Islands, of which the most valuable is a type of patchwork called *taorei* (handkerchief) in which several thousands of tiny rectangular pieces are sewn together (Figure 4.6). The pattern is constructed in triangles, after the coloured pieces, often more than 3,000 for a quilt, have been threaded onto a long string according to a numbered colours-string – '5 red, 2 blue, 6 yellow' for example. The example in Figure 4.4 shows a *taorei* made by Tokerau Munro of Arorongi on Rarotonga for her daughter's wedding. Another interesting example is currently under construction, worked upon by Vereara Maeva of Rarotonga, who borrowed the *tivaevae* from Kimi Semo of the island of Mangaia in order to remake the pattern she had earlier given to her associate. This new *tivaevae* is for her youngest son after the original version was placed into her husband's grave.

Figure 4.6 *Taorei* (handkerchief) quilt by Vereara Maeva, *c.* 2001, Rarotonga (photograph author's own).

Figure 4.7 *TaTaura* (piecework) quilt by Tukerau Munro, *c.* 2000, Rarotonga (photograph author's own).

Figure 4.8 *TaTaura* quilt, crocheted together by Vereara Maeva, Rarotonga (photograph author's own).

Figure 4.9 *Manu* 'Snowflake' quilt by Tungata Boasa, Atiu Island (photograph author's own).

The most popular *tivaevae* is called *Ta taura (piecework).* It is an appliqué work, usually of floral motifs, with detailed embroidery that gives the design a three–dimensional impression (Figure 4.7). The example is a depiction of a water lily made by Tungata Boasa of Atiu for one of her adopted sons, yet even butterflies and birds may be used as motifs. Another version of a *Ta taura* consists of embroidered squares, connected by crocheted grids as in the example by Vereara Maeva of Rarotonga (Figure 4.8).

Most closely resembling the snowflake designs of Tahitian and Hawaiian quilts, yet without the border, are so-called *manu* or 'bird' quilts. The use of bright colours against a dark background common to Hawaiian quilts tends to be reversed in the Cook Island version of the snowflake design, recalling the effect of bound cordage holding the feathers in *tapa*-bundles (Figure 4.9).

The recipient's popularity is a clear measure of the time needed to complete a quilt, but also of the type of social relations that it may accentuate. The snowflake design is considered to demand a specialist cutter, but is sewn by a single woman, quite in contrast to the *taorei* or patchwork quilt which demands the cooperation of many hands to complete the design. As piecework quilts are the fastest to produce, and allow for a mixture of individual and cooperative work, they are the most frequently made. The reason for the popularity of appliqué over the rather arduous snowflake, or patchwork, is the specialization it affords as well as the ease of both copying and design innovation.

Designs originally may have been owned by individual women, yet today so many women have exchanged designs, and quilts are exhibited in public on such a frequent basis, that there is no correspondence between locality and pattern. Both the hidden copying, by just noting and absorbing designs at one of the many exhibitions of *tivaevae* on the islands, and the overt copying as a stamp of friendship between women is accepted. In fact, one may say that traces of resemblance between different *tivaevae* manifest new networks of friendship that crosscut families, villages, islands and even countries. Such ties were created in the 1950s and 1960s by the work of women's associations, usually connected with the Cook Island Christian Church (CICC), who travelled around the islands teaching women sewing as well as other domestic skills. Today, through connections paved by these women, regular visiting takes place between islands, whereby entire villages prepare visits that may last up to a month. But women also go further away, to Hawaii, New Zealand or Sydney, and even China, as the leaders of scouts, accompanying a dance group or just to visit relatives. New flower designs as well as pattern books thus reach the islands regularly.

New designs are constantly innovated, often by talented younger women specializing in the cutting of designs into cloth. Good cutters and innovators of designs are often asked to create patterns for other women who are part of the same association, and in this way a pattern may quickly, at least for a while, become the hallmark of a village, before becoming more widespread.

Yet, while there are always new and innovative means of creating a layered and three-dimensional effect through the intricate use of coloured pattern, a quilt also allows ownership to be declared and restricted through stitches that tend to be passed down from mother to daughter. Experienced women, who frequently travel to neighbouring islands as part of their work for associations, can detect the hand of individual women in *tivaevae* exhibited en masse in the annual quilt show on the island of Rarotonga.

The lack of a border in Cook Island *tivaevae* reflects the fluidity of pattern transmission, while the cohesion of motifs which are visually attached to each other by an intricate symmetrical order manifests the salient impact of domesticity upon an otherwise unmarked visual landscape. Let me describe for the purpose of clarification the island of Atiu, the third-largest island of the southern group northeast of Rarotonga. Atiu is a high island with an area of not more than ten square miles, with a volcanic core, whose five villages are perched on the flattened top ridges. An obelisk-shaped monument stands on the Church parade ground in the heart of Atiu. The limestone monument was erected to the memory of the Atiuan high chief who assisted in the construction of the oldest and largest Cook Island Christian Church (CICC) in the 1850s; it is still standing today. Atiuans call this monument *Te Pito*, the navel, and consider it to mark the exact centre of the island, an impression confirmed as factual by a Surveying team employed for the restoration of the church in 1967 (Stephenson 1974).

Radiating outward from this centre, Atiu is divided into five villages, five districts, and three tribes. Yet, for an outsider there appears to be nothing but a sea of houses clustered along the roads which radiate outward from the centre like a star. It is only after having entered people's houses and having become accustomed to the movements of people around the island that one begins to realize that there is very little contact between inhabitants of different villages. The intricate pattern of sociality is envisioned in a hierarchical structure whereby each tribe is centred in a particular district, while the remaining two districts are loyal to one of the three ranked tribes. Yet the members of each tribe are scattered throughout the five villages. The village as a unit emerges only at the level of Church associations, so that one can say that a particular village is more or less Catholic, with its CICC followers living in houses situated in the direction of the CICC church, with other villages being predominantly Seventh Day Adventist or Bahai.

Women cooperate in matters of *tivaevae* at the village level irrespective of their membership in a particular religious organization, and may thus belong to more than association at any one time, working for a number of yearly competitions organized around village and Church. It is only at the yearly *Tutaka* event, believed to have been organized originally by the London Missionary Society as an inspection of health and household matters, that the village comes to the fore, leaving its trace for the remainder of the year in subtle differences in household possessions and decoration.

Once a year, usually in late November, a date defined today the president of the women's organization on each island, every household springs into feverish activity, cleaning and painting and taking out all the new and old *tivaevae* as decoration for beds and sofas, covering tables in crocheted cloth, and adorning chairs with embroidered pillows. A committee of women composed of the village association, in the past accompanied by the local health official, then moves from house to house. Collections are made and the proceeds given to women who are considered to require replacements or innovations such cookers or cutlery. The following day, the *tivaevae* are taken to the central square on the island, and each village is judged for both the number and completeness and care invested in its yearly *tivaevae* activities. Households are then returned to their normal state, with *tivaevae* and all the finery of tablecloth and embroidered pillows returned to treasure chests for another year.

Once, when a woman renowned for her activities in the women's association was being asked about her *tivaevae*, her son interrupted by pointing to the grave structure just next to the entrance of the house – 'we would have to open it for you to see. These are our bank accounts, you see?' Parallel to the monetary economy, there is thus yet another type of economy, one relying on recollection not accumulation, operating quietly and efficiently through the hands of women.

Why use cloth to make quilts, which then are never used as such? Clearly the story told here is just a brief snapshot of a complex scenario at the centre of which lies the relation between persons and a form of property that is not additive, but composite. Quilts, as layered, bound and olfactory things which can be recaptured over and over again, provide a striking visual analogue that allows for the translation of Christian dogma into a quintessentially Cook Island version to which all denominations can subscribe. While quilts may not themselves have engendered the acceptance of Christianity, having come last in a cycle of mediatory objects of far greater significance, they have secured a most successful accommodation of new spiritual and material resources, and proven ways of accessing them.

References

Arkana, E. (1986), *Hawaiian Quilting: a Fine Art*. Honolulu: Hawaiian Mission Children Society.

Babadzan, A. (1993), *Les dépouilles des dieux: essai sur la religion tahitienne à l'époque de la découverte*. Paris: Editions de la Maison des Sciences de l'Homme.

Baessler, A. (1899), 'Masken von Mangaia', *Ethnologisches Notiablatt* 2: 32–3.

Borofsky, R. (1987), *Making History: Pukapukan and Anthropological Constructions of Knowledge.* Cambridge: Cambridge University Press.

Buck, P. (1944), *Arts and Crafts of the Cook Islands.* Honolulu: Bernice Bishop Museum Bulletin 179.

Davidson, J. (1997), 'Cook Island Material Culture from the Christchurch Exhibition of 1906–07: Rediscovering A Forgotten Collection', *Baseler Archiv*, Neue Folge, Band XI. V. 159–80.

Gil, W. (1894), *From Darkness to Light in Polynesia.* London: Religious Tract Society.

Gilson, R. (1980), *The Cook Islands 1820–1950.* Ron Crocombe (ed.) Wellington and Suva: Victoria University Press/Institute of Pacific Studies of the University of the South Pacific.

Grimshaw, B. (1907), *In the Strange South Seas.* London: Hutchins.

Hammond, J. (1986), *Tifaifai and Quilts of Polynesia.* Honolulu: University of Hawaii Press.

Jones, S. (1973), *Hawaiian Quilts.* Honolulu: University of Hawaii Press.

Park, K. (1998), 'Impressed Images: Reproducing Wonders' in C. Jones and P. Gallison (eds) *Picturing Science, Producing Art.* London: Routledge.

Parker, R. (1984), *The Subversive Stitch, Embroidery and the Making of the Feminine.* London: Women's Press.

Poggliolі, V. (1988), *Patterns from Paradise: the Art of Tahitian Quilting.* Pittstown, NJ: Main Street Press.

Rongokea, L. (1992), *Tivaevae: Portraits of Cook Islands Quilting.* Wellington, NZ: Daphne Brasell Associates Press.

Shaw, R. (1996), *Hawaiian Quilt Masterpieces.* Honolulu: Hugh Lauter Levin Associates.

Stephenson, R. (1981), *Persistence and Exchange.* Honolulu: Pacific Sciences Association.

Thomas, N. (1999), 'The Case of the Misplaced Ponchos: Speculations Concerning the History of Cloth in Polynesia', *Journal of Material Culture* 4(1): 5–21.

Part III
Clothing and Agency

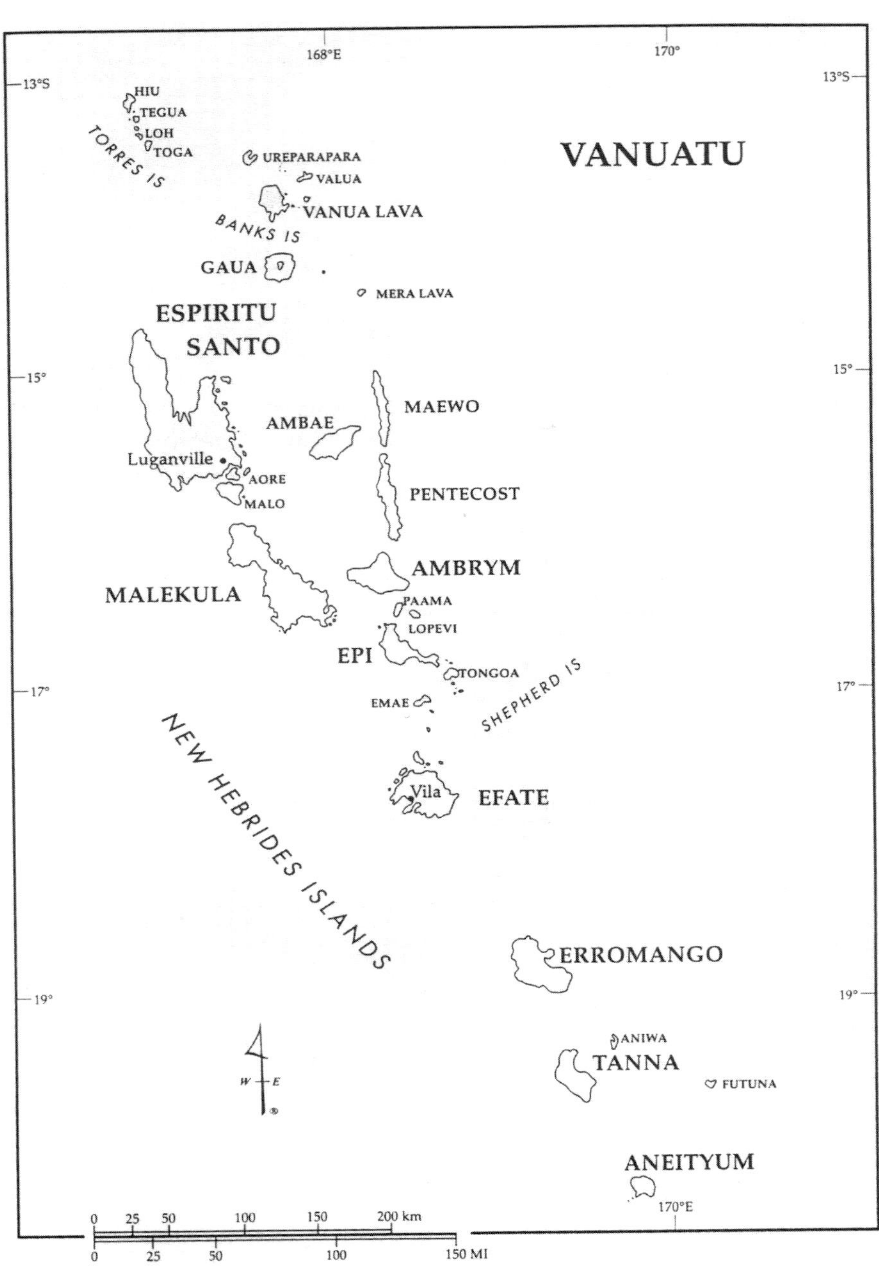
168°E
170°
13°S
13°S
VANUATU
HIU
TEGUA
LOH
TOGA
TORRES IS
UREPARAPARA
VALUA
VANUA LAVA
BANKS IS
GAUA
MERA LAVA
ESPIRITU
SANTO
15°
15°
MAEWO
AMBAE
Luganville
AORE
MALO
PENTECOST
AMBRYM
MALEKULA
PAAMA
LOPEVI
EPI
TONGOA
17°
17°
EMAE
SHEPHERD IS
NEW HEBRIDES ISLANDS
Vila
EFATE
ERROMANGO
19°
19°
ANIWA
TANNA
FUTUNA
W
E
ANEITYUM
170°E
0
25
50
100
150
200 km
0
25
50
100
150 MI

Figure 5.1

–5–

Gender, Status and Introduced Clothing in Vanuatu

Lissant Bolton

There is a story from Ambae in north Vanuatu about a woman who, brought up by her parents to be a man, was so successful as a man that she became a high-ranking and prosperous leader, and married ten wives, but was eventually exposed (literally) when climbing into a canoe. Her clothing was disarranged, and one of her wives saw her genitals. The wife asked the other wives if they ever received connubial visits from their husband, and when all replied negatively, they exposed the deception. Grace Molisa, a leading ni-Vanuatu feminist (and an Ambaean), wrote about this story in an article about women published to mark Vanuatu's Independence in 1980. For Molisa the story demonstrated 'that a woman coped as capably [as], if not better than, the orthodox male chiefs' (1980: 263). The story raises the question of what exactly gender difference entails. This woman, whom Molisa names as Vevineala, dressed and acted as a male for many years, and was, as Molisa points out, very successful as such. It was her physical body, and her inability to act as a man sexually, which in the end defeated her adoption of male gender.

A similar story from southwest Malakula in north-central Vanuatu, reported by Tim Curtis, focuses more explicitly on genital difference and sexual practice (Curtis 2002). This story is about a woman, Vin'bum'bau, who appears in many other narratives, mostly as a kind of female ogre, and who thus, unlike Vevineala, is not exactly human. The story reports that Vin'bum'bau dressed and acted as a male, and married ten wives. She was involved in the male status-alteration system *nimingi*, achieved the high status called *meleun,* and wore all the paraphernalia of a *meleun* on her body. Indeed she was the creator of the masks used in *nimingi*, and it was she who invented the *nambas*, or penis-wrapper, that men generally wear. Vin'bum'bau actually perceived herself as a man, but she was troubled by her own genitalia, which she thought of as a sore needing medicine. The story suggests that at this time people were a little uncertain about gender generally. Eventually one man looked at her genitals, recognized them, and had sex with her. He went on to take all her wives for his own.

Contemporary anthropological analysis has drawn attention to the degree to which gender is a metaphor, an idiom, of relationship in Melanesia. As has been persuasively argued, in much of Melanesia gender can be understood as a set of ideas about behaviour and practice which people deploy creatively in the negotiation of relationships (Strathern 1988). The metaphorical nature of gender, as a framework with which to think and act, goes beyond the simple constraints of biology: that is, men and women can act in relationships in ways gendered as male or female. In Melanesia gender is a powerful source of difference, and this is not a categorical difference so much as a context for creativity. In Vanuatu status is also an important context for relational creativity: if gender is one way in which people explore and negotiate their relationships, status is another. Vevineala and Vim'bum'bau each modified the difference between herself and other males through status-alteration achievements. In fact, focusing on the creative appropriation of gender, these stories treat as almost axiomatic the creative work of status-alteration.[1]

To some extent, these stories explore the limits of creative metaphorical practice with respect to gender; they describe a more radical and thoroughgoing appropriation of male-gendered practice than women usually enact. In doing so they locate a distinction between gendered practice and biological givens, identifying a point beyond which gender-as-practice cannot go. Both Vevineala and Vin'bum'bau dressed as men, the former by wearing a mat that passed between her legs and over a belt at the back and the front, the latter by binding her pubic hair in a penis wrapper. Both were high-achievers in the status-alteration systems that are the dominant focus of men's energies in both Ambae and south Malakula: their achievements are presented as a demonstration of their successful male practice. They entered into kinship relationships as males by marrying. But both had women's genitalia, and thus could not have sex as men.

What I focus on here, however, is not the identified point beyond which gender-as-practice cannot go, or even what the stories assume about the achievement of status, but rather what they reveal about the intersection in relationships between gender, status and clothing as an embodiment of difference. Clothing demonstrates, and also enforces, the distinctions within gender and status. It is thus a context in which to assert and explore those differences. Although the story of Vevineala does not specifically detail her wearing of the clothing befitting a high-ranking male in the *huqe*, a *ratahagi*, it is self-evident to any Ambaean listener that she did so. Vim'bum'bau's story outlines the clothing she wore to demonstrate her achievement: the evidence of Vim'bum'bau's successful adoption of maleness is that she was able to earn, and to wear, the paraphernalia of a *meleun*. What I focus on in this chapter is the effect that the introduction of European clothing had on ni-Vanuatu understandings, and expressions, of such distinctions of gender and status.

Figure 5.2 Macklin John and Dickinson Dick, from the Maskelyne Islands, north central Vanuatu, in contemporary ni-Vanuatu dress. Port Vila Vanuatu October 1998. Photo L. Bolton.

European clothing was part of a package of changes introduced into Vanuatu by expatriates after about 1840. It was by no means the most important or significant of those changes, and yet it had a subtle but enduring impact. The suggestion I make is that introduced clothing influenced the construction of difference in Vanuatu, and that it did so particularly along the axes of gender and status. In order to make this argument, I begin first with a discussion of indigenous clothing forms in Vanuatu, and then discuss the introduction of European clothing, moving on to discuss the effect of introduced clothing on difference.[2] This account is a survey, referring to examples from throughout the archipelago, and is thus generalising in effect.

Clothing in Vanuatu

Vanuatu, formerly the New Hebrides, is a Melanesian nation in the southwest Pacific, established across an archipelago of some eighty small islands (Figure 5.2). The archipelago lies roughly north-south over 850 kilometres of ocean, to the east of northern Australia. At the start of the twenty-first century, Vanuatu has a population of 200,000 people, who now call themselves ni-Vanuatu, and who speak 113 languages between them.[3] Almost all ni-Vanuatu also speak a neo-Melanesian pidgin called Bislama, the lingua franca, as well as either or both of the languages of their colonial experience: English and French. This extraordinary linguistic diversity reflects a greater diversity in knowledge and practice – many different ways of being in the world were and still are practiced by the archipelago's inhabitants.

Indigenous clothing styles varied greatly across the archipelago. In some areas men wore plaited pandanus textiles passed between their legs, as Vevineala did, in many other places they wore some type of penis wrapper, like Vin'bum'bau. Women's dress was more diverse. In much of south Vanuatu (Erromango, Tanna, Aneityum), for example, women wore some kind of multiple-fibre ('grass') skirt; in the central Shepherds they wore a textile passed between their legs; in the north (Ambae, Maewo, north Pentecost) they wore a plaited pandanus textile wrapped around their hips; in east Santo they managed with a single leaf suspended from a fibre band at the front and a bunch of leaves behind. In each case, both men and women's clothing was in some way distinctive to their place, so that no two clothing styles were the same.

Clothing was also a matter of ornamentation – of necklaces, armbands, head ornaments and other decorations – and of body modification, of tattooing, of piercing the nose or ear, of tooth evulsion, of head binding. It encompassed the treatment of the body, the application of coconut and other oils, of paint and other kinds of temporary marks, and hairstyles, the bleaching of hair, as well as washing and grooming. Crucially, in most parts of Vanuatu all these treatments and elaborations were not a matter of personal preference, but were rather controlled by a system of rights and privileges and by ritual proscriptions of various kinds. Maewo women participating as novices in the status-alteration system called *lengwasa* were secluded for a period of ten days in a special house, during which period they were not allowed to wash. In Maewo again, a small star-like splash was tattooed on the arm near the wrist in preparation for the life beyond death. The dead person, looking for a flame with which to light his or her fire in the land of the dead, needed to be able to show this tattoo to obtain the flame from someone else.

Clothing (broadly defined) also communicated much to the living, and very often indicated personal circumstances. On Erromango a girl's skirt was lengthened at betrothal, while widows ready to marry again shortened their skirts as a sign of their availability (Humphreys 1926: 144, 185). In eastern Santo a woman in mourning wore a long coconut cord dyed black, with shell beads at the ends, bound around the body from hips to breasts (Speiser 1991 [1923]: 170). On Tanna boys kept their hair cut short until puberty, at which time they began to bleach and bind their hair in whip-like strands, which, gaining length with age, became Felix Speiser reported, a sign of masculinity, dignity and age (ibid: 152).

Figure 5.3 A high-ranking Ambae man wearing a costume such as Vevineala would have worn. Photo: Felix Speiser c.1911.

The most significant variations in clothing and body treatment related to achieved status. If gender was indicated by a standard difference of form in dress (such as skirts versus penis wrappers), rank was indicated by elaboration and ornament, and depending on the context in which it was awarded, aspects of that

Figure 5.4 A woman from Erromango, southern Vanuatu. Women wore bark cloth as she does for special occasions; the length of her skirts indicates that she is married. Photo H.A. Robertson c.1900.

elaboration and ornament were worn by both men and women (Figure 5.3). In south Vanuatu status was dependent on the manipulation of inherited knowledge and on personal achievement, and was demonstrated in special clothing. On Tanna, for example, senior male leaders wore a special high headdress called a *qeria*. On Erromango women wore many long sweeping skirts (one on top of the other) and on special occasions wore a length of barkcloth, painted with freehand designs, draped or knotted across their shoulders (Figure 5.4). The wearing of a particularly beautiful cloth gave women increased status and prestige (Huffman 1996: 136; Lawson 1999). In central Vanuatu status was inherited, enabling long genealogies detailing the holders of chiefly titles. The inheritance did not necessarily follow strict rules, such as primogeniture, but allowed some negotiation in the selection of the holder of such a title. There, for example, high-ranking men and women had the right to wear special textiles made of barkcloth or plaited fibre and decorated with complex coloured designs (Huffman 1996: 132).

In north Vanuatu, status was achieved through participation in status-alteration systems like those mentioned in the stories of Vevineala and Vin'bum'bau. In a variety of related systems, men and women devoted their energies to marshalling the resources to mount ceremonies at which, often by killing pigs, they could achieve economic, spiritual, political and/or social benefits. The construction of these systems varied, but generally involved a sequential progression through a series of ranks. Status-alteration systems were gendered, providing linked but largely separate avenues for achievement for men and for women. The effect of this was to create distinctions among men and among women. In many places, the spiritual power accrued by men as they rose through the levels of such a system was so great that they actually became dangerous to each other. In systems such as the *nimingi* in which Vin'bum'bau participated, men of one grade or level cooked and ate together; to eat with others would be to jeopardize both them and those they ate with. Women were also significantly distinguished not only from men, but also from each other, by the power and status associated with their status-alteration system achievements. For example, Mary Patterson reports of the Ambrym women's status-alteration system *yengfa*, that 'Until its demise early last century, Yengfa offered women the major avenue for distinguishing themselves from other women that was not predicated on the status of their father or husband' (2001: 46).

Participation in public status-alteration systems generally granted a number of privileges of dress.[4] On Ambae the public status-alteration system (the one in which Vevineala participated) was the *huqe*. In this system the acquisition of a new rank involved such clear entitlements in dress that, in Bislama, they are described as *yunifom blong step*, the uniform for the grade. 'Uniform' elements include specific named textiles with nominated designs, beaded armbands, belt and headband (the bead designs replicating the designs on the textiles), red-feathered sticks to be placed in the hair, and certain decorative leaves (different species being linked to different ranks). Chief Rupert Garae, the highest-ranking chief on Ambae (who died in 2000), once showed me the paraphernalia of his rank, the beaded armbands, headband, belt, the feathered sticks, and the textiles. What was clear was that the ownership of, and right to wear, these objects was a source of pleasure and pride for him. They reminded him, and those who saw him in them, of his achievements and his power.

In north Vanuatu and specifically on Ambae, certain designs are applied across a variety of media. The designs associated with ranks in the *huqe* are applied to textiles, and to the beaded armbands, headbands and belts. Both men and unmarried women participated in the lower levels of the *huqe*, and the designs linked to these levels are worn by both men and women on their cloth. Although the textile forms, and the ways they are worn, are gender-specific, the designs marked upon them are not to do with gender, but rather with achieved status. A similar process occurred on Maewo, where men and women participate in linked but distinct status-alteration systems known as *kwatu* and *lengwasa*. Achievement is again marked by the right to wear certain designs, which are in some cases marked upon textiles, in others upon headdresses, and in others again upon the skin with paint. The designs are the same, even while the forms in which they appeared are context-, and hence gender-, specific.

Thus throughout Vanuatu indigenous clothing styles formalize gender. They also demonstrate, and elaborate, differences between people based on status. While in general achieved status is gender-specific (male and female achieve different kinds of status), where equivalence exists it is made evident in the sharing of designs that mark achievement or inheritance. In this sense, clothing itself reflects at a number of levels the creative play upon the nature of difference embodied in indigenous ideas of gender and status. Gender is both a given in matters of sex and reproduction, and an organizing principle and metaphor by which relationships were negotiated. Status is like another dimension added to the graph of gender. As in the relation of ornament to the basic items of dress, status embellished, and modified, the framework created by gender. And if status was an elaboration upon the basic structure of male and female, the elaboration seems to have interested ni-Vanuatu more than the structure on which it was founded.

Introducing European-style Clothing

As in Vanuatu, so in nineteenth- and twentieth-century Europe: clothing marked gender and status differentials. Male and female dressed differently, as did people in different social contexts. Significantly, of course, European understandings of gender and status, implicit in clothing forms, were different to those used by ni-Vanuatu. The introduction of European clothing, therefore, represented not just the substitution of one material form for another, but the importation of a different set of ideas and distinctions embodied in the specific material form of introduced clothing.

Europeans first appeared in the Vanuatu archipelago in 1606 when Fernandez de Quiros briefly attempted to establish a Spanish settlement on one island, which he named Australia del Espiritu Santo. Later European visitors hardly deviated from his precedent of itinerance. Captain Cook passed through the islands in 1774, mapping many of them, and naming the archipelago the New Hebrides. From the

1820s the islands were subject to the successive depredations of whalers, sandalwood traders, missionaries, labour traders and planters, but it was only toward the end of the nineteenth century that there was any significant European settlement in the region; the islands were never declared the colonial possession of any nation. In 1887 they became the subject of a Joint Naval Agreement between Britain and France; in 1906 this was reformulated as the Anglo-French Condominium Government of the New Hebrides. Independence was achieved in 1980.

While both de Quiros and Cook left small amounts of loom-woven cloth in the islands, it was only after the 1820s that cloth, among other trade goods, began to be more widely available in the archipelago. European-style clothing was introduced principally by missionaries. Missionary activity began from 1839 through the work of the London Missionary Society, while the first Presbyterian missionaries, John and Charlotte Geddie, arrived on Aneityum in 1848. The Presbyterians rapidly became the dominant missionary denomination in the archipelago, making conversions throughout south and central Vanuatu, and drawing 'native teachers' from their new congregations to work in unevangelized areas. The Anglican Melanesian Mission worked mainly in the north of the country, from 1849. Catholic missionaries joined the fray in the 1880s, the Church of Christ and the Seventh-day Adventists in the 1920s.

There is a growing literature about the changes missionaries sought to introduce in creating their congregations in the Pacific region. As many have observed, for missionaries, the adoption of European clothing was a sign of conversion (Jolly 1996: 271; Lawson 1994: 91f; Douglas 2002: 4). If it was generally true that missionaries saw the adoption of clothing as crucial, the specifics of how this was imposed and received varied greatly from place to place. Analysis of the effect of introduced clothing in the Pacific reflects the specific histories of colonialization and missionization across the region. Richard Eves' discussion of Methodist missions in New Britain, PNG, for example, highlights the various bodily disciplines the Methodists introduced, including not only clothing, but also physical activities such as 'drill' and plantation labour. Eves concludes that the impact of these introductions was only 'skin deep' (1996: 127). Nicholas Thomas argues for Samoa, by contrast, that local appropriations of introduced clothing (here barkcloth clothing from Tahiti introduced by mission influence) constitute 'a kind of technology towards a new way of being in the world' (Chapter 3 in this volume); specifically, he suggests that for Samoans these clothes 'were not just expressions of a new context, but technologies that created that context anew' (Chapter 3 this volume).

The Presbyterians in Vanuatu were as keen to see their congregations in European clothing as were their colleagues elsewhere. The John G. Paton Fund newsletter *Quarterly Jottings from the New Hebrides South Seas Islands,* in which, from the 1890s, news from Presbyterian missionaries was communicated to supporters around the world, contains continual pleas for clothing, for dresses for women, and for shirts, and either trousers, or more commonly, lengths of fabric to be worn as sarongs, for men. Missionary accounts often detail the putting on of clothing as a sign of conversion, reporting many stories in which a man's conversion is made public by the donning of a shirt and trousers. Missionary publications are also often illustrated with pictures of fully clothed converts. However, the photos that grace such publications picture an ideal, not an everyday reality. Describing his arrival in 1892 in an area of Ambrym where a native teacher was already working, the Presbyterian Robert Lamb comments on a group of men who greeted him: 'To honour the occasion they had hastily donned their five-year-old-shirts, sere and yellow with smoke and age' (1905: 43).

In 1895 a report was published in *Quarterly Jottings* detailing the visit of the missionary Fred Paton to a mission station at Belgaule in northwest Santo. Nearly two years earlier 'two native teachers and their wives' had been placed at Belgaule 'to encourage one another and hold the station until a Missionary could be found to take the lonely charge' (1895: 10). Arriving there, Paton was met by 'twenty or thirty *dressed* natives' (ibid.), but found one teacher and his wife dead, and the wife of the second seriously ill. The anonymous author of the article comments on the hardship suffered by these native teachers, who were drawn from congregations elsewhere in the archipelago, and goes on to ask 'And what fruits were seen of the Teacher's work?' (ibid.). Answering his own question, he continues:

> Thirty dressed natives carries little meaning to our minds at home. But it should be realised that a savage prides himself on nudity as a badge of heathenism. He needs the courage of conviction to adopt dress. Persecution follows. Caste is broken. The man who fears the Missionary's God wears the Missionary's gift of clothing. Was it not, after all, an act of spiritual import when our first parents clothed themselves? (ibid.)

The author of this report recognizes that to wear European clothes was not simply to demonstrate a new affiliation: it was not a neutral act, but was one that could invite hostility ('persecution') from others. He also recognizes what is erased by European clothing – 'Caste is broken'. While neither 'caste' nor 'nudity' is the best term for what he is describing, he acknowledges that the wearing of European clothing erases differences in status marked upon the body by traditional clothing. Introduced clothing effectively covered the greater part of both men's and women's bodies, obscuring in one action all the information about a person which they normally wore or embodied. If to wear the paraphernalia of status was to assert that achievement, to put off that paraphernalia was to lay aside that assertion.

The European clothing introduced into Vanuatu was different for men and women; it did not acknowledge any differences within each group based on individual status. While the kinds of clothing provided varied somewhat according to supply, the principal source of differentiation marked by clothes reflected missionary denomination. This was especially true for women's clothes. The Anglicans introduced blouses and skirts for women, a style that remained characteristic of women's dress in the Anglican north until independence (although sleeves and hems shortened over the decades). At the start of the twenty-first century Anglican women still wear t-shirts and skirts more commonly than dresses. The Presbyterians introduced dresses. A note published in *Quarterly Jottings* in 1896 specifies the style they preferred.

> An ordinary native dress is made yoke shape. Something like a lady's nightdress, but shorter, with elbow sleeves. Galatea, or good print, makes nice gowns – yoke lined. Two widths in skirt, three-quarters of a yard in length to come in under the knee. Plenty of room at neck *and arms* . . . Turkey red frill, or red braid, makes a nice gay finish. The natives dearly love bright colours. (*Quarterly Jottings* 1896: 7)

The revealing word in this description is 'native'. If ni-Vanuatu were being encouraged to wear European clothing, this was not exactly the same as the clothing worn by Europeans, but rather a kind of simulacrum of it. This was perhaps especially the case for women: ni-Vanuatu women were not provided with the elaborate garments that expatriate women wore. The description quoted above ends with an offer to send a paper pattern of the ordinary native dress to supporters prepared to make such dresses to be sent to Vanuatu. These loose dresses were often called 'Mother Hubbards', a designation that marked them as being specifically 'native' dresses. This is not a term used for European women's clothing. Thus, ironically enough, the introduction of European clothing actually signalled a specific distinction between expatriate and indigenous. This was the differential of race. The shirts and sarongs, the loose dresses, were European in character, and designed to meet European notions of modesty in appearance, but they made real, nevertheless, a categorical difference between ni-Vanuatu and Europeans.

Gender

From Captain Cook onward, expatriates have tended to interpret the status of women in Melanesia as unacceptably low. Captain Cook himself commented that men on the Vanuatu island of Tanna made women into pack horses, observing that while not beauties Tannese women were 'too handsome for the use that is made of them' (cited in Jolly 1991: 35). In 1910, a Presbyterian missionary, the Rev T.W. Leggatt, wrote of Vanuatu: 'the outstanding feature of Woman's position . . . is that of *Inferiority*' (1910: 23 emphasis in original). Leggatt saw women's acceptance of this situation as a species of false consciousness: 'if in course of generations they have reconciled themselves to the inevitable, and so fitted their necks to the yoke

Figure 5.5 Presbyterian converts from Epi and Paama, clothed in Sunday best. Photo Maurice Frater, pre 1920.

that it is really less galling than it seems to us, their condition is no less pitiable' (1910: 22–3).

While missionaries such as Leggatt saw indigenous women as existing in a subject relationship to men, they themselves brought their own ideals of appropriate gender behaviour with them to Vanuatu. As has often been argued, during the nineteenth century in both Britain and North America, transformations in agriculture and industry were accompanied by 'a radical shift in notions of family and femininity' which produced an ideal of women as tied to the home (Jolly 1991: 31; see also Eves 1996, Johnston 2000). Presbyterian missionaries brought with them the presumption 'that manual or physical work, especially in the fields or beyond the home, was in itself degrading to women' (Jolly 1991: 35). They held that women properly belonged in the domestic domain of the household, and deplored their participation in activities outside it.

This attitude enshrined a nineteenth-century European conviction of a bodily difference between men and women which related not just to the sexual act, but also to other physical capacities. Women were regarded as being physically weaker than men, and hence constrained in what they could or should do in the way of manual labour. The style of dress that missionaries imposed on ni-Vanuatu women reflected this bodily inequality. While men's clothes permitted physical labour, the long loose dress with sleeves described in the quotation above (or the encumbrance of a long-sleeved blouse and long skirt), was considerably more suited to sitting quietly at home than to digging in a garden, carrying loads of firewood, or harvesting shellfish on a reef.

If missionaries condemned indigenous societies as granting women an inferior position, they nevertheless almost universally enshrined their own assumptions about male superiority in the structures they introduced. As Churches were established, male missionaries were in charge, but their wives held no formal positions. None of the Churches permitted women to be ordained, or to hold positions of leadership above men. The Anglo-French condominium government took a similar approach, appointing ni-Vanuatu men as chiefs and assessors to broker relationships between specific communities and government agents. The condominium itself was staffed almost entirely by men.

Women were also excluded, although here very often by their own kin, from entering the other key context introduced by expatriates: the labour trade. Although some women did go to work in the Queensland sugar fields, and in plantations in New Caledonia, Fiji and other parts of Vanuatu, it was primarily men who participated in labour migration. By contrast, although some men were employed by expatriates as domestic servants, it was primarily women who became 'housegirls' for planters, traders, missionaries and government officials. For all their rhetoric criticizing the status of women in indigenous practice, it was expatriates who established a formal distinction between all women and all men, on the basis of the public/domestic division that they introduced with colonial structures.

Expatriates perceived a distinction between public and private/domestic contexts, and the interpretation of indigenous male contexts as 'public' and indigenous female contexts as 'private'. In many parts of the archipelago, indigenous practice allocated the domain of the *nasara*, the dancing ground and/or public plaza of a residential community, to men. Expatriates mistakenly perceived a spatial separation – between the men's house or dancing ground, and familial households – as a public/domestic segregation, but the spatial segregation did not exemplify a distinction between two such domains. In some parts of the archipelago women acted on the *nasara*, in others women had their own *nasara*; in all they had their own contexts of community action. Moreover, men were involved in what Europeans would regard as the domestic concerns of house and garden. As Jolly observes, among the Sa of South Pentecost 'the most central and public institutions revolved around the sacralisation of domestic life' (1989: 222). Significantly, for Europeans, the distinction between public and domestic involved a status differential, linked to an inequality of status between men and women. This model did not facilitate the creative deployment of gendered practice. It utilized a far less flexible allocation of gender roles, tied much more closely to the biological distinction between men and women.

As well as idealizing the domestic role of women, missionary endeavours actually enforced the association of women with house (as opposed to garden) labour, through the introduction of technologies to produce and maintain clothing. While both men and women were required to wear clothes, the production and maintenance of European clothing was introduced as a female responsibility. The evangelism of women was generally linked to instruction in sewing techniques (see Douglas 2002). Although in local practice many domestic tasks were and often still are shared (both men and women cook, for example), generally women were responsible for the production of indigenous clothing. In most areas it was women who made the plaited pandanus textiles or grass skirts people formerly wore. The production of those textiles was often linked to the seasonal cycle of the agricultural year. Sophie Nempan (an Erromangan), in describing the cool dry season indicators for yam planting on Erromango, records that time as being 'when women are cold and their grass skirts are ragged and broken, when they make barkcloth, mats, grass skirts and baskets because there is plenty of sunshine, when wild pigs are fat, and the creeks are dry so that it is easy to catch prawns, [and] when the leaves of the bluewater tree fall' (Nempan: n.d.). Sewing dislocated women from these cycles. Women were also charged with the laborious process of washing and drying clothes. The care of indigenous textiles was comparatively stress-free, whereas the introduction of European cloth meant a constant requirement to wash.

Accommodating European Clothing

European clothing was not adopted immediately and completely. Not only did limited supplies of cloth prevent people from dressing completely in European style, but for a number of reasons, people preferred to continue wearing local clothing. If expatriates found indigenous clothing horrifyingly immodest (penis wrappers in particular offended European sensibilities), European clothing also offended ni-Vanuatu proprieties. Speiser reports that even when wearing trousers, men accustomed to wearing penis wrappers 'retain . . . a strap to press the penis to the body. Otherwise, they would feel undressed' (1991 [1923]: 178). Bronwen Douglas draws attention to Lawrie's observation, made of Aneityum in 1880, that 'although every woman and girl wears a large print garment, she would have the feeling of being unclothed without the native-made fringes, of which three or four are worn together' (James Lawrie 1892: 305, cited in Douglas 2002: 5).

In southern Vanuatu, in Tanna and Futuna and Erromango, women continued to wear plant-fibre skirts (commonly known as grass skirts) on weekdays until about 1970, reserving clothes from the mission box for Sunday wear. A visitor to Erromango in about 1940, Kathleen Woodburn, describes women wearing a number of

Figure 5.6 Plantation workers on Erromango in about 1940. Women in southern Vanuatu were reluctant to give up wearing fibre skirts, and added European clothes over them. Photo: Kathleen Woodburn.

ankle-length skirts one on top of the other, surmounted by a Mother Hubbard (1944: 139). The last Futunese woman who wore grass skirts her whole life died in 1984. A Futunese woman (Vitu Magau) whom I interviewed in 2001, reported that she still makes herself grass skirts to wear to the garden and into the bush. Their practical qualities for this kind of work are enhanced by the fact that they are not complicated to care for. The good thing about grass skirts, Vitu observed, is that you can wash them in seawater.

Shortages of cloth also restricted the wearing of clothing until nearly the end of the twentieth century. A variety of clothing styles was dictated by such shortages. It was common, for example, for schoolgirls in the 1950s and 1960s to wear a triangle of cloth tied onto the front of their torsos, instead of a blouse or t-shirt. Underclothing was also a matter of approximation. For many years women seem to have worn a length of cloth passed between their legs and folded over a cord or belt at back and front. This may have been especially the case in central Vanuatu, where the traditional clothing for women was a textile worn in the same manner. While by the 1990s most men wore shorts or trousers, in previous decades they commonly wore lengths of calico as sarongs. Kathleen Woodburn reported that Erromango men wore 'a couple of yards of trade calico, twisted around their loins in apparently casual manner, but which has a knack of staying in place, however energetic the wearer, and generally a sleeveless singlet covering the torso' (Woodburn 1944: 140).

As in the narrative quoted above, putting on European clothing equated with putting off of the paraphernalia of status. Had Vim'bum'bau converted, she would have had to put off all the insignia that indicated her *meleun* status, and Vevineala would have had to relinquish those items that declared her a *ratahagi*. However, in practice, this relinquishment was not quite so complete as many expatriates may have imagined. Tattooing continued until the mid-twentieth century as a sign of status for Ambae women, for example. The *Quarterly Jottings* quotation cited above, 'the natives dearly love bright colours', suggests an infantile preference for brightness. However, colour was one of the privileges of status in at least some areas of Vanuatu. On Ambrym, for example, the wearing of both red and yellow was a right that had to be acquired. Up until about the 1960s Ambrym women were still constrained in wearing these colours on their dresses until they had earned the right to do so.

Other clothing privileges have been retained for a diminished range of occasions, relevant only for dances or other ceremonials. On Ambae the right to wear certain decorative leaves, acquired in the *huqe*, is maintained. Only when one has earned the right to do so may one wear a branch of such leaves in the back of one's belt in dancing. The right to wear a fowl feather in one's hair is similarly controlled. At the same time, the elaborate beaded armbands, belts and headbands that belong to the higher *huqe* ranks, such as Chief Rupert showed me, are now rarely acquired, as men decreasingly take on the difficulty and expense of achieving those higher grades.

However, among women, especially in central Vanuatu, the style of dress that developed from the Mother Hubbard, known in Bislama as the *ilan dres* (island dress), has been used to express regional differences within the archipelago. For some decades in the twentieth century, certain styles of island dress were characteristic of certain places. For example, one distinctive style until about the 1970s was the Paama style, named after the island where women wore it. Women from other islands who tried to copy and wear this style (distinguished by the way the skirt fabric was joined together), report that they felt uncomfortable wearing it, while I have recorded a number of stories of Paamese women living in other islands who resolutely wore Paama style all their lives, despite the prevailing fashions around them.

Since the achievement of independence the island dress has come to be regarded as the closest thing to a national dress. For women in Anglican areas, this has posed a certain problem. Most lack the knowledge and skills required to turn a length of cloth, bought in a trade store, into an island dress, and many report these problems in discussing the idea of island dresses as national dress. Presbyterian women, especially from central Vanuatu (where the island dress developed) see the dress as particularly their own, and notice when they see other women who have clearly purchased their dresses in a Chinese store in the towns of Port Vila and Luganville.

Figure 5.7 A group of women from throughout Vanuatu, taken in 1995. Generally speaking, Anglican women wear skirts and tops, while Presbyterians wear 'island dresses'. Port Vila, November 1996. Photo: L Bolton.

Figure 5.8 Sunday best: a choir from Lulep singing in the Presbyterian church at Liro, Paama, December 2001. Photo L. Bolton.

If island dresses signal regional differences in the archipelago, it may be that they are, in 2002, developing a further association. With the development of an urban population who wear Western-influenced clothing, which for women incorporates, for example, tight skirts, shoes with heels, and makeup, the island dress is also beginning to signify a kind of rural (island-based) conservatism.

However, ironically enough, one of the biggest gender issues for ni-Vanuatu at the start of the twenty-first century relates to clothing. Young women are increasingly seeking to wear loose wide *traosis*, rather like culottes. These 'trousers' actually facilitate modesty, enabling girls to sit, bend and jump without fear of skirts flying up, or falling back. There is, however, endless media coverage of male opposition to trousers, both on the grounds that they expose the contours of the female body, and that they are not *kastom*. *Kastom* is the Bislama word which ni-Vanuatu use to designate indigenous knowledge and practice in opposition to all that has been introduced. It is not a term which refers to a specific body of knowledge and practice as much as it is a form of classification. Not everything described as *kastom* is strictly indigenous: the term *kastom jif* (chief) for example, refers to a type of leadership which amalgamates both indigenous roles and colonial structures (Bolton 1998). In asserting that *traosis* are not *kastom*, however, opponents do not advocate a return to grass skirts and pandanus textiles. They want women to wear skirts or dresses. In particular, it is island dresses that are described as *kastom dresing blong yumi* – our traditional dress.

The extent of feeling on this matter is reflected by the fact that in some areas of Vanuatu, *traosis* for girls have been banned. While in some places women are able to wear *traosis* in the privacy of their hamlet yards, or in their food gardens, in others they are forbidden in all contexts. The chiefs on Paama island, for example, have ruled that women must not wear them at all.[5] In some places women returning home from a visit to town will don skirts or dresses almost literally as they cross the beach or airstrip.

The opposition to *traosis* could seem surprising, given how comparatively recently men worn sarongs on a daily basis. It can be understood as an expression of discomfort at the rapid pace of change in the country since independence, a pace people may find hard to manage. However, it is revealing that the issue which such anxieties have fastened upon relates to clothing. As I have argued, clothing in Vanuatu has always been a signifier of gender and status. Dresses do not only signify gender. They also signify the specific form of status difference between men and women that was introduced with clothing in the colonial era. The opposition to *traosis* has developed over the period when urban-based women's organizations have increasingly advocated women's rights, when women have started to seek election to Parliament, and when some women are achieving employment in government and business at higher levels. One of the most forceful advocates of women's rights in independent Vanuatu was Grace Molisa, whose story about

Vevineala began this chapter. For Molisa, it was Vevineala's ability to enact male practice that was significant: 'a woman coped as capably [as], if not better than, the orthodox male chiefs' (1980: 263).

Their position already diminished by the introduced status of race, and their authority eroded by the Church and condominium structures which have been maintained by the post-colonial state, it seems that the opponents of *traosis* are hostile to this claim against male practice. In other words, it is not just that women are seeking to wear 'male' clothes. They are also, increasingly, seeking to enact roles that in post-colonial Vanuatu have thus far been gendered as male. Without wishing to appear as men, as Vevineala and Vim'bum'bau did, these women are seeking to behave as men do. The opponents of *traosis* see the wearing of them as a claim to male practice. This is not a claim made in the context of indigenous practice, but rather a claim made against the gender relations introduced by Europeans, and in particular by missionaries. Hence it is expressed not in terms of a requirement that women should dress in the grass skirts and pandanus textiles that are the practice of the place, but rather that they should return to the dresses that embody the modest, domestic female practice introduced by Europeans.

Notes

1. I prefer to use 'status-alteration systems' as an umbrella term that includes all the various forms that these rituals take. Commonly, these rituals are described as either 'graded societies' or 'secret societies'. Graded societies are systems of ranked status grades through which men (and sometimes women) climb, commonly achieving each specified status position through rituals in which they kill or exchange pigs (see Blackwood 1981; Bonnemaison 1996). Secret societies often exist in tandem with a central public male-graded society, and offer other avenues for status enhancement through the performance of prescribed rituals; there are sometimes multiple secret societies in one small population (see Allen 1981; Vienne 1996).
2. In the early twenty-first century, ni-Vanuatu wore 'traditional' clothing primarily on special occasions, for rituals, celebrations and festivals. For this reason, I speak of everyday traditional dress largely in the past tense, but of special-occasion clothing in the present, such forms continuing today.
3. For the sake of clarity, I use the terms Vanuatu and ni-Vanuatu throughout this paper, whichever era I am discussing.

4. Participation in more secret status-alteration systems was not displayed on the body in the same way.
5. I did however observe a number of girls wearing *traosis* to play basketball one evening in Liro, Paama, in November 2001, suggesting that the Paamese ruling against *traosis* was, at that point at least, not very effective.

References

Allen, M.R. (1981), 'Innovation, Inversion and Revolution as Political Tactics in West Aoba', in M.R. Allen (ed.), *Vanuatu: Politics, Economics and Ritual in Island Melanesia*. Sydney: Academic Press.

Blackwood, P. (1981), 'Rank, Exchange and Leadership in Four Vanuatu Societies', in M.R. Allen (ed.), *Vanuatu: Politics, Economics and Ritual in Island Melanesia*. Sydney: Academic Press.

Bolton, Lissant (1998), 'Chief Willie Bongmatur Maldo and the Role of Chiefs in Vanuatu', *Journal of Pacific History* 33 (2): 179–95.

Bonnemaison, J. (1996), 'Graded Societies and Societies Based on Title: Forms and Rites of Traditional Power in Vanuatu', in J. Bonnemaison et al. (eds), *Arts of Vanuatu.* Bathurst, N.S.W.: Crawford House.

Curtis, T. (2002) Talking About Place: Identities, Histories and Powers among the Na'hai speakers of Malatula (Vanuatu) Ph.D Dissertation Australian National University.

Douglas, Bronwen (2002), 'Christian Citizens: Women and Negotiations of Modernity in Vanuatu', *Contemporary Pacific* 14 (1): 1–38.

Eves, Richard (1996), 'Colonialism, Corporeality and Character: Methodist Missions and the Refashioning of Bodies in the Pacific', *History and Anthropology* 10 (1) : 85–138.

Huffman, K. (1996), 'The "Decorated Cloth" from the "Island of Good Yams": Barkcloth in Vanuatu, with Special Reference to Erromango', in J. Bonnemaison et al. (eds), *Arts of Vanuatu.* Bathurst, N.S.W.: Crawford House.

Humphreys, C.B. (1926), *The Southern New Hebrides: an Anthropological Record.* Cambridge: Cambridge University Press.

Johnston, Anna (2000), 'On the Importance of Bonnets: the London Missionary Society and the Politics of Dress in Nineteenth Century Polynesia', *New Literature Review* 36: 114–27.

Jolly, M. (1989), 'Sacred Spaces: Churches, Men's Houses and Households in South Pentecost, Vanuatu', in M. Jolly and M. Macintyre (eds), *Family and Gender in the Pacific: Domestic Contradictions and the Colonial Impact.* Cambridge: Cambridge University Press.

—— (1991), '"To Save the Girls for Brighter and Better Lives": Presbyterian Missionaries and Women in the South of Vanuatu 1848–1870', *Journal of Pacific History* 26: 27–48.

—— (1996), 'European Perceptions of the Arts of Vanuatu: Engendering Colonial Interests', in J. Bonnemaison et al. (eds), *Arts of Vanuatu*. Bathurst, N.S.W.: Crawford House.

Lamb, Robert (1905), *Saints and Savages: the Story of Five Years in the New Hebrides*. Edinburgh: W. Blackwood.

Lawson, Barbara (1994), *Collected Curios: Missionary Tales from the South Seas*. Montreal : McGill University Press.

—— (1999), '"Clothed and in their Right Mind": Women's Dress on Erromango, Vanuatu', in R. Welsch (ed.), *Proceedings of a Special Session of the Pacific Arts Association Festschrift to Honour Dr Philip J.C. Dark: Working Papers*. Anthropology Department, Dartmouth College, Hanover: Pacific Arts Association.

Leggatt, T.W. (1910), 'The Position of Heathen Women in the New Hebrides', *New Hebrides Magazine* no. 38 (October): 22–4.

Molisa, G. (1980), 'Women', in W. Lini et al. (eds), *Vanuatu: twenti wan tingting long taem blong independens*. Fiji: Institute of Pacific Studies of the University of the South Pacific.

Nempan, Sophie (nd). Ms in Nempan's personal papers; also audiotape recording in Women's Culture Project Seventh Workshop Procedings (2000). In Vanuatu National Audiovisual Archives, Vanuatu Cultural Centre, Port Vila, Vanuatu.

Patterson, Mary (2001), 'Breaking the Stones: Ritual, Gender and Modernity in North Ambrym, Vanuatu', *Anthropological Forum* 11(1): 39–54.

Quarterly Jottings from the New Hebrides, South Sea Islands. 1895–1961. Woodford, England: John G. Paton Mission Fund.

Speiser, Felix (1991 [1923]), *Ethnology of Vanuatu: an Early Twentieth Century Study*. Trans. D.Q. Stephenson. Bathurst, N.S.W.: Crawford House.

Strathern, M. (1988), *The Gender of the Gift: Problems with Women and Problems with Society in Melanesia*. Berkeley: University of California Press.

Vienne, B. (1996), 'Masked Faces from the Country of the Dead', in J. Bonnemaison et al. (eds), *Arts of Vanuatu*. Bathurst, N.S.W.: Crawford House.

Woodburn, M. Kathleen (1944), *Backwash of Empire*. Melbourne: Georgian House.

–6–

God's Kingdom in Auckland: Tongan Christian Dress and the Expression of Duty

Ping-Ann Addo

Contemporary Tongan formal dress is more than the sum of its European-Christian and pre-Christian Tongan parts; it is a set of acts whereby one assumes values inherent in Christianity and the Tongan way of life. It is a means of melding these values into an ethos for living – and for thriving – in Tongan communities all over the world today. Looking at Tongan clothing necessitates an examination of Tongan textiles and textile-related practices, as well as at the practices that have become central to the expression of national Tongan identity. In the Kingdom of Tonga, dress has enabled the expression of respect, duty and social conformity to permeate most aspects of everyday life. However, despite the value that people attach to expressing conformity through dress, clothing styles are not static but are subject to subtle adaptations. Cities in the Tongan diaspora are frequently cited by kingdom-based Tongans as sources for innovations in dressing styles and practices. Most of these innovations do not involve a break with tradition, however, but typically involve the elaboration of traditional forms. In Auckland, for example, where over thirty-five thousand Tongans now live, the significance of traditional-styled textiles is continually being bolstered and expanded.

Formal dress is composed of a combination of foreign and indigenous cloth. Beaten barkcloth and woven mats are draped, wrapped and tied over tailored Western-style garments (Figure 6.1). These dress compositions are now considered appropriate to wear at events of religious, political and cultural significance. What interests me is how formal dress helps to foster a way of being in the world, and more specifically, of inculcating a sense of duty and respect. For, by means of combining foreign and indigenous cloth, Tongans wrap themselves for presentation to God, believing that they are clothing their spiritual essence appropriately before God and the Tongan community. This chapter will discuss how contemporary clothing styles bridge the distance between the Tongan Islands and the Tongan diaspora, relating innovative self-expression to abiding mechanisms for showing loyalty to the religious hierarchy. I will begin with an examination of shifts in Tongan cloth-related practices during the period of missionization, in order to reveal how perceptions of the body, social rank and material wealth were interconnected. I will then assess how notions of duty and respect are expressed through diasporic Tongans' contemporary dress.[1]

Clothing Tongans: Assuming New Layers of Religious Practice

Dress compositions provide the clearest manifestation of political, social, religious and aesthetic interactions between Tongans and people from overseas. Christian missionaries have had a lasting influence on the basic form of Tongan dress, since they introduced tailored clothing that was to become the basis of daily wear for virtually all Tongans (Helu 1999: 290). When Europeans first met Tongan *hou'eiki* (high-ranking Tongans) they were wearing rectangular pieces of painted barkcloth and woven pandanus mats wrapped around their bodies. *Tu'a* (Tongans of lower rank) wore either loincloths of plain white barkcloth, waist mats, or a girdle of *si* leaves (Ferdon 1987: 7). Although most people went topless, these waist-to-hip wrappings rendered them properly dressed. It is significant that neither plain white barkcloth nor leaf skirts were considered appropriate for commoners to wear in the presence of *hou'eiki* on their own; they had to be worn together, with a leaf skirt worn on top of the barkcloth. Only then were *tua* respectably attired to meet their social superiors. Layering was therefore already an established part of formal dress prior to the establishment of the mission (James 1997: 39).

European garments were quickly embraced by high-ranking Tongans as signs of their distinction, and of their new modern selves. Missionaries facilitated the acquisition and making of tailored clothes with long sleeves, high collars, long skirts, trousers, hats and shoes that would accomplish the task of religious transformation (Helu 1999: 290). Most lower-ranking Tongans, constrained by lack of resources to dress likewise but needing to show their abiding respect for their chiefs, began to layer traditional textiles with garments introduced by the mission.

Many of these imported garments were white, which was considered to be comfortable in the tropical heat and to convey proof of cleanliness, for missionaries considered that the work needed to keep white clothes clean provided a necessary lesson in industriousness. It is possible, however, that from the Tongan point of view, plain white clothing could have been associated with the white barkcloth worn by commoners. This could explain why Tongan Christian converts wanted to continue to wear woven-fibre waist ornaments over the plain white clothes introduced by missionaries.

Respectability was more generally associated with wearing mats or various forms of woven covering around the hips (Kaeppler 1999: 172; Teilhet-Fisk 1992: 53). Many photographs taken by European and Australian photographers in the late nineteenth and early twentieth centuries show women posing in *palangi* clothes with a woven or intertwined layer of plant fibres around their waists, a Bible in one hand (Helu 1999: 291).

Indigenous cloth, such as fine mats embellished with red parrot feathers, also played a key part in rites of installation. Yet it was the ritual trappings of foreign, European monarchs – the crown, the throne, an ermine cape and other royal insignia – which were to play a key part in legitimating the first King of Tonga. King George Tupou I has long been lauded as the man whose military prowess and political astuteness saved the Tongan islands from formal colonization. In 1875, he consolidated the Tongan islands into a constitutional monarchy, dedicated to God and Tongan cultural values.[2] While assuming the ritual trappings of the British monarchy at his installation, his reign was further legitimized through long-held Tongan beliefs in the power of lineage to endow individuals with inherited *mana* and rights to power. Tupou I had all of these by virtue of his being descended from the feathered god Tangaloa who, like the Christian God, ruled over the heavens. The European-style ermine robes that all four Tupou monarchs have worn at their coronations became the means of assuming titles with rights to power over the kingdom and of protecting the society; a shield so to speak, which kept colonial forces at bay. Today, the current King of Tonga, who has been described as the highest-ranking chief who has ever lived because three kingly lines are consolidated in his blood, continues to demand his respect and tribute.

Textile-related practices in the kingdom of Tonga have long been associated with the state of the soul, the sacred Tongan polity, and the health of the body (Young Leslie 1999; Kaeppler 1999; Herda 1999; James 1997; Teilhet-Fisk 1992; Gailey 1987). Varieties of painted Tongan barkcloths (called *ngatu*) and mats woven from bleached, dyed or softened pandanus leaves, have historically been used as bedding, clothing and burial wrappings, or to form pathways several hundred yards long in ceremonial contexts. They are often presented as gifts, or displayed as potential gifts, in life ceremonies.[3] Collectively called *koloa faka-Tonga* (treasures of Tonga) their value is realized on a social level through their organization into ranked categories that reinforce the pervasive sense of hierarchy in everyday life. Because unstitched textiles constituted the earliest forms of clothing, even barkcloth and mats that have no history of being worn are still commonly referred to as *vala faka-Tonga*, meaning clothing in the manner of Tonga.[4]

Dressing in tailored clothing is known as dressing *faka-palangi* (in the manner of foreigners) but dressing *faka-Tonga* incorporates aspects of *vala faka-palangi* in many specific ways. Whether barkcloth, decorated mats, appliquéd quilts or printed cottons are tightly wrapped, casually draped or worn as stitched clothing on the body, all these forms of 'clothing' index the use of traditional forms of cloth wealth (Herda 1999: 162). Contemplation of these national and heirloom textiles connects contemporary Tongans to a cultural history that remains a point of pride regardless of their religious or political convictions (Figure 6.2). While printed and painted barkcloths (*ngatu*) commemorate aspects of the royal dynasty through the

Figure 6.1 Women wearing '*ta'ovala*' and '*kie kie*' over western-style clothing fasten *ngatu* around the waist of another woman in preparation for the wedding of her female relative. Auckland 2002 (photograph author's own)

use of certain standardized designs, and are commonly worn for dancing and on particularly festive occasions like weddings, waist mats (*ta'ovala*) are far more commonly used as clothing today.[5] *Ta'ovala* are short mats that are worn wrapped

Figure 6.2 In the Tongan diaspora quilts have begun to be used in ceremonial contexts as cloth wealth, alongside more 'traditional' forms of cloth, Auckland 2002 (photograph author's own).

about the midriff and fastened with a braided cord at the waist. They have become a standard aspect of Tongan Christian Dress.

The term 'clothing' is an imprecise translation of the term *ta'ovala*; 'wrapping' or 'covering' are better, though these terms also fail to convey the associative richness of these garments. The term *ta'ovala* is derived from *tata'o*, which refers to the practice of covering freshly slaughtered pig or taro in order to bake it in an earth oven. So a *ta'o-vala* is a *vala* that covers or overlays one's other clothes, or which is worn as the outermost layer, wrapping the offering that it contains.[6] Certain *ta'ovala* are indeed 'baked'; for example, *ta'ovala lokeha* are customarily soaked in seawater and then buried in the ashes of burnt lime coral to give a yellowish tint to the light brown fibres, which are soft to the touch and acquire a smoky smell.

In etymological terms, *vala* can be interpreted as a composite of *va*, 'distance apart' or 'relationship' according to Churchward (1959: 528) and *lâ* (a sail from a boat, the older forms of which were closely woven pandanus mats). *Vala* may therefore be interpreted as a kind of motion that creates the relationships that demarcate social space. In keeping with the hierarchical principles that physically separate *tu'a* from *hou'eiki*, wearing *ta'ovala* can be seen as a way of reinforcing hierarchical distinction (Churchward 1959: 528).

The relationship between *vala* and sails finds some corroboration from oral tradition. According to a Tongan story from the *tala tupu'a* genre of oral Tongan literature, the custom of wearing waist mats was derived from sails on Tongan fishing boats. A group of fishermen was lost at sea for several weeks. In time, their white *tapa* wrappings became tattered and torn. So when they finally drifted to shore they decided to wrap themselves in their sails (*lâ*) before meeting with their chief who had gone down to the shore to lay his eyes on the men whom fate had returned (Helu 1999: 288).[7]

Even after the Constitution and the introduction of European dress when, as a result of missionary impositions, the production and use of all Tongan cloth treasures became the prerogative of all social classes, wearing waist mats was generally reserved for ceremonial occasions. It is a popular perception that Tonga's Queen Salote Tupou III, the great-granddaughter of George Tupou I, made the practice of donning plaited waist ornaments over tailored clothing part of everyday practice (Helu 1999: 291). Today, the basic work dress of civil servants now commonly includes *tupenu* (mid-calf-length wraparound kilts made of viscose or cotton) and waist mats for men, while women tend to wear *kiekie* over their ankle-length *vala,* or wraparound skirts. *Kiekie* are woven belts with several vertically dangling rows of decoratively braided fibre which, like waist mats, envelope the area between the waist and the hips while allowing for more freedom of movement (Teilhet-Fisk 1992: 52). These waist ornaments rank lower than other components of Tongan formal dress, but they are often called waist mats, suggesting that their use as wraps is more important than their specific design. Thus woven and braided waist ornaments have become a standard feature of formal Tongan attire, and are be worn to events of religious, state and community significance. Today, 'Tongans perceive the wearing of a *ta'ovala* as a way of binding their country around them' (ibid. 62). The story of the origin of the waist mat indicates that it is a garment that is associated with respect, rank and duty: three key components in Tongan social interaction (James 1997: 12).

Woven mats were seemingly unaffected by the imposition of sumptuary laws that banned the making and wearing of certain indigenous cloths in the late nineteenth century. Pressure from the Methodist mission to form Church-based women's groups to make indigenous cloth had ostensibly led to the democratization of indigenous cloth production. This was a period when aspiring Tongans, who just a short time before had relied upon Tongan dress and regalia to transmit and sanction political and religious power, viewed indigenous clothing as an encumbrance. By appropriating European forms of dress and rejecting indigenous clothing, they wanted to convey the civility of the Tongan polity to the surrounding colonial powers. Moreover, it was in Tupou I's interest to suppress native cloth production so that he could be seen to be working with, rather than against, the Methodist Mission. The 'Law on *Tapa*' was issued together with the Constitution

Figure 6.3 Young woman buying fish on Vuna wharf, Nuku'alofa, Tongatapu, wearing a *kiekie* waist ornament, 1987 (photograph Chris Spring).

of 1875. It stipulated that, 'between 1876 and 1878, the manufacture and wearing of the native cloth was to be progressively eliminated' (Rutherford 1996: 82). The sumptuary law was drawn up by Rev Shirley Baker, a Wesleyan missionary and Tonga's first Prime Minister, to the advantage of a particular textile firm who sought a market for cotton cloth, 'on the sale of which Baker was supposed to receive a commission' (ibid. 82–4).

The sumptuary law primarily had an impact upon people of rank. Wearing painted barkcloth (*ngatu*) was outlawed, and its production was restricted to one day a week, yet mat weaving seems to have remained relatively unrestricted. Because of the fact that it was less noisy than the sonorous beating of paper mulberry bast on wooden anvils, and given the nature of the group assembly of *ngatu* that often involved singing, mat weaving seems to have been more acceptable to missionaries. It has been suggested that in the eyes of Methodist missionaries 'mat-making [was] a work of patience', capable of teaching Melanesian women control over their hands and bodies, a necessary precursor, it was thought, to their training in sewing which would further provide them with clothing (Eves 1996: 110). Thus making and wearing mats became a means of allying Christianity with older Tongan religious practice.

Tongan women's agency has long been connected to their status as the makers and preservers of textiles that were imbued with the *mana* of the pre-Christian spirit world (Filihia 2001: 387). After conversion, Tongan waist wrappings acquired newer meanings of decent Christian dress. The persistence and elaboration of *koloa faka-Tonga* forms show that people have come to use these clothing forms to generate an abiding sense of the Tongan way of life.

Dressing Subjects

When I ask Tongans why they wear waist mats (*ta'ovala*) or waist ornaments (*kiekie*) over their clothes, they refer to the importance of showing respect (*faka'apa'apa*) and manifesting a sense of duty (*fatongia*). Waist mats have come to be equated with showing one's love for Tonga and one's obedience to its rulers. As a result of Queen Salote Tupou's influence, waist mats have enabled all Tongans to be dressed as subjects whose daily tasks can be perceived as acts of duty. Many different kinds of work come under this rubric. Even in the early 1990s, one could still see men working in their bush gardens dressed in tailored clothes, over which would be tied a tattered waist mat.[8] Dressed in waist mats, the person is no longer simply a labourer, but a spiritual subject, performing acts of love for the kingdom of Tonga and the kingdom of God. Thus, national duty embraces religious piety, respect for ranked persons, and work (James 1997: 7). Celebrations for the Tongan hierarchy, such as the King of Tonga's birthday, call for modes of dress similar to those worn for dedicated work and for going to church and to events of political and national significance.

In the diaspora, however, formal dress is becoming confined to ceremonial occasions and cultural festivals. Tongans who live abroad often feel that it is

Figure 6.4 Tongan woman wearing a calico blouse and Tongan-style barkcloth skirt overlaid with a fibrous waist ornament, *c.* 1890 (Lister Collection, British Museum OC/B48/12-GN673).

Figure 6.5 Tongan woman carrying a Bible and wearing a locally made blouse and a girdle made of local plants around her midriff (Lister Collection, British Museum OC/B53/18).

inappropriate to wear waist mats to their wage-earning jobs in the mainstream community. Yet if they are in mourning they will wear customary black clothes and even waist mats, especially if the deceased relative has not yet been buried. Even in Auckland it is widely held that a Tongan's body is the 'temple of the Lord', a manifestation of the glory of God and the Kingdom, and funerals, together with other life ceremonies, continue to be occasions for exaggerated public gifting of Tongan cloth treasures (*koloa faka-Tonga*). Thus, migrant Tongans proudly proclaim themselves to be part of a culture whose basic ethos is generosity. Although all Pacific cultures are based upon an ethos of reciprocity, Tongans believe that they give away more cloth wealth and money at their funerals and weddings than any other Pacific island community. They are fiercely proud of their distinctively patterned barkcloth, which island-based Tongan women have to produce continuously in order to supply demand from Tongans and tourists as well as from Samoans and Fijians (Neich and Pendergrast 1997: 20). For Tongans believe themselves to be the guardians of Pacific cultural patrimony based upon the intense production, export and gifting of cloth.

Tongans also believe in openly showing their respect through their demeanour and mode of speech[9] as well as through their dress. Many Tongans overtly display positive emotions like joy and gratitude through spontaneous gifting actions, words of thanks and praise and even spontaneous tears, indicative of Wesleyan revivalist worship (Campbell 1992: 99). Sadness, too, is shown with tears, and Tongan women are known for leading a congregation's weeping at funerals with their high-pitched, mournful wailing with prescribed forms of speech (Kaeppler 1978: 74). Family members who rank below the deceased (called 'being *liongi*') are especially duty-bound to wear black clothes and dishevelled hair, and to wrap themselves almost completely in large, tattered *ta'ovala* which are really nothing more than old, dirty floor mats. The following section will demonstrate how cloth and clothing are conventionally used to express and to evoke appropriate emotions.

'You Can Have All the Money You Want but You Can't Wrap a Dead Body in a Dollar Bill'[10]

The cash economy is not antithetical to presenting gifts of Tongan clothing. Whether they are based in the islands or in New Zealand, Tongans continue to pursue money, and they continue to pursue Tongan cloth treasures. As the above quote from the Tongan woman shows, barkcloth and mats are vital for the performance of burial rites. Here again, Tongan and European clothing are worn layered on top of the other, but the order is reversed. Among Tongans in Auckland, the bodies of the dead are initially wrapped in a layer of barkcloth or matting, over which Western-style garments are added. Barkcloth and mats are not outer wrappings for public display. This is not simply because these forms of cloth wealth embody family and cultural values, but because they are believed to facilitate journeying, the passage from one state to another (Filihia 2001: 383). Today, wearing Tongan cloth wealth *under* European tailored garments is meant to facilitate the deceased's final journey to God and marks a final, secret entreaty that they may be found worthy of eternal life.

Tongan funerals are euphemistically known as *me'a faka'eiki,* literally things of the high-ranking, for 'as [a] proverb says, a man becomes a chief when he dies' (Kaeppler 1978: 174).[11] Once again, dress is involved in indicating submission. Women who are ceremonially lower than the deceased are expected to wear their hair untied, leaving it dishevelled should it become so. After the burial their long hair will often be cut in honour of their deceased relative and as a further sign of

Figure 6.6 Tongan woman dressed in typical Tongan mourning clothes, seated on a pile of folded *ngatu* recently gifted by several families at a funeral in Auckland 2002 (photograph author's own).

their remorse and respect, further changing their appearance so that their status as mourners remains apparent. Sometimes, hair from these hair cuttings will be braided into a thick belt, several metres long, called a *kafa* which is used to bind a waist mat in place (Teilhet-Fisk 1992: 48). *Kafa* celebrate women's sacrifice, for these items of clothing are, quite literally, extensions of the self. Even *kafa* that are made for daily use with waist mats must be wrapped many times around the waist, the horizontal rows being spread out so that they form an ornate brown band, which is several inches thick, in a process which is known as *ha'i ta'ovala* (literally 'that which is bound round and round'. Churchward 1959: 216)

The colour of mourning dress makes sense in both Tongan and European systems of representation. Black has long been regarded as a sacred colour, and the highest ranking barkcloth is called *ngatu 'uli* (blackened barkcloth) which is heavily charged with blackened clay and tree sap. When the younger brother of the king of Tonga, Prince Fatafehi Tu'ipelehake, died in 1999, Auckland-dwelling Tongans wore the customary all-black funeral clothing with waist mats for the many days it took to complete his funeral observances. In Tonga, many people anticipated the clothing needs of the customary six months of mourning for the highest-ranked of *hou'eiki* that was to be observed, and quickly depleted the kingdom's many small shops' supply of black clothing and black fabrics.[12] The several hundred diaspora-based Tongans who returned to Tonga for the Prince's funeral were asked by relatives to bring home remittances of black fabric and clothing (Figure 6.3).

Figure 6.7 Women and girls on their way to a funeral wearing mourning dress and *ta'ovala* (waist-mats), Tongatapu, Tonga, 1987 (photograph Chris Spring).

Clothing, Church, Hierarchy and the Appeal of Foreign Clothes

When the first big wave of Tongan migration to New Zealand began in the late 1960s (facilitated by work visas offered by the New Zealand government), many

Tongan men travelled abroad alone, working to save money so that their families might join them in New Zealand. New Zealand, the location closest to the home islands in the Tongan diaspora, soon started to serve as a stepping-stone to places like Australia, Honolulu and the mainland USA. Now, almost forty years later, New Zealand is home to many Tongan communities that are predominantly situated in and around Auckland and the capital city Wellington. Research and census data shows that, in 1996, over one-third of the Tongans living overseas had been born in Tonga, suggesting that as fast as Tongans are being born abroad, native Tongans are still emigrating at fairly rapid rates (Spoonley 2001: 83). Between 1996 and 2001, the registered Tongan population in New Zealand grew from just over 31,000 to over 35,000 (Didham and Bedford 2001: 28). Based on the 1996 census figures, over 80 per cent of New Zealander-Pacific Islanders were avowedly religiously affiliated (ibid. 41), which at current Tongan-New Zealand numbers suggests that there may be some 28,000 Tongans involved in religious activity in New Zealand. Clothing operates as an immediate visual indicators of cultural, and in some cases, religious devotion, working to the advantage of newly arrived Tongan immigrants and of short-term visitors from Tonga who rely on these established communities for social, spiritual and even economic support.

Tongan churches in Auckland usually have their own Tongan administrators who come under the auspices of the larger churches that are based in Tonga. Church activities provide situations in which the hybrid cultural identities of young diasporic Tongan people are standardized. Churches are cultural enclaves, providing a point of stability for Tongans in all parts of the diaspora. Young Tongans are encouraged to marry other Tongans and, usually, a woman will become active in her husband's church even if she marries a man who attends another Tongan congregation or belongs to another Christian denomination.

Within the Tongan community, the presence or absence of *koloa faka-Tonga* (Tongan clothing treasures) serves as a marker of religious affiliation or rank. Tongans who are simply passing through Auckland will usually attend church in full formal dress. As in Tonga, Methodists, Catholics and Anglicans will wear waist ornaments or waist mats layered over a full set of long, decent Christian clothes.[13] Men regularly wear slacks to church, but for funerals and other important religious family occasions they inevitably appear in a tailored sarong (*tupenu*) and a waist mat. Even members of the Mormon Church, who typically dress in European clothes for worship, will wear formal Tongan dress for funerals and extended periods of mourning. Generally speaking, however, most Mormon Tongans and their religious leaders believe that too many resources – time, money, and faith – are invested in Tongan clothing treasures, which they believe to be superfluous to true worship and devotion.[14] Yet out of respect for the deceased, native cultural practice – and many of the things for which its rituals and material culture stand – is allowed to prevail.

Living in the diaspora affords greater access to cutting-edge fashions, which means that people of lower rank are able to dress in the same way as their superiors. Nevertheless, many Tongans living in the diaspora continue to cherish the ability to assess other people's economic and social status by observing the kinds of *koloa faka-Tonga* they wear. I know a Tongan woman who recognized another Tongan, who must have been a woman of rank, by the shape and mode of wrapping of her waist mat. It turned out that the second woman *was* a relative of the Queen of Tonga and had dressed, for a special church service, in an older form of a very high-ranking waist mat called a *falavala* that had been bound over her clothes in 'the *hou'eiki* manner'. This meant that the *ta'ovala* had more a diagonal than a horizontal orientation, so that all four corners of it were visible and one corner was folded halfway up the back of her bodice. So, despite some levelling of access to European garment styles over social class, ceremonial dress continues to denote social status and one's commitment to pursuing Tongan values in a different homeland. Conversely, Western clothes can also be read for indications of one's access to global commodities, money and culture flows, to which the diaspora is often local people's strongest initial link.

The diaspora has long facilitated access to clothing in island Tonga, and has directly influenced the clothing styles that are considered modern and therefore desirable by many who live there. A favourite pastime for young people on the main Tongan island of Tongatapu is to spend Saturday mornings at the local *fea*, or flea market, where many people buy their clothes, shoes and cosmetics. Most of the clothes are second-hand garments provided by relatives living abroad who send clothes home in shipping containers. It is the foreign origin of the clothes sold at *fea*, most of which are originally from Britain and the United States, that attracts people.[15]

Second-hand clothing is popular with people of all age groups given its cheaper price, the excitement that comes with making a bargain find, and the opportunity for small enterprise that it offers women. The *fea* affords young Tongans, whose 'new clothes' normally constitute hand-me-downs from relatives, a rare chance to experience browsing and shopping. For schoolchildren and workers, Saturday mornings are one of the few chinks in time when they do not have to wear school or work uniforms, or other forms of formal dress. Saturday mornings, in particular, are among the rare occasions when girls are allowed to wear jeans and jewellery in public. Dressed in their best casual wear they board the minibuses from various villages and travel into the capital for the *Tu'imatamoana fea* where they can browse and socialize to develop their own sense of style. Tongan youth are the 'living vortex in the present revolution in style' (Helu 1999: 291). It is said that the monarch's grandchildren, who have studied and travelled abroad, also enjoy a morning out to look around the *fea* in Nuku'alofa.

To island-based Tongans, dressing in *palangi* clothes usually denotes modernity. Young, unmarried women are now wearing clothes made out of sheer fabrics, layered for both modesty and stylish effect, along with their waist ornaments and waist mats to church. Acquiring new *koloa faka-Tonga* – which are either bought for cash or acquired through a series of reciprocal exchanges of food, clothing, island foods and money with family members back home – is also a facet of Tongan modernity. For it marks one's place in trans-Pacific networks linking the islands to the diaspora.

Innovation in the Hands of Old Women

Both traditional Tongan cultural forms and clothing styles are, for the most part, controlled by the female gerontocracy. Older Tongan women are usually the ones in charge of the family's clothing choices, telling younger women and girls what to wear. It is they who adapt the form of Tongan traditional textiles to meet the needs of Auckland city-dwellers, and they who either sanction or condone shifts in attitudes to clothing and dress in Tongan communities in Auckland. Yet, as the people with time and skills on their hands and with honour for Tonga in their hearts, it is they also who come up with interesting approximations to island-based Tongan dress compositions that later become standard wear.

'Keli' is a 67-year-old Tongan spinster who has lived for the past twenty-two years in Auckland. She retired from working at an Auckland fish-processing factory seven years ago and now helps to organize the activities of a group of eleven elderly Tongan women who meet weekly to produce *koloa si'i*, that is, 'small treasures'.[16] The group is modelled on the women's groups in Tonga, which meet regularly to produce Tongan barkcloth and to weave waist-mats and other pandanus mats. They refer to their communal sessions of embroidering pillowcases and braiding hair belts or waist ornaments as performing their *fatongia,* or duty. 'Keli' is the descendant of one of the most famous Tongan Methodist missionaries to Fiji, Joeli Bulu, and is a devout member of the Free Wesleyan Church of Tonga. She often acts as the family representative at religious cultural events, such as funerals and birthdays, that occur all over Auckland.

I was therefore surprised to see her on her way to choir practice dressed in something other than her usual ankle-length sarong, knee-length dress and waist ornaments (*kiekie*). Instead she was wearing a long black skirt and a long-sleeved shirt made of brown and white printed cotton fabric along the hem of which, starting at the waistline, were attached a dozen double-layered, dangling strips of matching brown and white fabric. These strips were patterned with vertical rows of Xs, reminiscent of braided strips of dried plant fibre, and functioned as an attached *kiekie.* 'Keli' called the garment a *kofu kiekie* (literally a '*kiekie* dress') and said that it was one of two such garments that she owned, one of which she had been given by a woman friend who had had them made by a seamstress in Auckland.[17] Besides going to choir practice in them she has worn her *kiekie* dress to pay a home visit to her pastor, and on a church-group visit to two young Tongan princesses who are being schooled in Auckland.

One would expect 'Keli', who speaks little English, and who seems to be minimally integrated into wider New Zealand society, to follow conservative cultural prescriptions to the letter.[18] When I asked her why it was appropriate to wear the *kie kie* dress on these occasions, she replied: 'These [occasions] are not the same as going to church'. Her *kiekie* dress allowed her another way of visually expressing the notion that religious worship is the pinnacle of her cultural activities, over and above choir practice and visits with the pastor.

From Cloth Wealth to Cotton Prints

Any discussion of the presence of the Kingdom of Tonga in Auckland must necessarily cover the transposition of barkcloth designs to cotton and viscose fabrics. Cotton and viscose imitations of Tongan-style barkcloth (*ngatu*), printed with distinctive motifs (using *kupesi* pattern boards), have become ubiquitous in the outdoor markets and fabric shops in Auckland (Thomas 1995: 140). Commissioned by Fiji-Indian traders who have them printed in Japan (where they have the necessary expertise to replicate the painterly qualities of Tongan barkcloth) they are an interesting example of the transcultural traffic in ideas.[19]

The clothes made from these fabrics are called *vala tapa'i ngatu,* or '*ngatu*-design-based clothing'. Barkcloth imitations have made Tongan prints as widely appreciated and as accessible as island and Hawaiian Aloha prints. They are bringing barkcloth into everyday use, thereby echoing Queen Salote's achievements with *ta'ovala*. The designs feature motifs from modern chiefly motifs, such as the *kupesi* of the Tongan monarch's crown, the royal seal and coat of arms called *Sila 'o Tonga* (Figure 6.4).[20] Apart from indexing Tongan patriotism these designs are a source of pride because they index the widening influence of their homeland.[21]

Tongans frequently express their pleasure that 'even *palangis*' (foreigners) are buying their barkcloth and wearing Tongan-print shirts. Furthermore, many Tongans now concede that dressing up in tailored outfits made of these fabrics constitutes another version of dressing *faka-Tonga,* although 'barkcloth-design-based clothing' is not referred to as *vala faka-Tonga* (dressing in the manner of Tonga) per se. People can wear such garments and be considered appropriately dressed for most church services, in both Tonga and in New Zealand, if they layer on waist mats or waist ornaments. Through these designs, cotton has been appropriated as a distinctively Pacific material. For whereas cotton clothes were initially

Figure 6.8 Women wearing viscose shirts printed with the Tongan Royal Coat of Arms '*Sila 'o Tonga*', Auckland 2002 (photograph author's own).

embraced *because* they were foreign and indexed foreign religious resources, barkcloth imitations are now embraced because they signify patriotism to the homeland. This is yet another example of the way in which Christianity has become naturalized as a dimension of Tongan cosmology.

Conclusion

I have attempted to show that Tongans have not been blind followers of other people's religious and cultural beliefs. Dress is an integral part of how Tongans have always defined themselves to themselves, as well as to others. By continuing to be makers of treasured textiles, low-ranking Tongan women have ensured that the guiding construction of the Christian Tongan self has maintained standards of decency and respectability that are also visual markers of Tongan identity. Like 'Keli', some individuals are changing their own modes of dress according to personal and cultural values, and varying them just enough from the conventional practices that they remain salient, in increasingly more qualified ways, both in meaning and function.

Socially high-ranking Tongans have often been the first to innovate new clothing styles. They were the first to embrace European styles of dress when missionaries first introduced them in the early 1800s. One trend in the physical form of *ta'ovala* that I have witnessed recently seems to have just begun to trickle down into the practices of non-chiefly Tongans. On Sunday in April 2001, King Taufa'ahau Tupou IV and his daughter, Princess Salote Mafile'o Pilolevu Tuita, both arrived for a special church service wearing what seemed, from a distance, like shiny black and gold *ta'ovala* over their well-tailored garments. What they actually wore were cloth substitutes woven with gold-coloured thread. Both designs were culturally resonant: the king's waistcloth was woven with floral patterns; the princess's was embellished with thick stripes. When I later remarked on this to an Auckland-dwelling Tonga woman, she thought that this substitution was 'a good idea . . . it's cooler for [the king] that way because it's not as heavy as a *koloa faka-Tonga*.' She averred that since he was king it was 'up to him' to wear what he wanted, but also remarked that he was 'still doing the right thing' by wearing a waist-to-hip wrapping.[22] In January 2002, I saw something similar in Auckland when an elderly Tongan man attended a special church feast at a local Free Wesleyan Church of Tonga, dressed in a 'waist mat' made of dark green yarn which had been knitted into a rectangular textile that resembled a shawl and which was fastened on his waist with a braided coconut fibre *kafa*.

The waist wrappings of these three people were all made from non-native Tongan materials, highly processed thread or textile, quite different from the usual Tongan *ta'ovala*. Nevertheless, these innovations in dress composition did *not* formally break with the traditions established by a long-standing practice of bodily adornment that are said to foster the ideal inner emotions and attitudes that a person should have before God and monarch. Partly owing to mythical, historical, and contemporary cultural and religious reinforcement, this creed continues to be lived out by a majority of Tongan people, during their entire adult lives, whether they are in Tonga or in other lands. The act of dressing *faka-Tonga* (in the Tongan manner) becomes, then, a technique of the body that is based on the abiding value of doing all one can to ensure physical and cosmological protection for the bounty of the Tongan kingdom, from wherever one may dwell in the world.

Notes

1. The research for this chapter is part of an on-going research project on the contemporary significance and influence of traditional Tongan textiles in the lives and aspirations of Tongans in New Zealand. It has been funded by the Wenner-Gren Foundation for Anthropological Research and the Yale Centre for International and Area Studies. I thank Dr Chloe Colchester for helpful planning suggestions, Jane Horan for editing help, and Dr 'Okusitino Mâhina for academic support and for his personal insights on what it means to be a Tongan in Auckland.
2. I have heard Tupou I cited by several religious leaders of Tongan congregations in New Zealand as the person, guided by God, who was responsible for ensuring the Christian spirit of Tonga. He offered the islands to God and made his kingdom with this motto: 'Koe 'Otua mo Tonga, Ko Hoku Tofi'a' ('God and Tonga are My Inheritance').
3. Life ceremonies create the arenas in which these transmissions of power happened, and still happen, when textiles are customarily gifted upward, from people of lower status to people of higher rank in various ceremonies of religious, political and social significance.
4. In etymological terms, *vala* can be interpreted as a composite of *va* – 'distance apart' or 'relationship' according to Churchward (1959: 528) – and *lā* (a sail from a boat, the older forms of which were basically tightly woven pandanus mats). *Vala*, therefore, can be seen as textiles that cordon off space for the wearer's personal essence and Tongan *ta'ovala* as functioning to defining one's personal space, separating it from the public space around. In keeping with the hierarchical principles that physically separate *tu'a* from *hou'eiki*, wearing *ta'ovala* can be seen as a way of essentializing class distinction (Churchward 1959: 528).
5. *Kupesi* are the designs – and the patterned design boards that are used to make them – on *ngatu*.
6. I am indebted to Max Tu'itahi of the department of Pacific Studies, Auckland University for these etymological insights.
7. See '*Tupu'anga 'o e Ta'ovala*' – 'The origin of the *Ta'ovala*' in Moala 1994: 183–5.

8. Heather Young Leslie, February 2002; personal communication.
9. It should be noted that there are several dialects of the Tongan language, with one reserved for speech to *hou'eiki*. This is also the dialect in which prayers are said, since one would be addressing the highest-ranked being of all. I have met many Tongans, both diasporic and island-based, who claim that their knowledge of this dialect is scanty. Not wanting to appear disrespectful to *hou'eiki* whom they do have to address, many of them opt to use English.
10. 'Olivani', Auckland, New Zealand: March 2001.
11. Cited in Adrienne Kaeppler's description of the mourning rituals for Queen Salote. The full import of this statement, however, is debatable and highly context-dependent ('Okusitino Māhina: personal communication).
12. Six months was the length of Prince Fatafehi Tu'ipelehake's mother's (Queen Salote) funeral, which, Kaeppler comments, also saw the shops 'in chaos with the frantic buying of black cloth' (1978: 180).
13. From my random sampling of the religious affiliations of Tongans in three communities in Auckland, about half seem to belong to some branch of the Free Wesleyan Church of Tonga, the state Church back in Tonga. About one-third are Church of Tonga affiliates, 10 % Roman Catholic, 10 per cent Mormon and 10 per cent belonging to any one of several religious groups that range from Bahai to Assemblies of God. This investigation is part of my ongoing research in Tongan communities in Auckland.
14. 'Pisila', Auckland, February 2001: personal communication.
15. Karen Tranberg Hansen's work is a key discussion of the social, economic and political implications of a nation whose clothing is largely supplied by imports of second hand clothing from Britain and the United States (Hansen 2001). I am indebted to Niko Besnier for insights into behaviour and attitudes connected to flea-market shopping in Tonga.
16. Herda (1999: 162) explains that quilts and embroidered pillowcases – ostensibly *palangi* textile products – tend to complement, rather than form the core of a major gift presentation of *koloa faka-Tonga*. '*Koloa si'i*' means 'small *koloa*'. A genre of 'value added' Tongan mats (a term I borrow from Janet Davidson, Curator of the Pacific Collection at Te Papa Tongarewa Museum of New Zealand) is also popular among groups like 'Keli's' who obtain undecorated mats and *ta'ovala* from Tonga and decorate them with yarn and feathers, in much the same way as it is done in Tonga.
17. The classification of the garment as a dress, rather than a shirt, suggests its appropriateness, since women necessarily wear dresses for church-related activities. Shirts are shorter and do not necessarily fall past the hips.
18. In 1996, 15 per cent of New Zealand-based Tongans were adults who had not yet learned English (Macpherson et al. 2001: 61).

19. Pramika International Ltd is an Auckland-based textile design firm which prints hundred of different designs based on *ngatu* at factories in Japan. The aesthetics of Tongan *ngatu* have now begun to make their mark on a global, commodified scale, opening up questions of indigenous rights and copyrights of culturally coded designs that cannot be discussed here.
20. To Thomas, out-migration from the islands suggests that there is considerable unease with the domination of the homeland by the extremely powerful and influential royal family. However, my investigations reveal that there still exists, among Auckland's Tongan population, a loyalty, at least at discursive levels, for Tonga's royal Tupou dynasty and a rather strong disdain for the pro-democracy movement.
21. Aesthetic shifts have been integral to the continued relevance of *ngatu* since the earliest *kupesi 'I ngatu* were geometric in composition, shifting sometime in the last two hundred years to more literal designs, from abstraction to representation ('Okusitino Māhina: personal communication).
22. 'Filisi', Auckland, New Zealand, February 2002; personal communication.

References

Campbell, I.C. (1992), *Island Kingdom: Tonga Ancient and Modern*. Christchurch: Canterbury University Press.

Churchward, C.M. (1959), *Tongan Dictionary*. London: Oxford University Press.

Didham, R. and Bedford, R. (2001), 'Who are the "Pacific Peoples"? Ethnic Identification and the New Zealand Census', in C. Macpherson, P. Spoonley and M. Anae (eds), *Tangata o te Moana Nui: the Evolving Identities of Pacific Peoples in Aotearoa/New Zealand*. Palmerston North: Dunmore Press.

—— and Cook, L. and Khawaja, M. (2001), 'The Shape of the Future: The Demography of Pacific People', in C. Macpherson, P. Spoonley, and M. Anae (eds), *Tangata o te Moana Nui: the Evolving Identities of Pacific Peoples in Aotearoa/New Zealand*. Palmerston North: Dunmore Press.

Eves, R. (1996), 'Colonialism, Corporeality and Character: Methodist Missions and the Refashioning of Bodies in the Pacific', *History and Anthropology* 10(1): 85–138.

Ferdon, E. (1987), *Early Tonga As the Explorers Saw It 1616–1810*. Tucson: University of Arizona Press.

Filihia, Meredith (2001), 'Men are from Maama, Women are from Pulotu: Female Status in Tongan Society', *Journal of the Polynesian Society* 101 (4): 377–90.

Gailey, C.W. (1987), *Kinship to Kingship: Gender Hierarchy and State Formation in the Tongan Islands*. Austin: University of Texas Press.

Hansen, K.T. (2000), *Salaula: The World of Second-hand Clothing and Zambia*. Chicago: University of Chicago Press.

Helu, I.F. (1999), 'Tongan Dress', in I. F. Helu (ed.) *Critical Essays: Cultural Perspectives from the South Seas*, Canberra: Journal of Pacific History.

Herda, P. (1999), 'The Changing Texture of Textiles in Tonga', *Journal of the Polynesian Society*, 108 (2): 149–67.

James, K. (1988), 'O, Lead Us Not Into "Commoditization" . . . Christine Ward Gailey's Changing Gender values in the Tongan Islands', *Journal of The Polynesian Society* 97 (1): 31–49.

—— (1997), 'Reading the Leaves: The Role of Tongan Women's Traditional Wealth and Other "Contraflows" in the Process of Modern Migration and Remittance', *Pacific Studies* 20 (1): 1–27.

Kaeppler, A. (1978), '*Me'a faka'eiki*: Tongan Funerals in a Changing Society', in N. Gunson, (ed.), *The Changing Pacific: Essays in Honour of Henry Maude.* Melbourne: Oxford University Press, 174–202.

—— (1999), '*Kie Hingoa*: Mats of Power, Rank, Prestige and History', *Journal of the Polynesian Society* 108 (2): 168–231.

Macpherson, C. (2001), 'Pacific Islanders', *Asia Pacific Viewpoint* 42(1): 27–33.

Macpherson, C., Spoonley, P. and Anae, M. (eds) (2001), *Tangata o te Moana Nui: the Evolving Identities of Pacific Peoples in Aotearoa/New Zealand.* Palmerston North: Dunmore Press.

Moala, M. (1994), '*Efinanga: Ko e ngaahi tala mo e anga fakafonuo 'o Tonga*', *Kolomotu'a.* Tonga: Lali Publications

Neich, R. and Pendergrast, N. (1997), *Traditional Tapa Textiles of the Pacific.* London: Thames & Hudson.

Niessen, S. (1993), *Batak Cloth and Clothing: A Dynamic Indonesian Tradition.* Kuala Lumpur: Oxford University Press.

Rutherford, N. (1996), *Shirley Baker and the King of Tonga.* Auckland: Pasifika Press.

Spoonley, P. (2001), 'Transnational Pacific Communities: Transforming the Politics of Place and Identity', in C. Macpherson, P. Spoonley, and M. Anae (2001), *Tangata o te Moana Nui: the Evolving Identities of Pacific Peoples in Aotearoa/New Zealand.* Palmerston North: Dunmore Press.

Teilhet-Fisk, J. (1992), 'Clothes in Tradition: The "*ta'ovala*" and "*kiekie*" as Social Text and Aesthetic Markers of Custom and Identity in Contemporary Tongan Society Part II', *Journal of Pacific Arts*: 40–65.

Thomas, N. (1995), *Oceanic Art.* London: Thames & Hudson.

Weiner, A. (1989), 'Why Cloth: Wealth, Gender, and Power in Oceania', in A. Weiner and J. Schneider (eds), *Cloth and Human Experience.* Washington DC: Smithsonian Institution Press.

Young Leslie, H. (1999), 'Tradition, Textiles and Obligation in the Kingdom of Tonga', unpublished PhD. Thesis. Toronto: York University.

Part IV
Clothing the Diaspora

–7–

T-shirts, Translation and Humour: on the Nature of Wearer-Perceiver Relationships in South Auckland

Chloë Colchester

It is six o'clock on a Saturday morning in mid-August. The sky is grey and overcast and sleet is falling, the ground is wet and my feet are freezing. I am at Otara, Auckland's main Polynesian market in a distant city suburb. The market is full of Maori and Pacific Islanders, the local community. People pass by wearing sports gear and baseball caps, or with the hoods of their tracksuit tops raised against the wet and the cold. The market is filling up. Maori are selling fruit and fresh vegetables that they have grown at their farms. A few Pacific Islanders are selling fruit and taro tubers from Niue and Tonga. There are stalls selling cheap foreign clothing. I stop to look at a shell suit made for a toddler that has the Carlsberg logo on it, and move on.

The stalls run by Fiji-Indians are full of 'island prints' – versions of Pacific *tapa* and former colonial fabrics designed for the Pacific market that are printed in acrid colours: acid yellow, maroon, ochre, viridian green and black. Some have been made up into dresses, ties, shirts and waistcoats (Figure 7.1). Older women from the islands are also running stalls. Tongan women have stalls selling large lengths of *tapa* with the Tongan royal seal or images of fish printed upon them. Maori women are selling baskets. Two women from the Cook Islands are selling huge family sacks of doughnuts. One woman is selling *tapa* souvenirs that have ink drawings of sentimental scenes of island life on them: a boat, some coconut palms, a beach, and a sunset. It is a scene that, like many of the other things here, seems to belong to a different world from the asphalted market place on this dull grey morning.

I begin a second round of the market, and register the sounds. There is a street preacher, a gospel choir, a group of fund-raisers; and there are music stalls with island-style music blaring from their speakers. A T-shirt grabs my attention. It is a rip-off of an American Express card that reads 'Samoan Express' (see Figure 7.2). In place of the warrior there is a drawing of a Samoan. It has also been made for a child. Where the name would be printed it says **'JUNIOR AFRO'**; the expiry

Figure 7.1 Otara Market, South Auckland, August 2001 (photograph author's own).

Figure 7.2 'Samoan Express' T-shirt design by Pacific Gear, Auckland, *c.* 2001 (photograph author's own).

date reads '12-2000' – possibly a millennial reference? But I am particularly struck by the pattern that has been substituted for the normal background design, a distinctive Samoan *tapa* or *siapo* pattern. The T-shirt is an intriguing thing, and I am not sure what to make of it, but it seems to capture the feeling of in-betweenness about this place. I start to look more closely at the other stalls and I become aware that the Samoan Express T-shirt is indicative of a genre. Many of the other T-shirts that I had taken to be foreign are only apparently so. That is the hook. Five weeks later I am on my way back with a suitcase full of T-shirts.

Had I not spent the past three months looking at lengths of *tapa* in the British Museum I might not have spotted this. However, studying *tapa* had involved working with Rosanna Raymond, a woman of both Maori and Samoan descent. While we had both been struck by the optical charge of Samoan *siapo* patterns, we had both found the designs baffling and difficult to fathom. She urged me to go to New Zealand for my research. Accordingly, I had set out with the intention of studying the ways in which *tapa* is being translated by people of Pacific island descent who are living in the midst of larger settler communities.

Auckland

Auckland has now become the largest Polynesian city in the world. Half of New Zealand's population of Pacific Islanders (roughly 200,000 people of Pacific descent were recorded in the 1996 census) is based there. Polynesians from islands under New Zealand administration such as Samoa and the Cook Islands, Niue, as well as other islands within the Tokelau group came to New Zealand during the post-war boom in manufacturing and agriculture in the 1950s and 1960s. These early migrations set up a chain reaction. During the 1970s and 1980s other islanders came to join their relatives, and they chose to stay in spite of the imposition of tougher immigration laws. Then, as ethnic nationalism became more pronounced in Fiji, as well as other Pacific islands, another wave of migrants and political dissidents came to New Zealand.

The 1990s witnessed the growth of recognition of contemporary Pacific culture in New Zealand. The critical acclaim with which *Te Maori*, a blockbuster exhibition of traditional Maori art and culture, was greeted in the United States spearheaded growing emphasis upon the redefinition of New Zealand as Aotearoa, a bicultural Pacific Island nation. Aotearea-New Zealand's status as a bicultural, as opposed to a multicultural, nation in certain ways made it harder for newer migrant populations to find a voice; and this may have been why people of Pacific Island descent began to achieve a more prominent exposure in the public domain in a number of different areas of *contemporary* cultural activity. Artists of Pacific island descent began to make an impact in the contemporary art scene, rap crews began to develop a distinctive Polynesian version of hip hop, and playwriting, fashion and performance provided other means of exploring Pacific Islanders' urban experience.

A new cultural festival, called *Pasifika* and a TV youth programme, called *Tagata Pasifika* (transmitted early on a Sunday morning) provided new arenas for the celebration of both traditional and contemporary forms of expression. As public attention was drawn to past misappropriations of Maori art, wealthy white New Zealanders turned to the apparently less politically contentious art from the Pacific. *Tapa* started to feature in their interior decoration schemes. This 'Pacific accent', to use Nicholas Thomas's formulation, became more entrenched as *tapa*-derived motifs spread from contemporary art to be used in murals, in signage and even in corporate art, where they served as a cliché for signifying Pacific presence (see Thomas 1996, 1999).

To a certain extent, fine art, fashion and rap have attracted different audiences. While contemporary Pacific art remains directed at the largely white, or *palagi*, gallery-going public, and is focused upon the city centre, Polynesian hip hop culture has developed out of the suburbs of South Auckland and is primarily directed at a 'brown', or largely Polynesian audience. Yet one can make too much of such distinctions. Recently, some prominent Samoan artists such as Feu'u and Tuffery have gone out of their way to bridge this divide by doing outreach programmes in schools and art centres in the suburbs. And, given that an increasing number of Polynesians have achieved professional positions in the art world, there is a growing degree of overlap between the two communities.

The mid – to late 1970s had witnessed the relocation of more than half the Pacific community to a newly built city suburb, called Manukau, which grew from a settlement used by the Polynesian builders who worked on the construction of Auckland's main power station. Prompted by the formation of the European Common Market, the deregulation of the economy and the downturn in manufacture, the area achieved some notoriety for inter-community violence as unemployment soared. Relations between the Samoan and Tongan communities, the two largest expatriate communities of Islanders in Auckland, were particularly strained, and led to gang violence. During the 1970s, the imposition of spot checks and dawn raids by the police to locate and deport illegal migrants added to a sense of embattlement. All of these factors may have made the Polynesian community receptive to the messages and cultural strategies of hip hop.

Polynesian Hip Hop

Hip hop was taken up by Maori and by young Pacific Islanders living in the southern suburbs of Auckland in the 1980s. Although Pacific Islander engagement in hip hop developed on the back of Maori rap, the emergence of this movement was in many ways symptomatic of the development of a more youth-oriented culture by the second-or third-generation descendants of Pacific Island migrants. The efflorescence of Pacific youth culture has been linked to the decline in the Pacific gerontocracy's control of cultural forms, which has been attributed, in turn, to the in-between status of Pacific Islanders in Aotearoa. Islanders are acutely sensitive to their status as visitors in the homelands of the Maori, and the fact that their distance from their own homelands – and the land in particular – is undermining the authority of traditional cultural practice in everyday life. For as family life changes orientation, the younger generation's respect for their elders has become an increasingly contentious issue among all the diaspora communities (Spoonley 2001).

The Samoan novelist, Albert Wendt, has shown how Church and sport provided alternative focal points for migrants' lives that helped them to cope when they first moved to New Zealand in 1950s and 1960s. Up until the 1980s, sport and the Church were the linchpins of tightly knit enclaves that circumscribed Samoan, Tongan and Cook Islanders' separate social worlds. These communities remained largely oriented to the islands – home was elsewhere – and links to it were maintained through fund-raising and the return of remittances. The long list of different churches, distinguished by denomination, country, region, and later splinter groups, grew and grew in Auckland's Yellow Pages. By the end of the century reaction against these claustrophobic self-contained church communities, as well as a gradual decline in the new generation's attachment to the islands was becoming increasingly evident in the Samoan expatriate community.

Sociologists working in Auckland have suggested that modernist ideologies of education, cross-community marriages and the growing independence afforded by welfare provision are leading the Pacific communities to alter their bearings (Macpherson et al. 2001). But it is my purpose here to describe how such changes are being realized through shifts in the control, nature and orientation of cultural forms. For hip hop is symptomatic of a more outward-looking, youth-oriented culture which is turning to other Pacific diaspora communities, as opposed to the home islands, for inspiration. (An estimated further 200,000 people of Pacific descent live in other parts of the new world [ibid.: 83]).

Kirsten Zemke-White has suggested that the Samoan community has played a leading part in the development of Polynesian hip hop in Aotearoa-New Zealand. Migrants from Western Samoa, a former New Zealand dependency, are by far the oldest and largest expatriate community in the country. Their identification with American Samoan rap crews, such as Boo Ya tribe from Los Angeles (who came to prominence in the mid-1980s) has played a part. But if the turn toward American hip hop is an indication of Samoans' growing openness toward modern life, it also has a dimension of fantasy. Like churches, hip hop is a cultural form that means that Western Samoans can feel at home in an imagined landscape that is both here and elsewhere at the same time; only partially anchored in Auckland. As if to emphasize its in-betweenness, South Auckland has been renamed 'Southside' as migrants from Western Samoa match their urban experiences to the experiences and struggles of American Samoan expatriates living in Southside Los Angeles.

American Samoans are not the only point of identification. The experiences of intimidation by the New Zealand government have meant that both Maori and Pacific rap crews are sympathetic to the struggle of African Americans living in the Bronx, or downtown Los Angeles and Washington. Nevertheless, Pacific islanders have adapted hip hop culture in a specific manner. They are less overtly political than Maori rappers (such as Dam Native or Upper Hutt Posse) and do not identify with American gangster rap, emphasizing that their aim is not to dwell on the negative aspects of their experience but to use past suffering to provoke a more positive cultural attitude in the future (Zemke-White 2001).

Since the early 1990s, artists of Pacific descent have used different aspects of hip hop culture such as rap, graffiti ('tagging' or 'bombing') and T-shirt design to promote cultural pride and awareness. The auditory or visual collages such as mixing, sampling and wordplay that are a key feature of all these genres have enabled artists to draw upon Pacific cultural referents as well as the signs, words and images which encapsulate more recent shared experiences of colonialism, migration, dislocation and urban experience.

How these elements are brought together can serve to shift the contexts of people's thought. For example, the meaning of terms of abuse can be reworked through recontextualization and reappropriation. The use of the term 'coconut' is a case in point. In the recent past, Samoans, Tongans and Niueans were painfully reminded aware of their rootless, marginal status as newcomers by being collectively called 'coconuts' – a term with distinctive Polynesian resonance. By the mid-1990s Pacific rap artists had begun to reappropriate this term, however, as a way of proudly reaffirming their position.

> I ain't black and I won't take it back.
> I'm brown like my daddy who was proud to be a coconut
> Don't get me wrong cause I'm down with the black watch
> But you need 2 get your culture straight
> B 4 it's 2 late. Otara 4 eva
>
> (Paully Feumana of OMC in Frizzel, 1994, cited by Kirsten Zemke-White 2000)

'Otara for ever': a common feature of Polynesian hip hop is the emphasis upon place providing a primary point of reference. It is an approach that encourages a more pan-Pacific approach toward cultural forms. But place, as we have seen, is a complicated thing: a landscape that is both inside and outside Aotearoa-New

Zealand at the same time. Dawn Raid is a cooperative of rap musicians, designers and clothes retailers whose members are descended from Irish as well as different Pacific Islander communities. A recent CD cover for Dawn Raid's album, *Southside*, illustrates how urban American and south Auckland landscapes can be spliced together. It pictures a road heading to Otara via Brooklyn Bridge and route 66 to Oakland, California. T-shirts produced by Dawn Raid also reference place. The name, 'Dawn Raid', derives of course from the early morning raids that were staged by the immigration services in the late 1970s and 1980s with the aim of deporting Pacific islanders who had over-stayed their permits. Dawn Raid's T-shirt designs, printed with slogans such as 'Overstayer', 'Cocoland', 'Southside' or 'Otara' are a way of reworking an image bank of trauma and turning it in to a more positive thing to mark their affiliation to place.

Hip hop is not the only aspect of American counter-culture, however, that has gone into Otaran T-shirt design; the visual idioms of surfing and skateboarding have also played a part. A significant number of T-shirt designers working in Otara are members of the Mormon Church, which has strong links with America. The Kennerly brothers, among others, began by importing T-shirts from Hawaii in the early 1990s when they were studying at the university department of Brigham Young in Honolulu. Some of the T-shirts bore Samoan catchphrases; others had slogans that were intended to convey a sense of collective cultural pride, with expressions such as 'Polynesian Strength' or, 'Don't Mistake our Quiet Ways for Weakness' or 'Samoan, Built to Last'. A design bearing the legend 'Super Samoan', using the *Superman* lettering, shows how collective affirmation had begun to be expressed through appropriating features of American popular culture.[1]

Outwardly many T-shirts produced in Otara would appear to draw very heavily upon different aspects of American popular culture. Indeed, the emphasis upon urban commercial visual culture would seem to distinguish T-shirt art from work by the Pacific and Maori contemporary artists who achieved prominence in the 1980s. Nicholas Thomas has shown how the first generation of contemporary fine artists were encouraged to play up their Pacific roots. They drew on traditional arts from the islands such as *tapa* (barkcloth), or much older and supposedly more widely dispersed visual traditions, such as Lapita pottery decoration, in order to develop a pan-Pacific indigenous idiom that could describe some kind of relationship with the ancestral past and the traditional culture of the islands (Thomas 1999). By contrast, Polynesian hip hop places greater emphasis upon islanders' contemporary experience. What Polynesian rap artists refer to as 'knowing where you are from' does not only require some awareness of ones culture or tradition it increasingly involves developing an attitude or a relation to place (Zemke-White 2001).

In this respect T-shirt art has made a significant contribution. Because artists' designs draw upon concrete visual details of the immediate environment, they are playing a vital part in the development and dissemination of shared cultural perceptions of place. The foreign appearance of the designs is deceptive, in fact, for T-shirt art is an exercise in allusion in which you are challenged to see the connection between familiar commercial imagery and Pacific cultural referents.

T-Shirt Design in Otara

To visit the suburbs of South Auckland is to understand why it has been so important for islanders to express their subjective responses to this place. Manukau city suburb (whose name means 'many birds', or 'the flock of birds' in Maori) has a transitory feeling. It is spacious and clean but also impersonal and functional. Neatly painted timber houses set in lots stretch out mile after mile repetitively. The houses have been put together from prefabricated sets. It is a man-made, purpose-built, rationalized environment in which zones have been allocated for dwelling, commerce and entertainment. The focal points are provided by the beer factory, the freezing plants, the abattoirs and the Tiptop factory (which converts animal render into ice cream) as well as the retail centres – with their supermarkets and 'drive-thru' takeaways – and the car showrooms, whose forecourts are strung with bunting and flags. 'Ornament' is also supplied by loud signage, or promotional posters announcing price discounts and special offers; these can be read from a car. It seemed typical that when I asked for directions to get to Otara, Auckland's principal Polynesian market, I was told to look out for the McDonald's sign.

There are now eight different T-shirt producers operating from Otara market. Some of the larger players such as Urban Pasifika, Dawn Raid and Pacific Gear also run clothes shops in other Pacific urban centres. The other stallholders produce their own designs from their own backyards. All of the designers are youngish men, aged between twenty and thirty, and the majority are either Samoan or of Samoan descent. With the exception of Siliga Setoga, who has received some training in graphic design, the other T-shirt artists have had no formal training, and have to rely upon illustrators and printers to execute their ideas. What they all share is street knowledge – they are 'down with the brown'. Some T-shirt artists started out as graffiti artists, or 'bombers'. However the cost of spray paint was constraining, and although funds for paint could be acquired via community arts projects, they tended to commission murals of traditional island scenes. By developing T-shirt designs for sale at Otara market, these artists have found a way of conveying their experience of their surroundings to a predominantly brown audience. How the designs 'go down', with the other T-shirt artists, as well as with the visitors to Otara, is the important issue here. Even the larger outfits, such as Dawn Raid, make the effort to put up a stall at Otara to see how the market-goers respond to their work. 'It's our market research' said Danny Leosavati of Dawn Raid. In fact, most outfits were selling several thousand T-shirts each year.

Engagement is sustained through the rapid-development T-shirt design. Because the designs are funny, they are also short-lived: jokes go stale as a new design, by a competing T-shirt artist, gives a joke a new twist, another dimension, meaning that new designs have to be brought out every month. Some of the older designers claimed that their ideas had been misappropriated, and there is a sense in which all the designers seem to work and rework similar elements. Yet the work of younger designers was often wittier or more elaborate, and it was my impression that T-shirt design had developed into a virtuoso form by the beginning of this century. What follows is an attempt to convey how my investigation into the collaborative development of Otaran T-shirt design has progressed.

One way to begin is to consider the core elements. The coconut has become a leitmotif of T-shirt art, and as competition between Pacific T-shirt artists has intensified, the way in which it is used to convey jokes has evolved in an interesting way. Perhaps this can be best illustrated by contrasting an early T-shirt design, made by a company called Coconut Apparel (founded in 1996), with a couple of more recent designs from a new design company called Nektar (founded in November 2000). Coconut Apparel's design consists of a series of cartoon drawings of a flip-flop, a coconut, a machete and a taro root. All of these objects are set in a series of frames and the design carries the tag line 'Coconut Essentials' (see Figure 7.3). If one was to interpret the design, one might say that the low-tech, anti-materialistic culture of the Pacific islands is being affirmed through the implicit reference to foreign materialism, 'essential leisurewear' and McDonald's multiple-choice meals (which uses a similar graphic format to display a choice of burgers, cola, ice cream, and chips). This would be a familiar strategy in Pacific cultural politics where cultural difference is often stereotyped and polarized through the caricature and the oversimplification of us/them distinctions.

It is interesting to contrast this design with the version produced by Nektar that approaches similar subject matter by a different tack. The Nektar design resembles the Coconut Apparel design in both format and content: the design is also about Pacific material culture. It features three black-and-white photographs depicting a coconut, a coconut grater and a stream of coconut cream being poured into a bowl. The photographs are superimposed against a background image of a pandanus mat and the images are set in a slick, 'techie' chrome frame. 'I wanted to find a frame that looked really urban' says Dean Purcell, Nektar's designer. In this case, the tag line, 'bump n' grind island style' alludes to dance culture. Such simple devices are sufficient to open up some discursive space between urban experience and that of everyday life in the islands.

Perhaps it is the interpretation of the viewer that counts. In later designs Purcell seems to have shifted from using frames to using titles to condition the viewer's perception of an object to elicit the points of view that condition the viewer's perception of a subject. As Purcell puts it, 'What inspires the designs is the people,

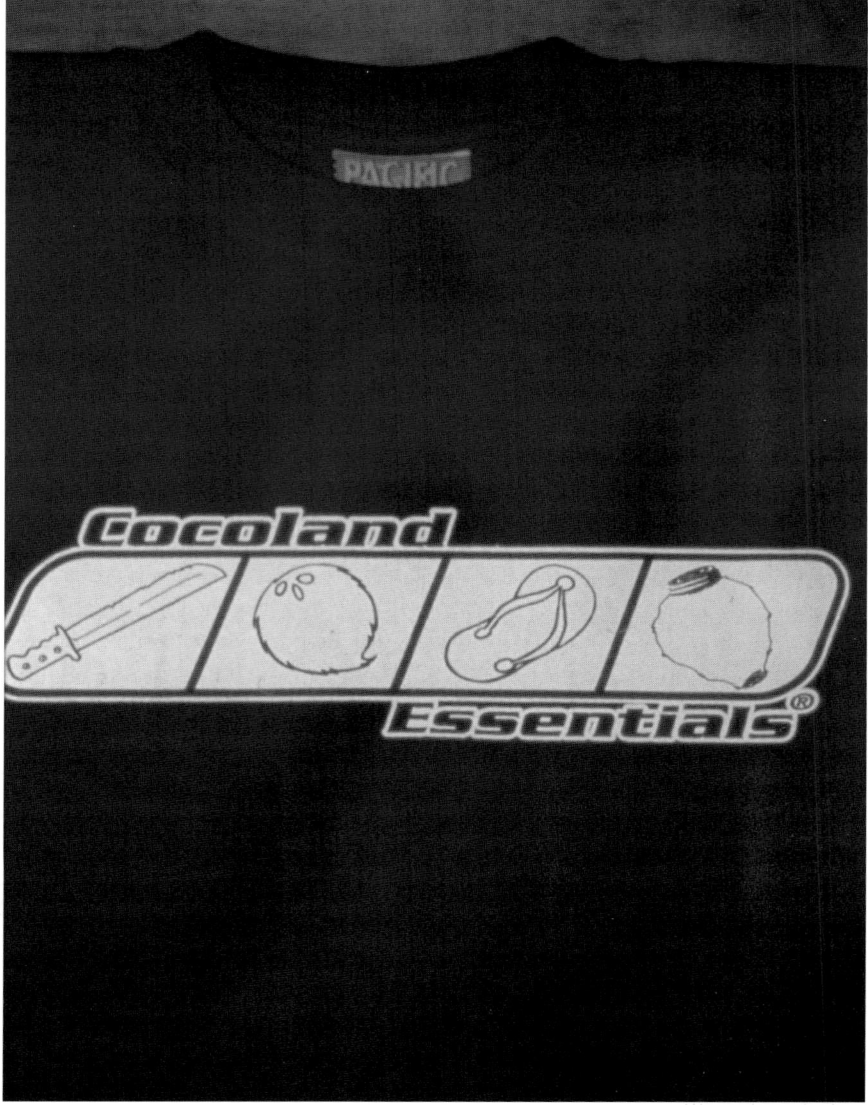

Figure 7.3 'Cocoland Essentials' T-shirt design by Coconut Apparel, *c.* 1999 (photograph author's own).

it's everyone around us'. An engaging design encourages Maori and *Pakeha* to exchange perspectives with the wearer of the T-shirt. The design seems to indicate how a T-shirt can be used to squelch an opponent in a battle of wits. The yellow triangle of a warning sign is fitted with the caption 'Caution! Coconut Approach-

Figure 7.4 'Coconut Approaching!' Dean Purcell modelling one of his own designs under Mangere Bridge, South Auckland, 2001 (photograph author's own).

ing!' (see Figure 7.4) It is an image that forces itself upon the audience. The design does not serve as a vehicle for self-identity; instead, it anticipates (and parodies) the perspective of the viewer, seeming to require a new response.

F.O.B. (as in 'Fresh off the Boat') is another term that was used to poke fun at newly arrived Pacific migrants' provincial ways. George Pritchard, one of the pioneers of Otara T-shirt design, whose company is called Island Wear, said that his most popular design was one that reads 'FOBU XXL'. The relationship between island life and physical appearance is condensed into a formula: 'Fresh Off the Boat Unlimited' equals 'Extra Extra Large'. Another of his designs features a globe set against a strip of either Tongan or Samoan *tapa* motifs, and is subtitled 'Planet Pollywood'.

Both of these designs contain jokes that are implicit, meaning that the viewer is lifted from his or her passive role and compelled to cooperate, to repeat to some extent the process of inventing the joke, to recreate it in his or her imagination (cf Koestler 1989 [1964]: 86). T-shirt artists do not explain their leaps of thought – one is left to fill in the gaps oneself. What is one to make of these designs? I now regret that I bought the T-shirt in a downpour and did not stop to talk to the designer or to study other people's reactions to his work for long enough. Is my interpretation worth anything? I want to know how these T-shirts engage with knowledge on the street.

The play on the word 'wood' *could* serve to highlight the difference between two incompatible visual cultures that have shaped people's perceptions of Pacific island life. Hollywood's version of the South Seas contrasted with another kind of visual economy that is based upon the circulation of patterned imagery carried by wooden cloth or *tapa*. I began this chapter by describing how *tapa*, an object that has long held an important place in Pacific kinship economies and religious practice, has been translated in T-shirt design. References to cultural history are so economic and implicit, however, that it was some time before I became aware that a large number of T-shirts alluded to the history of exchange in the Pacific. Pritchard's designs would seem to encourage one to consider the connection between exchange and appearance. Perhaps this may help to explain this T-shirt design: the F.O.Bs are oversize because kinship in the Pacific involves eating on behalf of others. But I have to admit that this is speculation. When I ask George Pritchard he points out that the joke has another aspect: FOBU is the logo of the black American company, *For Us By Us* that supplies clothing for the hip hop scene. So oversize T-shirts may be seen as encouraging self-determination. Like the analogy between *tapa* and Hollywood movies it encourages the viewer to imagine a 'What if?' scenario: a counterfactual world in which the Polynesian visual economy defines the dominant world-view.

So much depends on the way in which things are perceived and reinterpreted. Dean Purcell has created a design that uses an impersonal government-issue object to explore the relationship between cultural perception and different domains of Samoan and Maori experience. His 'found object' is a fluorescent orange road sign that warns drivers that there are labourers at work on the road. The road sign shows a man digging an oblong hole in the ground. Both the man and the hole are silhouetted against a fluorescent orange field. Purcell has managed to connect this image to shared cultural perceptions by adding three subtle modifications to the design. The changes are almost imperceptible: a few wisps are added to indicate steam; the design's title, UMU WORKS, or HANGI WORKS (that is, 'Earth Ovens Work', *umu* is a Polynesian term for 'earth oven', while the Maori term is *hangi*) and the fluorescent orange field, which by being printed on blue or green T-shirts, has altered the relation between figure and ground. These three devices create an interpretive screen which comes between the everyday object, the wearer and the perceiver, thereby prompting the audience to consider its cultural resonance. It is doubtful whether most Pacific islanders would have spontaneously seen the road works sign in the way that Dean Purcell has, but once the analogy is pointed out it would strike many of them as both provocative and self-evident.

Does the design invite the viewer to make a positive or negative reading of ceremonial exchange? It would seem to provoke both. This time I am determined to investigate other people's responses to this shirt, not merely the designer's or my own. As an experiment I wear the T-shirt during a visit to Ta Te Hou, the Maori Pacific department of the Elam Faculty of Arts at Auckland University, and I am struck by the diversity of response it provokes. A Maori Artist-in-Residence, studying for a PhD, sees the design in a negative light. 'I'd say that's typical', he comments, 'every time you find road works you see a brown face; that's what this design means'. But then I talk to a Samoan artist who suggests that the image can be seen in a number of different ways.

I advance my own interpretation. Might the designs reveal the inadequacy of the realist structuring of experience? Perhaps; for the relationship between figure and ground in Purcell's design – where the digging figure and the hole are rendered counter-intuitively *as a hole* in the middle of a luminous field of brilliant orange (a hole which covers the body of the wearer) *could* suggest that ritual can reveal the existence of a hidden layer of reality beyond that of the everyday world as the *palagi* (white foreigners) perceive it (see Figures 7.5, 7.6). I suggest all of this to the Samoan artist; he looks at me, and answers carefully: 'Do you mean that you are interested in the indigenous view of things? I suppose you could see that in it if you wanted to.'

Perhaps the ambiguity of this image, its capacity to provoke questions rather than to advance a definitive interpretation, provides the key. For whatever the situation in the past, it has been several generations since it could be assumed that adult Samoans held the same explicit beliefs. Now in the Diaspora, Samoans are torn between maintaining the old ways and embracing modern consumer culture. Ritual practices, however, especially formal exchange, still bear a great deal of authority and command the respect of members of different Christian denominations who stand in different relationships to the market economy.

The following week I stand by Purcell's stall watching people as they pause to look at his T-shirts. A Tongan girl has brought some of her friends to see his stall, and they are all giggling together in the rain. They seem excited and happy: Nektar have recently launched a new T-shirt for the Tongan market. I ask Purcell about the UMU T-shirt, explaining that I am interested in people's response to it. 'I'm very interested in their response too!' he says, adding that he had chosen to use the word UMU in a design once he had found that the Samoan, Tongan and Niuean terms for 'earth oven' were the same. 'A lot of the old island designs had muscle men on them with tag lines saying "Samoan Power" and so on. We've got our own style. We are just trying to do things that everyone can relate to, we want to cater to all the people here.' This involves taking risks. For example, no other designer had ever tried to make a T-shirt design for the Maori market before, and some of Purcell's friends had prompted caution. But the experiment has proved to be a success: the *Hangi* T-shirt has sold consistently well. Purcell agrees that the UMU design can be seen 'in two or more ways and you can get a laugh out of that' but rather than offering his own interpretation he says, 'You have got to be urbanized

Figure 7.5 'Umu Works' T-shirt design by Dean Purcell for Nektar, Auckland *c.* 2001(photograph author's own).

to get these jokes . . . When you live in NZ you realize that you have to mix the custom, and sometimes it works and sometimes it doesn't. The main thing is that we want to build up hope. We are all trying to move forward together, but everything is happening so fast.' The T-shirt designs seem to help: 'Our parents are starting to pick up on how we think and how we relate to the past', he comments.

Figure 7.6 Works sign, South Auckland (photograph author's own).

Siliga Setoga, the graphic designer who started a one-man band company, called Popo Hardwear (lit. 'Coconut Hardwear': *popo* means coconut in Samoan) in 2000, also works with imagery in mass circulation. His designs use the commercial imagery of the fast-food industry to alert viewers to the complexities and contradictions of their current predicament. Brand subversion dates back to the 1970s in America, where it emerged in reaction to the use of T-shirts for commercial advertising. Since then it has become an established genre that has spread via the surfing and skateboarding scenes to Europe and the New World. It is a comic form that is beginning to seem a little overplayed, giving the gags a sense of ennui (see Figure 7.7). Yet Setoga has reanimated this genre by working with brand logos in a way that prompts the viewer to contemplate hidden analogies between American commercial imagery and Pacific traditions. His trademark – the 'face' of a coconut with its brows drawn together in concentration – is indicative. It is a reference to a widely known Pacific myth that describes how the coconut got his face. But it is drawn to resemble the mask used by Herbie Hancock (one of the founding fathers of rap) as a device for his band, 'The Headhunters'. This synthetic device seems to indicate how current ways of thinking are shaping how Islanders relate to the past.

In 2001, Setoga's best selling T-shirt featured the Kentucky Fried Chicken logo. In the design Colonel Saunders has been given an Afro and the epithet KFC is translated as '*Kalo* and Fried Corn Beef' (that is, 'taro and fried corn beef'; see Figure 7.8).

Figure 7.7 'High Again' (photograph author's own).

Figure 7.8 'KFC – Kalo and Fried Corn', T-shirt design by Siliga Setoga for Popo Hardware, Auckland, Spring 2001(photograph author's own).

You need to appreciate the changing material culture of gift exchange to appreciate this joke. When global trade and commoditization began to have an impact upon Pacific Island economies, newly introduced cattle and machine-made cloth began to be substituted for the pigs, *tapa* and finely woven pandanus mats that would have been exchanged at ceremonies that marked the departure or return of kin. The second half of the twentieth century was marked by the growing economic dependency of Pacific island economies; this was a period when tinned fish and tinned corn beef and taro became standard items of gift exchange. Siliga's joke about KFC resonates well among the Samoan expatriate community because it presents yet another example of the way in which Samoan traditional culture has registered American influences. I show the T-shirt to a Samoan photographer. 'Everyone loves KFC,' she says, 'we are all asked to bring family boxes of KFC when we visit the family in the islands.'

Yet there is another dimension to this joke. As it transpires, T-shirts bought in the stalls at Otara are starting to form part of a new gift economy interlinking the diaspora community. It is eight o'clock on a Saturday morning. I am sitting at the Popo Hardwear stall and two Samoan women are looking at Setoga's T-shirts. They single out the KFC one, pick it up and start to laugh. They say they are over from Sydney and looking for some gifts to bring back to their relatives. As they leave, Setoga points out that the KFC design is often bought by expatriate Samoans to take to their relatives in Australia or the United States: 'it would not work back in Samoa, they'd think it's just another T-shirt'.

This is a revelation because it shows how his design both comments upon – *and is directly implicated in* – the changing imagery of gift exchange in the Samoan diaspora. The T-shirt design enables the buyer/donor to present a gift that will invite the wearer recipient to consider the current state of gift exchange among the Samoan diaspora community and its relation to the power of global corporations. By the time that I start to consider these implications I have left New Zealand and am surrounded by my books at home. They tell me that a characteristic feature of gift transactions in both Polynesia and Melanesia is that some reference is made to prior interactions between parties to an exchange. Indeed, the way in which past interactions are represented provides the means of modifying and altering relationships in the future. Exchange is more than just swapping because the speeches, together with the things exchanged and even the arrangement of offerings, create an *image* that allows people to reflect upon the relationship between contemporary developments and the ancestral past (see Gell 2000). Therefore the process of mentally juxtaposing a contemporary image of a relationship with other, preceding images of exchange relations is a key dimension of displays of cloth and food. Setoga's designs are true to this tradition, which they continue, albeit in a tragicomic manner.

Another of Setoga's designs with McDonald's giant yellow 'M' carries the substitute message 'Mulipipi, health hazard, Samoan delicacy': he explains that turkey tails (*mulipipi*) were exported by Americans to Samoa. Here is Setoga talking about them on tape: 'You know they are like these offcuts these bits that they would throw away normally or turn into dog food and instead they sold them all to us, knowing very well that they were bad for our health, and we ate them all the time. You know turkey tails were in the feed every second day. It was the same with lamb flaps, they were sent over from New Zealand.' He makes the analogy with McDonalds. Yet the criticism does not appear to be directly levelled at McDonald's or even America; Setoga is using his stall and the wearers of his T-shirts to hunt for Samoan heads, challenging them to think about the accommodations that they are making. These designs do not simply bemoan the loss of a rural way of life in which art and speech were more robust, and not yet gelded by advertising, rather Setoga challenges his audience to examine their entrenched and unexamined habits of mind, to move onward in a state of critical awareness.

Dean Purcell has also made designs that challenge the unthinking appropriation of American mass culture, although he focuses upon clothing. He has imitated the boxy lettering of USA athletic leisurewear to write the message 'U*SO CRAZY'. This is a multi-dimensional joke. It can be read as 'you so crazy', in an imitation of a black American brother, or it can be read as '*uso* crazy', which means 'brother', or 'sister' in Samoan. The target of the joke could also be the unthinking Samoan who walks around Otara wearing a t-shirt that says USA.

To understand how a design like this can be elaborated, one needs to consider the issue of wearer-perceiver relations. Talking to Dean and his wife Cathy Purcell at their home near Mangere Mountain makes me aware of how much Cathy contributes to Dean's designs. 'These designs are something that you really have to work on,' Cathy explains. 'You have to be creative; you can't just make a design without thinking – someone might buy a T-shirt for their wife, or their cousin – you have to understand your culture to be able to think about all of this. It's common knowledge that a large percentage of island men have a healthy appetite for the girls but it is still taboo to say that women have any appetite themselves. Island girls can't dress in short skirts, they've got to be covered up in South Auckland. You can use T-shirts to imply things in a subtle way that it would be impossible to say directly.' Dean continues, 'When a boy wears the USO T-shirt it can seem to mean one thing, like he's a crazy brother roaming the streets. But when a girl wears it, well you could think that she was boy crazy, or something'.

When I show Rosanna Raymond an early version of this chapter, she says that I have focused too much on the conceptual side of the jokes and should consider how clowning, parody and impersonation have always been central to the way that Islanders perform with clothing at ceremonies and with clothes in everyday life.

Her point is that, like *tapa* or fine mats, wearing a T-shirt elicits performance – it enables people to act out impersonations, in a shadowy subjunctive world where the literal is eschewed and everything is played out in a game of 'as if'. This multilayered approach to reality, now heightened by the contrast of traditional and modern life, is an important source of the comic force that sustains the Pacific Diaspora community. The records show how women used to impersonate the ancestors as they completed a mat, by weaving red feathers into it, for example. These impersonations were often hilariously licentious and served to express something that the missionaries had suppressed, but in a way that was acceptable, at a remove (see Hereniko 1992, 1995). Referring to this kind of humour Cathy comments, 'It has always been there, but no one has put it on a T-shirt before'.

Given that they have put so much effort into working with sensitive issues relating to sexuality and appearance in an oblique manner, both Dean and Cathy are uncomfortable about explaining these things so baldly. It is noticeable, in fact, that as T-shirt humour has become more contentious or provocative it has also become more implicit, more folded-in: harder to follow or unfold. The attempt to find a solution to a joke exposes the viewer's perspective, not the logic of the artist, making one question what one is laughing at. A design by Setoga, for example, reads 'Coconuts, harder than the real thing', and is rendered in the Coca-Cola graphic. It is a design that acts as a trigger – initially provoking and then making the viewer question his or her response. For it seems that Pacific T-shirt art is not about creating a vision of the world and man's place in it but about working with the relationships that can be perceived from a particular standpoint, rendering them visible and thereby challenging wearer-perceiver relations. And it is the verbal and visual analogies – or rather the nexus of interpretation that they provoke – that links the T-shirt artist and his audience, or the wearer and perceiver together.

Now it is my turn to present an analogy. When one comes to think of it there are certain similarities between T-shirts and a blank canvas or a white gallery: all are generic formats that can be used as a vehicle of expression. However, although humour and visual analogy are often ingredients of concept art, the gallery-canvas implies a relationship to an audience whose cultural references remain tethered to the Western art historical tradition. Setoga was uninterested in *exhibiting* his work in a gallery; he said it would attract the wrong kind of people. By making T-shirts in Otara, he can work with the market-goers to develop and broaden the kind of contextual resonances to which they are sensitive. Trying to explain this to me Setoga contrasts his work with fine art. 'Art is in a box; it's away from life', he gestures with his hands. 'If I did work there no one would see it. This is like art' he adds, indicating the display of T-shirts on his stall and the small crowd of people who have come to look at his work on this chilly midwinter morning. 'It doesn't bother me if they don't buy them.'

When T-shirts are exposed to a predominantly white audience, the designs are different. In the year 2000 the Samoan-Japanese fashion stylist Shigeyuki Kihara stirred up a media storm with a collection of T-shirts that subverted the logos of well-known brands, and drew attention to some of the more ludicrous commercial images of Pacific Island life. Initially the T-shirts were put on show at a hairdresser's. She treated them like meat, displaying them vacuum-sealed on styrofoam trays in a refrigerated cabinet. The collection was bought by the Te Papa Museum, New Zealand's national museum of Maori and Pacific Culture, and was put on display in 2000, where it provoked an outraged response.

The commercial imagery that Kihara drew attention to was well targeted. One T-shirt featured the visual guide on the back of a box of soap powder called Cold Power that shows Pacific women how to use washing soap! Her subversions of logos were more iconoclastic, designed to shock: the epithet KFC was translated as KKK; a New Zealand store called Warehouse was translated as Whorehouse. Both designs seemed to reflect some of the cultural violence that had been achieved through the misappropriation of Pacific artefacts in the past. The provocation worked. In the extensive coverage of her show, both companies were reported to be considering legal action for what they regarded as the misuse of their brand identity, but of course, given the negative reaction that such a move would make, they never presented a case (New Zealand Herald)

Self-parody is a popular genre of humour. Last year the Kennerly brothers issued a T-shirt which adapted the logo of Nestlés *Milo* brand (a malted drink that is very popular in the Pacific) to read 'Samoan KOKO ®' and added a quote from the Samoan boxer David Tua who, when asked to pick a letter for the American game show *Wheel of Fortune,* is said to have selected 'O as in awesome'. Setoga responded with a design that aped the graphics of a well-known New Zealand fruit-flavoured drink called Freshup, whose catchphrase goes 'Freshup. It's got to be good for you! ' For that tag line he substituted the words, 'Freshy ! I'm got to be good for you! ' This T-shirt uses self-parody to flatten the opponent by raising the moral tenor of the joke: by demonstrating the Samoan community's capacity to laugh at themselves, the design implies that it is in poor taste to laugh at a foreigner's awkwardness. The Freshy T-shirt was worn by a leading Samoan rap artist called King Kapisi (King Cabbage), at his concert in the summer and went on to become one of Setoga's best selling T-shirts. Broken English had now joined the other voices, cultural stereotypes and catchphrases that made up the widening pool of speech genres that T-shirt artists have spliced together.

Yet I was interested to note that Kihara's work had prompted T-shirt designers to reconsider their audience. In the same year as Kihara's T-shirts went on display at the Te Papa Museum, a Samoan journalist called Lisa Taouma made a documentary about Otara market for prime-time New Zealand television; it was the first time that a programme had been shown on the contemporary life of the Pacific

2. In many parts of Polynesia, it is boys who are charged with the work of preparing earth ovens to bake ceremonial feasts of root crops such as taro, and pig. Women's ceremonial duty is to prepare cloth. The design is witty in a self-reflexive way, because it highlights the topsy-turvy character of the contemporary situation where men have turned to T-shirt design.

References

Douglas, Mary (1968), 'The Social Control of Cognition: Some Factors Regarding Joke Perception', *Man* 3: 361–76.

Gell, Alfred (2000), *The Art of Anthropology: Essays and Diagrams.* Eric Hirsch (ed.) Monographs on Anthropology. London: London School of Economics.

Hereniko, Vilsoni (1992), 'When She Reigns Supreme: Clowning and Culture in Rotuman Weddings', William E. Mitchell (ed.) *Clowning as Critical Practice: Performance Humor in the South Pacific.* ASAO Monographs (13), Pittsburgh: University of Pittsburgh Press.

—— (1995), *Woven Gods, Female Clowns and Power in Rotuma.* Honolulu: University of Hawaii Press.

Koestler, Arthur (1989 [1964]), *The Act of Creation.* London: Penguin Arkana.

Morton, Helen (1998), 'Creating their Own Culture: Diasporic Tongans', *Contemporary Pacific* 19(1): 1–30.

Spoonley, P. (2001), 'Transnational Pacific Communities: Transforming the Politics of Place and Identity', Macpherson, et al (eds), *Tangata O Te Moana Nui: The Evolving Identities of Pacific Peoples in Aotearoa New Zealand.* Palmerston North: Dunmore Press.

Strathern, Marilyn (1990), 'Artefacts of History: Events and the Interpretation of Images', in Jukka Siikala (ed.) *Culture and History in the Pacific.* Helsinki: Finnish Anthropological Society.

—— (1999), 'The Ethnographic Effect, Parts I and II', in Marilyn Strathern, *Property Substance and Effect.* London: Athlone Press.

Thomas, Nicholas (1996), 'The Dream of Joseph: Practices of Identity in Pacific Art', *Contemporary Pacific*, 8(2): 291–317.

—— (1996), 'From Exhibit to Exhibitionism: Recent Polynesian Presentations of "Otherness"', *Contemporary Pacific*, 8(2): 319–348

—— (1999), *Possessions: Indigenous Art/Colonial Culture.* Interplay Books, Thames and Hudson: London.

Wendt, Albert (1973), *Sons for the Return Home.* Auckland: Longman Paul.

Zemke-White, Kirsten (2001), 'Rap Music and Pacific Identity in Aotearoa: Popular Music and the Politics of Opposition', in C. Macpherson, P. Spoonley and M. Anae (eds), *Tangata O Te Moana Nui: The Evolving Identies of Pacific Peoples in Aotearoa New Zealand.* Palmerston North: Dunmore Press.

–8–

Getting Specific: Fashion Activism in Auckland during the 1990s: A Visual Essay

Rosanna Raymond

I spent the 1980s modelling in London, Milan and New York. When I came back home to New Zealand I found that a renaissance of Pacific culture was under way. Maori and Pacific Islanders had started to make an impact in the music and contemporary arts scenes, but Pacific Island street styles and fashion was being overlooked.

Fashion is part of everyday life but Pacific Islanders seemed to be cut off from it, and from other parts of consumer culture as well. In the early 1990s you never saw a brown face in advertising campaigns. It was as though the Polynesian community still occupied certain boxes: church; museums and festivals; crime statistics – but could not contribute to other aspects of contemporary life. What follows is a visual summary of my attempts to change this state of affairs. The text illustrates the images; it is an edited version of the many conversations and written exchanges that I have had with Chloë Colchester over the past few months.

This first picture looks staged and planned but it wasn't. You have to understand that Pacific Islanders never featured in the New Zealand fashion press in the early 1990s. The fashion editors looked to Italy for inspiration; they had not thought of developing a Pacific fashion aesthetic, or of working with the people around them.

We had been talking about the way that the old colonial photographs and the tourist literature had helped to fashion a Polynesian stereotype. *Papapalagi* (foreigners) have pretty fixed ideas of Polynesian women – they have an image that they can picture in their mind's eye that seems to overshadow everything they see. Working as a catwalk model in Europe had given me first-hand experience of the power of stereotypes: no matter what I said or did, people still labelled me as exotic. When I returned to Auckland I found that I had some authority with the fashion community and I set out to find a way of reworking these images of 'the exotic dusky maiden'. She was part of our heritage after all. I wanted Pacific islanders to be able to reclaim her, to bring her back under our control.

These issues may have been in the back of my mind when Greg Semu, a Samoan photographer, and I were working on this image, but really this photo just turned out in the way it did. You analyse it after you have done it, when you see

Figure 8.1 Fashion shoot for *Planet* magazine, 1992 (photograph Greg Semu, stylist Rosanna Raymond).

that it fits. Bonny Proctor had a Samoan and Maori background. Greg spotted her on the street and we asked her to sit for us. She had never modelled before and she had this respectful, dignified bearing that seemed to be very typically Polynesian. Maybe this was why Greg asked her to close her eyes and fold her hands like a good island girl in church.

The styling was all about juxtaposition: the gloves were very quaint and the feather jewellery and the poncho were quite tribal but they seemed to 'fit'. That was the main thing – finding the things we thought went together and showing them in the way we wanted to see them. We wanted to show that there could be more to our culture than museums or cultural festivals, we wanted to show that it was relevant now.

Figure 8.2 Fashion shoot for *Stamp* magazine, 1992 (photograph Greg Semu, stylist Rosanna Raymond).

In the first photo the model's face is partially hidden. This second photo draws attention to the face. Greg Semu and I liked to choose islanders with strong faces; you rarely saw these in the mainstream media in New Zealand at the time. Greg was trying to develop a new genre of Pacific fashion portraiture. We wanted to challenge the mainstream fashion media's idea of beauty by presenting islanders

Figure 8.3 *G'nang G'near*, Customized Levis by Rosanna Raymond, 1993 (photograph Greg Semu, 1997).

in new ways. Style magazines like Planet and Stamp helped us by letting us manage the casting, styling and photography.

We used *lavalava* (sarongs) to encourage people to be proud of island styles. Up until the early 1990s island dress was regarded as provincial, 'fresh' or 'fobbish' in New Zealand; most islanders thought that American culture was cool. Then, as Pacific expatriates began to affirm their 'islandness', island prints started to appear on the streets and in clubs in central Auckland, where they were worn as bandanas or made up into Hawaiian-style island shirts. I wanted to take this further: I wanted to re-empower islanders by re-empowering the *lavalava*! I styled them over jeans to give them a more contemporary edge.

The *lavalava* in this photo were designed and made by a man called Louis Fesolai who ran a stall in Onehunga Market, out in the southern suburbs. He had started to work with a wide range of *tapa* and Maori *koru* motifs to develop a pan-Polynesian look. He knew his market, and although the idea of Pacific fashion was new to him he had agreed to participate in the first Pasifika fashion show. This photo was commissioned by *Stamp* to promote that event: it helped to spread the net to a wider audience.

People see different things in this image. Some people think that the model is mimicking an Elvis pose. (Elvis is really big in the Polynesian community – think of all those Hawaiian films.) Then again, islanders often talk of facing the past, going back to the future, moving onward that way: some people like the fact that we chose a back view for that reason. So you can see that this photo works. In fact this was another image that seemed to fall into place.

The photograph's title, *g'nang g'near*, is taken from the slang that spread with the new Pacific gay scene. The pose came from the clothing. In the late 1970s Maori began to form gangs in the suburbs of Auckland and Wellington. One gang, called the Mongrel Mob, used to patch their jeans with leather: getting your 'patch' allowed you entry into the gang. I'm part Samoan, part Maori, part Tuvalu, part French and part Irish – so you see, I'm a bit of a mongrel myself. I wanted to make my own mongrel gear by customizing a Levis suit with pieces of *tapa* (barkcloth). *Tapa* is used as a ceremonial valuable that is used in many parts of the Pacific. A lot of *tapa* is exported to New Zealand from Tonga, for ceremonial use by the expatriate community living there. I used to drive around the suburbs collecting the pieces that had been used in an exchange and were being turned out with the rubbish. The mats we used as a backdrop are also used as *taonga* (valuables) in ceremonial exchange. Most of the older islanders in New Zealand will keep some under their beds in preparation for the next big family occasion, while the younger islanders like to display them prominently on their walls, as they are here.

I began making the *tapa* jeans when I was a stylist. I was trying to create the garments that I needed to see. They were patched over the following six years. My *tapa* jeans were used out clubbing, in fashion shoots and in a window display

Figure 8.4 Pasifika 1994, fashion editorial for *Stamp* Magazine (photograph Greg Semu, stylist Rosanna Raymond).

before being re-patched and bought by the National Gallery of Victoria, Australia. Greg Semu shot a front and back view of the suit for our own records and for some reason the front view got lost.

Figure 8.5 *Niwhai Tupeaea* 1994 (photograph by Rosanna Raymond).

A fashion shoot of Tongans, Cook Islanders, Samoans and Maori wearing customized clothing and tailored *tapa* garments would hardly surprise many New Zealanders now. But in 1994, at a time when our multicultural society was only just beginning to come to terms with bicultural politics, these photo shoots helped to develop people's awareness of the variety in Polynesian culture in New Zealand.

In the early 1990s, Auckland City Council had asked me to organize a Pacific fashion show to coincide with Auckland's new festival of island culture called Pasifika. I looked hard and found eight designers to enter the first show in 1993; by the second show this number had doubled; by the third we had 150 entries.

The shows provided a bridge between different generations and between the Polynesian and *palagi* (white) communities (see Figure 8.4). This was not always easy to pull off. The urban Pacific vision that I wanted to promote went against the ideas of modesty that we had inherited from the missionaries, and the Pacific Islander community leaders gave me a roasting after the first two shows. But they could see that a growing number of young second- or third-generation Polynesians were keen to join in. In retrospect, I would say that many of us were trying to break away from the stronghold of the church and its colonial past.

Figure 8.6 Hand Maiden Aotcaroa, Promotion for *Motu Tagata* (Island People) 1996, (photograph Terry Klavenes).

My collaboration with The Pacific Sisters developed from the Pasifika fashion shows. Niwhai was one of the founding members of The Pacific Sisters. To begin with they were a group of designer makers who produced feather and tapa jewellery. But Niwhai was a great performer and she inspired the rest of us to get more involved in costuming and performance. This was the first costume she made, and it inspired much of The Pacific Sisters' future work (Figure 8.5).

In New Zealand the elders saw performance as being separate from everyday life; this allowed us to convey punchy messages while maintaining the involvement of the wider community. We wanted to develop our own way of working, but at the same time we wanted to show respect – and this meant treading a fine line. We found that staging performances and making our own costumes helped. The effort we put in to learning traditional skills and oral tradition got us involved with a range of people in our communities. I think they were impressed: we were working with eight-strand plaits and *pu'a* (carob) seeds at a time when most people were only thinking about getting hold of the next pair of Nikes.

This image (Figure 8.6) was used to promote the Pacific Sisters at *Tala Measina*, the Seventh Polynesian Festival of the Arts in Samoa.

We had been invited to hold a fashion show and to stage a performance at the festival. It was a breakthrough: this was the first time that a contemporary multicultural group from New Zealand had been invited. These festivals typically provided a platform for celebrating the traditional arts. At *Tala Measina* the other groups were representatives from various parts of Papua New Guinea and from the different islands in the Pacific, and each of them was displaying its own specific cultural traditions. Inevitably the organizers had difficulty entering us into one of the festival categories. After all, what did we represent? We wanted to use dress and performance to challenge the position and image of women in both *palagi* (foreigner) and Polynesian society. We did not claim to be cultural representatives in the old-fashioned sense: we represented our 'eyeland' – our vision of Aotearoa. We called the fashion show *Motu Tagata*, which means 'island people' in pidgin Polynesian. People laugh at islanders' Pidgin English in New Zealand. We were trying to turn this around by having a bit of a laugh at ourselves, since most of us were *afi kasi* (mixed blood) second- or third-generation New Zealanders, and few of us were fluent in our native tongues.

Taina had just returned from doing the Paris fashion shows, so she was ready to take risks that other Polynesian girls would have found impossible. The core group of Pacific Sisters – Suzanne Tamaki, Niwhai Tupeaea, Jeanine Clarkin, Ani O'neill and myself – made her gear. We called our composite sister 'Hand Maiden Aotearoa'. She was our way of responding to colonial photography. Photographers came to the islands several years after the missionaries had started to change the way we dressed. They used to get island girls to pose for them semi-naked in 'native dress' order to sell saucy photographs and postcards of 'dusky maidens'. We grew up with these images. Well here was our version of a dusky maiden – with attitude!

People without any Pacific background find it hard to understand how we feel about clothing. For example, to wear traditional clothing we believe you need to be able to demonstrate your respect for its *kaupapa* (cultural foundations and value) through movement and performance.

Figure 8.7 *Pingau* costumes, by Cherie Te Rore, 1996 (photograph Greg Semu).

The two costumes in Figure 8.7 are made from *pingau* (a kind of flax). *Pingau* grows in the coastal areas; it is one of the Maori's traditional weaving materials and today only certain people have access to it through their cultural ties. Cherie Te Rore was able to use it because she had maintained her links with her tribe.

This photo was taken backstage at the fashion show in Samoa. The performers presented the costumes on the catwalk by using a number of *kapahaka* moves. Now this had never been done before at a fashion show. I was taking elements of Maori ceremonial performance out of their customary context. Some people found this shocking; others could see that sashaying down the catwalk would hardly suit clothing inspired by Maori traditional dress. I used to talk of '*kaupapa*-driven frocks' in order to convey the idea that the cultural foundations to Polynesian dress meant that it had to be presented in a different way. I used to play a CD called *Kaupapa-Driven Rhymes Uplifted* by a Maori rap crew called Dam Native at a lot

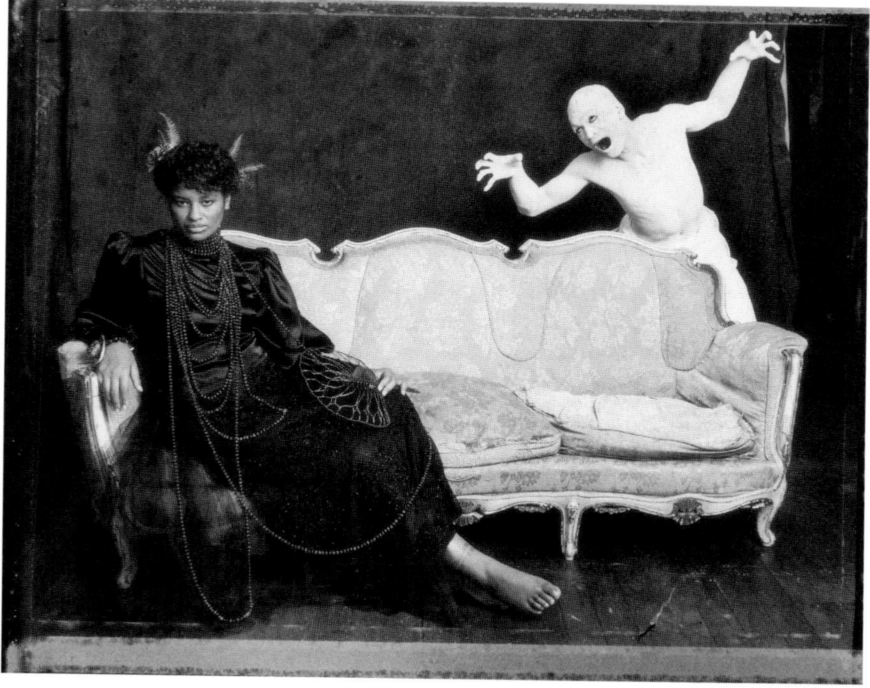

Figure 8.12 Shigeyuki Kihara and Chris Lorimer, styling for Pulp Magazine issue 22, Autumn 2001 (photograph Duncan Cole) Reproduced by permission of Pulp Magazine.

to this feedback. It was also my parting shot before moving to Britain. I knew that in Europe the Internet would have to provide the new context for my work. Now the challenge was to learn how to use it. The Full Tusk Maiden is dressed in many of the things that Polynesians associate with strength – *pua* seeds, boars' tusks – and her posture is defiant. She is my way of confronting the dusky-maiden imagery that I had tried to rework throughout the 1990s.

I have included this last image, Figure 8.12, as a postscript. Although it mimics the dress and posture of colonial photographic portraiture, it also embodies the confidence and sophistication that islanders have started to achieve in New Zealand. Anyone who is familiar with Pacific colonial photography will immediately recognize that there is something quite new to this model's expression.

Teremoana Rapley is part Cook Islander, part Kiribati. She is a modern media icon in contemporary New Zealand as she is a working mother, a musician, a director and a leading presenter on the Maori youth programme *Mai Time*. Shigeyuki Kihara is a part-Samoan, part-Japanese stylist and visual artist who has said that she feels she is continuing my work in New Zealand. The Pacific Sisters' presence is acknowledged in the form of the shell-flower on Rapley's wrist, showing that the influence of our work remains strong in the visual landscape of our community. This brings me full circle because in a lot of Pacific creation stories the earth and sky emerged as two sides of an original shell, so for the purpose of this visual essay, at least, it seems a good place to stop.

Index

Index

Index